LITTLE GIANT® ENCYCLOPEDIA

NUMEROLOGY

DANIEL HEYDON

STERLING

New York / London
www.sterlingpublishing.com

Library of Congress Cataloging-in-Publication Data Available

2 4 6 8 10 9 7 5 3 1

Published 2007 by Sterling Publishing Co., Inc.
387 Park Avenue South, New York, NY 10016
© 2005 by Daniel Heydon
Distributed in Canada by Sterling Publishing
c/o Canadian Manda Group, 165 Dufferin Street
Toronto, Ontario, Canada M6K 3H6
Distributed in the United Kingdom by GMC Distribution Services
Castle Place, 166 High Street, Lewes, East Sussex, England BN7 1XU
Distributed in Australia by Capricorn Link (Australia) Pty. Ltd.
P.O. Box 704, Windsor, NSW 2756, Australia

Author's note: The general meanings and characteristics of the 26 letters
of the alphabet discussed in Chapter 4 were partly derived from the collected works of Florence Campbell, to whom I am greatly indebted.

Sterling ISBN-13: 978-1-4027-5082-3
ISBN-10: 1-4027-5082-X

For information about custom editions, special sales, premium and
corporate purchases, please contact Sterling Special Sales
Department at 800-805-5489 or specialsales@sterlingpub.com.

In Memoriam

For Sheila Anne Barry, my beloved editor, who was truly the power behind the throne where this book is concerned. She inspired me to do my very best and believed in this book with her heart and soul. Sadly, she passed away before *The Little Giant Encyclopedia of Numerology* reached publication.

For Lloyd Cope, astrologer, numerologist, and close friend, who first introduced me to the study of numerology and astrology.

For Julia Wagner, former editor-in-chief of Dell *Horoscope*, who was my mentor, editor, guardian angel, and, above all, a true and dear friend.

CONTENTS

CHAPTER 1

NUMEROLOGY: WHAT IS IT?

Some ancient writings show that the science of numbers (numerology) dates back to the beginnings of history. These writings include the Hebrew *Kabbala*, the Indian *Veda*, the Chinese *Circle of the Heavens*, and the Egyptian Book of *the Master of the Secret House*.

History's Most Celebrated Numerologist

Without question, history's most celebrated numerologist was Pythagoras, a Greek philosopher who lived in the sixth century B.C. Today, he is chiefly remembered for his mathematical theorem; the square of the hypotenuse of a right-angled triangle is equal to the sum of the squares of the other two sides. Few people are aware that this same man is also considered the father of numerology.

Some historians say Pythagoras learned of numbers while in Egypt. Others say it happened while he visited India. In any case, Pythagoras brought the study to the Greeks and made it the basis of a new religious philosophy.

Pythagoras believed in reincarnation, vegetarianism, and the equality of women. He and his followers lived together in a community where they shared all property and contemplated the mysteries of the universe. They were known as the Brotherhood and were considered both a religious order and an academy of science.

Pythagoras believed that "all things are numbers." He was the first person to hold the belief that mathematical relations held the secret of the universe. In some ways, modern science has proven him to be right. Few modern scientists, however, share his belief that scientific investigation should and will lead to spiritual revelation.

To the Pythagoreans, both music and astronomy have their basis in mathematics, and the highest vocation is the study of numbers. Numbers were held to be sacred because they can exist without matter. Pythagoras was led to this belief when he discovered the harmonic intervals that underlie the production of musical sounds. No matter what materials the strings of a musical instrument are made of, their sound will be the same as long as the mathematical proportions are preserved among them. The pitch depends on the length of the string that is producing the sound.

In the Pythagorean vision of the universe, numbers become the basis of all art, science, and music, and the key to the spiritual life. What determines the sound of a piece of music are the ratios between numbers, and what governs the heavens are mathematical laws. Numbers allow us to perform mental operations that are not dependent on our five senses. Numbers are not of the external world, but of the mind, and reflective of the spirit.

The Pythagoreans believed that by contemplating numbers, a person's soul would be purged of earthly passion. Through numbers, a way to God could be found.

The idea of numbers as a link between heaven and earth may be unfamiliar to most of us. Yet we hear echoes of Pythagoras in the thinking of the psychologist Carl Jung, who once wrote:

> *The opposition between the human world and the higher world is not absolute; the two are only relatively incommensurable, for the bridge between them is not entirely lacking. Between them stands the great mediator, Number, whose reality is valid in both worlds.*
>
> —*Civilization in Transition,* p. 409

The Basis of Numerology

Like astrology, numerology is based on the rhythms of your birth date, but includes in addition a study of your name. Each letter of the alphabet has a matching number (from 1 to 9). Here is a table showing the number value of each letter:

```
1 2 3 4 5 6 7 8 9
A B C D E F G H I
J K L M N O P Q R
S T U V W X Y Z
```

The practice of correlating numbers with letters dates back to ancient Chaldea, where the same symbols were used for both numbers and letters. Modern numerology, though, begins with the work of American music teacher Mrs. L. Dow Balliet, who around 1903 applied the principles of Pythagoras to the English language. It was she who determined that each letter of the alphabet has a number value based on its position in the alphabet. A is the first letter and is given the value of 1; B is the second letter and receives a value of 2; and so forth until we come to J, the 10th letter. Here we drop the 0 and treat J as 1, the first letter of a new cycle from 1 through 9.

We do this because (as Mrs. Balliet explained) Pythagoras taught that there are nine basic numbers—all else is repetition. In numerology, whenever we encounter a compound number, we reduce it to a single digit by adding the numbers together. For example, 14 becomes 5 by adding the 1 and the 4.

This may seem to be a strange way to treat a number, but the practice is as old as numbers themselves and dates back to Arabia. By reducing a number this way, we find the root digit in which a larger number had its origin in a series of ninefold progressions.

For example, 204 reduces to 6. If you subtract 9 from 204, you will get 195. If you subtract 9 again, you will get 186. Repeat this process 20 more times, and you are left with a remainder of 6. Obviously it's much simpler to reduce the number immediately than to go through this tedious process.

According to Pythagoras, there are nine basic experiences common to humanity as represented by the numbers 1 through 9. A mastery of these nine principles encompasses the totality of what it means to be a person.

Master Numbers

Yet throughout history there have been certain people, such as Jesus Christ and Buddha, who seem to have been more than human and have offered to humankind a vision of the future beyond what is commonly thought to be within human capacity. Thus, in numerology, two numbers have become associated with revelation and the implementation of revelation for the benefit and progress of all humanity. These numbers are 11 and 22, and they are called Master Numbers. The name *Jesus* adds up to 11, and *Buddha* to 22. These two men were truly Masters, teachers at whose feet many sat awaiting instruction.

When we encounter the numbers 11 and 22 in numerology, we may reduce them for the purpose of addition. But for interpretation, we always keep in mind that 11 is not simply 2, but has the *higher potential* of 11. If a name or birth date adds up to 11 or 22, we write it 11/2 or 22/4.

Soul Urge

To find out how you, or any person, views life, we look at the number of your *soul urge*, which is found by adding up just the vowels of your name. The soul urge tells us the motives that lie behind your acts. In your soul urge is revealed your heart's desire, your attitudes toward things and people, and what you consciously want out of life.

The Quiet Self

The sum of the consonants in a name is called the *quiescent* or *quiet self*. It tells of your daydreams, your fantasies, and what you're like when you're alone. It is you in a state of rest, devoid of ambition and aspiration. As soon as another person enters the room, you are no longer your quiescent self.

The Expression

The full name, including both vowels and consonants, is called the *expression*. It is the you that the world sees and judges. Its number tells how you characteristically express yourself. As the sum of all the letters in a name, the expression shows natural abilities and indicates the kinds of things you can do most easily.

Some Things to Remember

• In addition to the vowels A, E, I, O, and U, Y is a

vowel when there is no other vowel in the syllable, as in *Mary*. *Y* is also a vowel when preceded by another vowel and pronounced as one sound, as in *AY, OY,* and *EY*.

• Most people don't know that in English, the letter *W* is sometimes also considered a vowel, as in *AW, EW, OW*. Both *Y* and *W* are always vowels when they end a word. *Y* is a consonant in *Yonkers*, as is *W* in *William*.

• Always use the full name at birth (including your middle name) when analyzing a name. Do not include titles such as *Jr., Esq., Mr.,* or the *2nd*. Abbreviated names, such as *Tom Smith* for "Thomas John Smith," show what qualities you are accenting at present. Nicknames show how your friends think of you. The real you, though, is found in your original name.

• The simplest way to chart a name is to write it in full on a piece of paper, leaving space above for the number values of the vowels and below for the number values of the consonants.

• After you have written in the number values of the vowels and consonants, add the *vowels* of each name separately and reduce to a final digit. Then add these digits together and reduce the sum to a single digit. The result is your *soul urge*.

• To find the quiescent self (or quiet self), add the *consonants* of each name separately and reduce these totals to single digits. Then add these digits together and reduce the sum to a single digit. The result is your quiescent self.

• On a separate line below your name, write down all the digits of your first name, including both vowels and consonants. Then add and reduce to a single digit. Do the same with the middle name and the last name. When you have found the numbers of the individual names, add them together and reduce to a single digit. The result is your expression.

• Do not take the shortcut of adding the numbers of the quiet self and the soul urge to find the expression, as you may come up with an 11 or 22 that doesn't belong there.

Example: Jack Lemmon

Here's how a numerologist would chart the name of beloved actor Jack (Uhler) Lemmon.

6 +	8 +	11/2	= 16/7 soul urge
6	3 5	5 6	
JOHN	UHLER	LEMMON	
1 85	83 9	3 44 5	
14/5 +	20/2 +	16/7	= 14/5 quiet self
1685	38359	354465	
20/2 +	28/1 +	27/9	= 12/3 expression

With 5 as a quiet self, when Jack Lemmon was by himself he dreamed of travel, adventure, sex, and the freedom to enjoy life to the fullest.

With 7 as a soul urge, Jack was a private person who

did not wear his heart on his sleeve. It was his 7 soul urge that enabled him to play such serious dramatic roles as Lee Remick's alcoholic husband in *The Days of Wine and Roses*; the conscience-stricken nuclear power plant executive in *The China Syndrome*; and the disillusioned middle-aged executive in *Save the Tiger*.

With 3 as an expression, Jack was a natural-born comedian, with a gift for self-expression—talents that were much in evidence in such films as *Some Like It Hot,* in which he played a cross-dressing musician who dances a sidesplitting tango with millionaire suitor Joe E. Brown; and *The Odd Couple,* in which he costarred with Walter Matthau as the slightly neurotic anal-retentive but lovable Felix Unger.

To find out what path Jack Lemmon had to travel in life, we need to look at the numbers of his birth date. It is not enough to know what the name reveals about a person. What a person *wants to do* and what a person *can do* means little if life does not provide the right opportunities. The name signifies character, the birth date—destiny and character in the making.

Jack Lemmon was born on February 8, 1925. To find his life path number, we reduce the digits of the month, day, and year to single digits. Then we add these digits and reduce again. Here's how a numerologist would set up Jack Lemmon's birth date:

2 / 8 / 1925

$2 + 8 + 8 = 18/9$ life path

The life path number tells us of our chief opportunity to find meaning and purpose in life. Its number indicates our goal in life and the type of achievement we may expect to accomplish. By learning all we can about the principles that lie behind our life path number, we can better fulfill our destiny.

The life path describes the type of people who will help us along the way, as well as what we must learn from experience to lead a fulfilled life. It represents what we must do with our life.

With a 9 life path, Jack Lemmon's destiny was to find meaning and purpose in life through experiences that would help him realize the common humanity we all share. This Jack did in his film career, perhaps like no other. As critic Judith Crist once noted: "As Chaplin's clown in his time embodied the commonality of the common man, so Lemmon's everyman has provided an empathetic symbol for mid-20th-century man." Whether through humor (his 3 expression) or pathos (his 7 soul urge), he excelled at illuminating the struggles of average men (his 9 life path) against a callous world.

Also important for Jack was his birthday number of 8, the number of material success. Jack was raised by his parents to go into business (to which the number 8 typically relates). Instead, however, he chose an artistic career. Ironically, but quite in keeping with his birthday number of 8, Jack was often called upon to play businessmen in his film career, most notably an uptight millionaire in director Billy Wilder's *Avanti!* and a fading, high-strung real estate salesman in playwright David Mamet's *Glengarry Glen Ross*. The question remains, though: How was Jack, without actual experience in the business world, able to give us truly believable portraits of businessmen at play, at work, in sadness, and in joy? That, of course, is what good acting is all about!

The birthday number tells us of the principles that we will be called upon to utilize in our career. It is especially important from ages 28 to 56.

In the next chapter, you'll find brief descriptions of all nine numbers, plus 11 and 22. In chapter 3, you will find in-depth descriptions of these same numbers when found in the soul urge, quiet self, and expression. Remember to qualify your interpretation of the numbers with the following guidelines:

- Your *soul urge* tells what you want out of life.
- Your *expression* tells what you can most easily do with your life.
- Your *life path* tells you what you need to do with your life.

in your dreams, inspirations, and visions. You look for opportunities that match your ideals. You relish being in the limelight.

22/4: Opportunity to you is the chance to find practical ways to implement your visionary ideas and ideals.

To obtain a greater in-depth understanding of your Key, a look at the numbers that it is made up of will yield important insights. For example, if your first name is Mary, which adds up to 21, read in chapter 8, "The Day You Were Born," what is written about the 21st birthday. Also read in this chapter about the qualities of the letter *U*, the 21st letter of the alphabet.

If the Key is the same number as your birthday number unreduced (if, for instance, your first name is Brian—which adds up to 26—and you were born on the 26th): You can push your luck too far and need to learn moderation in all things. Though your capabilities are fine, you have a joie de vivre that can cause you to be carefree, careless, and extravagant. The number of your Key reduced to a single digit indicates the types of risks you're prone to take. If your Key is 8, you might be extravagant or careless with money; if your Key is 5, you may have a hectic love life.

The Point of Security

Add up the total number of letters in your full name at birth—the result is your *Point of Security* (sometimes called the *Name Characteristic* or the *Habit Challenge*).

For example, there are 14 letters in the name Mary Alice Smith.

The Name Characteristic is a part of you that you take so much for granted that you don't even think about it. The Name Characteristic represents a natural talent that manifests as *habitual behavior,* but it becomes a *challenge* when used negatively, and may even become an annoying personal characteristic—an *idiosyncrasy.* It manifests in everyday living in both positive and negative ways.

It assumes special importance, though, if the Name Characteristic adds up to 11 or 22, or to one of the *karmic* numbers: 13, 14, 16, or 19. (These four karmic numbers are discussed in detail in chapter 11.)

Mary Alice Smith adds up to the karmic number 14. To learn more about Mary's 14 Point of Security, familiarize yourself with the qualities of *N,* the 14th letter of the alphabet. Also, look up the 14th birthday in chapter 8, "The Day You Were Born."

If your name characteristic equals a number from 2 to 26, learn about the qualities of the letter of the alphabet that corresponds to that number. Also, learn about the birthday number that matches your name characteristic in digit. If your full name at birth equals a number higher than 31, reduce that number to a single digit. Then examine the corresponding letter or birthday number. For example, if you have 36 letters in your name, reduce 36 to 9, then read about the 9 birthday and the letter *I,* the 9th letter.

Of primary importance in terms of the overall life is the number of the Point of Security *unreduced*. In daily behavior, however, we often express this number in its reduced state. The examples given below will show you how easy it is to slip from a positive to a negative expression of this number. For these examples, we'll call the Point of Security by one of its other names, *the Habit Challenge*.

If your Habit Challenge is:

1: You have great ideas, but be careful not to become overbearing and dominant in expressing them because of a one-track mind.

2: You handle matters properly and well, but be careful not to become faultfinding and a fussbudget about little things.

3: You have many creative talents, but be careful not to become vacillating or procrastinating instead of doing.

4: You are a careful, serious, hard worker, but you'll have moments when you put things off or perform at less than your best.

5: The whole world is your oyster, but at times you can screw up opportunities by being too changeable, fickle, or irresponsible.

6: You can create beauty and harmony in your environment, but you can also be dominating, interfering, and too possessive.

7: Your perfectionism gives you specialized skills, but be careful not to let inner resentment or being aloof separate you from others in spirit.

8: Your ability to see both sides of the question is a valuable business asset, but refrain from complaining at the wrong time or relentlessly.

9: Others will find your ability to add color and drama to your undertakings to be heartwarming, but they won't appreciate those up-and-down moods.

CHAPTER 5

THE RULING PASSION AND KARMIC LACKS

The Ruling Passion

Earlier in this book, you learned how to find the expression. This number tells you what you do most easily and spontaneously. To find out about other strengths and weaknesses of character, look at all the individual letters that are included in your name and note how many duplicate digits appear. For example, the table of the alphabet in chapter 1 tells us that the letters *A, J,* and *S* all have a number value of 1. If you have 3 *A*'s and 2 *J*'s in your name, then you have five letters of the 1 vibration in it. In simpler terms, you have five 1s in your name.

The number that appears most often in your name is called the *ruling passion*, and this tells us what you enjoy doing most. If you do not have the letter *A, J,* or *S* in your name, then you have no 1s in your name. Missing numbers are called *karmic lacks*: Their absence suggests weak links in the character that, if not strengthened, can cause all sorts of problems.

Let's take a look at the birth name of Leonardo DiCaprio. First we want to know the numbers of his expression, soul urge, and quiet self. If these numbers are the same as one of his karmic lacks or his ruling passion, it would modify our interpretation.

```
    18/9    +   14/5   +    25/7    = 21/3 soul urge
 5 6   1   6   9   5   9 1   9 6
L E O N A R D O  W I L H E L M  D I C A P R I O
3   5  9 4    5 3 8  3 4  4  3  7 9
    21/3    +   23/5   +    23/5    = 13/4 quiet self
 3 5 6 5 1 9 4 6    5 9 3 8 5 3 4   4 9 3 1 7 9 9 6
  39/12/3   +   37/10/1  +   48/12/3  = 7 expression
```

The simplest way to set up a chart for all the letters that are included in a name is to list the numbers 1 through 9 in a column, leaving a space whenever we confront a missing number. This chart is called the *inclusion*.

```
11
no 2
3333
444
5555
666
7
8
99999
```

With two **1s**, Leo has leadership qualities and is able to stand on his own two feet.

No **2s** may indicate a need for Leo to develop tact and consideration for others' feelings.

Four **3s** intensifies the desire of his soul urge to express himself creatively and gives him the ability to do so.

Three **4s** shows self-discipline, a willingness to work hard, and an ability to be patient and to envision long-range goals.

Four **5s** gives him a zest for living life to the fullest—a love of travel, change, sex, and the exploration of the five senses.

With three **6s**, he has a good sense of responsibility and can be depended upon. He enjoys family life and the comforts of domesticity, and has a willingness to bear others' burdens.

One **7** adds to his 7 expression abilities to be discriminating, to think deeply, and to get at the heart of the matter. 7 is also indicative of spiritual strengths and shows that he can be happy with his own company. All people with 7 as an expression are private people, secretive, and disinclined to wear their hearts on their sleeves.

One **8** shows that money and material success are not the end-all of his existence, yet the one 8 ensures that he can make things pay.

Five **9s** makes 9 the number of his ruling passion, indicating that he has genuine concern for the welfare of others in this world; is generous and humanitarianly inclined; has a good understanding of the emotional reactions of others, but may be extremely emotional himself; and is highly dramatic.

More About the Ruling Passion

1 as your ruling passion: You enjoy being your own person and doing your own thing; you're self-reliant, with leadership abilities.

2 as your ruling passion: You enjoy working with others, collecting things, partnership activities, music, and dancing; you enjoy artistic appreciation.

3 as your ruling passion: You enjoy expressing yourself with the written and spoken word; have a capacity for joy; are inspired, imaginative, enthusiastic, cheerful, creative, and spontaneous.

4 as your ruling passion: You enjoy work for its own sake; take pride in doing a good job; have a love of order and are industrious, dutiful, and conscientious.

5 as your ruling passion: You enjoy living life to the fullest.

6 as your ruling passion: You have a love of home and family; enjoy being the shoulder that others lean on; are loving and dependable.

7 as your ruling passion: You derive satisfaction from intellectual interests, studying, exploring the mysteries of life, counseling, contemplation, and reflection.

8 as your ruling passion: You think big and enjoy large enterprises; have a strong drive for material success; enjoy prominence and the things that money can buy.

9 as your ruling passion: You enjoy doing for others; have artistic, cultural, and political interests.

The Karmic Lacks

Missing numbers are called *karmic lacks*; their absence suggests experiences that you have consciously avoided or misused in former lifetimes. Missing numbers represent weak links in the character that, if not strengthened, can cause all sorts of problems.

A belief in reincarnation, though, is not necessary for an understanding of why a person will have problems with the principles that a missing number represents. Each of us identifies with the numbers (letters) that make up our full name at birth. They are a part of us, just as much as our skin and bones. Numbers that are missing from our name seem foreign to us, and we may even have a conscious or unconscious dislike for names that begin with these numbers. Some of us may even have a dislike for the persons who bear these names, largely because they are projecting—or, rather, are visible manifestations of—principles and qualities that we lack in ourselves.

For example, if you are missing the number 8 in your name, you may not be particularly fond of the names *Henry, Harry, Hope, Hank,* and *Heather,* all of which begin with the 8th letter of the alphabet. And if you are missing 2 in your name, to hear the name Barbara with its two *B*'s (*B* is the 2nd letter of the alphabet) may be like hearing chalk screeching against a blackboard.

What's more, people missing 2 in their names will probably at some point in their lives be put in the position where it will be necessary for them to cooperate with a Betsy, a Bob, or a Bill. If that is indeed the case, chalk it up to karma!

However, if you're missing 2 and you find yourself happily married to Betsy or your best friend's name is Ben, know that you have come a long way in dealing with and understanding the principles and challenges of your missing number.

Missing 1: You have a lack of ambition, plus a dread of being first and making beginnings. Life will force you to make your own decisions, to face issues squarely, *to take a stand—so dare to be original and creative*. Cultivate initiative, and never delegate to another what you can do for yourself. Often you do not know what is owed the self. Know that you have a right *to be*. Overcome self-distrust and overcaution. Become your own person. Find and then do your own thing! Learn to speak up for yourself. Fight for your rights. Don't settle for second best—or second place.

Missing 2: Little things are always getting in your way. Without patience and attention to detail, you will never get around to more important things. Your bad sense of timing is in part due to your lack of patience, tact, and consideration for others. At times you need help, which you won't get from others until you learn how to get along with them better. Always look before you leap; weigh your words carefully before you speak; think before you act—lest you give offense in situations where diplomacy and friendliness are called for. If you're a compulsive shopper, know that this is your way of trying to compensate for your missing 2—but it is not the best way.

Missing 3: Sometimes when you try to be carefree, you are awkward. Idle chatter and clichés can bore those who otherwise would be interested. Your words are often inappropriate to the social situation. You tend to wear an apologetic air, and this invariably defeats you. Life will force you into situations where you'll need the ability to advertise and sell—developing a sense of humor will also help. In creative areas, you can be all technique with little heart and soul. Strive to put your originality into your work. Don't mimic others, but find your true voice—then you'll be successful.

Missing 4: You resent hard work and can think up all kinds of excuses to avoid it. Your plans fall apart when you try to escape reality. Recklessness on your part may lead to accidents. Often you are shortsighted. Life will show you that you can accomplish nothing without patience, effort, and careful planning. Overcome a tendency to take shortcuts and to avoid effort. Cultivate practicality. Life will put you in situations where you need to deal with inescapable obligations. You'll have to graciously accept and conscientiously discharge them. This will happen over and over again, until you get the hang of it. Above all else, learn the joy that comes from doing a job to the best of your capabilities, and learn to take pride in your work.

Missing 5: Life will throw you off the routine you've set up for yourself with unexpected changes. You tend to block out the new, the progressive, and other people through your fear of taking chances. A fear of the new and untried in experience can cause you to stay in a rut, resisting all changes that may intrude in your life. You have little taste for the challenge of discovery, no thirst for the joy of adventure. Sex, too, may be a question mark—either too little, too much (not as likely), or too perfunctory. In your case, you will have to learn to give in to temptation and experimentation in order to come to terms with your own human nature and also to learn about your fellow man. To live life, you must experience it. You'll be faced with many emergencies until you learn how to adapt, to be innovative, and to profit and grow from your experiences.

Missing 6: You tend not to finish things you start. You dislike domesticity, are somewhat childish, and expect others to care for you. You resent family problems, yet you'll learn you must make adjustments in your relationships with children, parents, and marital partners. Life will force you to replace irresponsibility with a sense of responsibility toward loved ones. There will always be people who depend on you, and in these relationships you will have to give far more than you get—that is, until you learn that the receiving is in the giving. Love must rule your heart.

Missing 7: If the slightest thing goes wrong, you expect the worst to happen. You worry too much and need to learn that this, too, will pass—that tomorrow will be a brighter day. Life will give you the opportunity to replace fear with faith. Poverty, loneliness, and isolation may be yours to face until you realize that what happens to you in the material world is but a reflection of your own lack of faith. You'll have your times of crisis when you'll be thrown on your inner resources and forced to develop a workable philosophy of life and also to discover the meaning and purpose of your life.

Missing 8: At some point in life, you will be put in the position of having to take responsibility for your own financial affairs. Your hands will be tied until you learn some business know-how and the wise management of your own funds. Money is apt to come in and then quickly go out. Too much emphasis on money and financial concerns, though, can lead to health problems. Like Scrooge, you may forget the meaning of Christmas. Missing 8 per se does not deny money—indeed, many millionaires and billionaires are missing 8. Some of these people who have ruthlessly strived for money have felt the burden of it—being deprived of health, happiness, or the gratification of other desires. Others, though, through their missing 8, have learned ambition: how to make tough decisions; how to hone their talents; how to achieve, develop, and use their power and authority wisely—indeed, how to become a power for the good.

Missing 9: You'll meet up with people who act irrationally and go to emotional extremes until you gain an understanding of the full gamut of human emotions. You'll be placed in emergency situations where only you can help. A stranger has a heart attack on your doorstep and you are the one who must call 911; or you are the only eyewitness to a crime and are called on to testify. The outside world in some way will come knocking on your door, placing you in situations requiring sympathy, compassion, and involvement with the problems of humankind. Life will force you to *become involved*—to learn that there is a bigger world out there than the one that revolves around just yourself.

No missing numbers means you've done everything in life at least once. Unless you have a Master Number in either your name or your life path, you may tend to get bored with life. In your case, full attention must be paid to the opportunities of the life path.

Chapter 6

LIFE—WHAT DOES IT ALL ADD UP TO?

The birth name reveals valuable insights about your character and abilities, but you need to examine your birth date to find out what path you must travel in life. Most important is the life path number, which is found by adding up the numbers of the month, day, and year of your birth.

The life path number tells you of your chief opportunity to find meaning and purpose in life. Its number indicates your goal in life; by learning all you can about the principle of the number that governs your life path, you will be better able to understand and fulfill your destiny.

Finding the Life Path Number

Mary Alice Smith was born on March 5, 1942. To find her life path number, we reduce the digits of the month, day, and year to single digits. Then we add and reduce these digits again. Here is how a numerologist would set up Mary's birth date:

MARCH 5 1942
3   + 5 +   7 = 15/6
MARY ALICE SMITH has a life path of 6

The 1 Life Path

> *"If a life can have a theme song—and I believe every worthwhile one has—mine is [best] expressed in one word: Individualism."*
>
> —**Ayn Rand,** novelist-philosopher, February 2, 1905 (2 + 2 + 6 = 10 = 1 life path)

If 1 is your life path, you need to:

Learn to be independent and to stand on your own two feet; to find and do your own thing.

Attempt an undertaking that's never been tried before.

Develop leadership qualities, self-sufficiency, and a take-charge attitude.

Put your personal stamp on what you do.

Have the ability to go it alone.

Your destiny is:

To become your own person—to be unique.

To cultivate your originality.

To become the rock that others can lean on.

To be independent in thought and action.

To create, develop, and pioneer new ideas.

To instill new life into old ideas.

Your success:

Depends on the courage to think freely.

"Independence is happiness."
> —**Susan B. Anthony,** suffragist, February 15,
> 1820 $(2 + 6 + 2 = 10/1$ life path)

"First in war, first in peace, and first in the heart of his countrymen."
> —words of Henry (Light-Horse Harry) Lee,
> spoken on the news of the death of
> **George Washington,** the first president
> of the United States, February 22, 1732
> $(2 + 4 + 4 = 10/1$ life path)

"Golf is not everything. It never will be. The most important thing is furthering yourself, making yourself a better person."
> —**Tiger Woods,** golfer, December 30, 1975
> $(3 + 3 + 4 = 10/1$ life path)

Celebrated Persons with a 1 Life Path

Horatio Alger, writer	1/13/1832
George Clooney, actor	5/6/1961
Mikhail Gorbachev, Soviet leader	3/2/1931
Rita Hayworth, actress	10/17/1918
Eartha Kitt, singer	1/17/1927
Golda Meir, Israeli prime minister	5/3/1898
Jack Nicholson, actor	4/22/1937
Florence Nightingale, nurse	5/12/1820
Georges Seurat, painter	12/2/1859
Spencer Tracy, actor	4/5/1900

The 2 Life Path

"Romeo and Juliet, they never felt this way I bet."
—from "Cherish," **Madonna,** singer, August 16,
1958 (8 + 7 + 5 = 20 = 2 life path)

If 2 is your life path, you need to:

Learn to be a peacemaker, a diplomat.
Be sensitive to others' feelings.
Learn how to please through charm, sweetness,
friendliness, helpfulness, and consideration.
Learn how to be efficient with details.
Learn to be a good listener.
Learn to be patient, modest, and thoughtful.
Learn how to give and receive.

Your destiny is:

Often intertwined with a significant other.

Often affected by the friends in your life who can be counted on to do your fighting for you.

To be loyal, devoted, and supportive.

Often to follow rather than to lead.

To know when to speak, and when to be silent.

To attract rather than pursue what you need.

Your success:

Depends on the ability to downplay your ego and work in cooperation with others.

Henry Kissinger, U.S. Statesman, May 27, 1923 (5 + 9 + 6 = 20/2 Life Path)

Known for his political savvy and intellectual prowess, Henry Kissinger was a trailblazer for every diplomat who came after him. As President Nixon's national security adviser and secretary of state, Kissinger was the go-between in the secret negotiations that eventually opened relations between the United States and communist China. He also was the chief architect of the policy of détente with the Soviet Union and shuttle diplomacy to the Middle East. In 1973, he received the Nobel Peace Prize for his role in arranging a cease-fire in North Vietnam. His 1994 book, *Diplomacy,* secured his place in history as one of the greatest diplomatic thinkers of our times.

Jean-Paul Belmondo, actor	4/9/1933
Danny DeVito, actor	3/17/1944
Kirk Douglas, actor	12/9/1916
Isadora Duncan, dancer	5/27/1878
Jerry Lee Lewis, rock star	9/29/1935
Gustav Mahler, composer	7/7/1860
Alexander Pushkin, poet	6/6/1799
Keith Richards, rock star	12/18/1943
Jason Robards Jr., actor	7/26/1922
Diana Ross, singer	3/26/1944

The 3 Life Path

"Can we talk?"

—**Joan Rivers,** comedian, June 8, 1933
(6 + 8 + 7 = 21 = 3 life path)

If 3 is your life path, you need to:

Learn to be a gracious host or hostess.
Develop an appreciation for beauty and beautiful things.
Not scatter your energies or waste your talents.
Develop showmanship and versatility.
Cultivate social contacts.

Your destiny is:

To make other people smile, to spread joy, to entertain, to shed light in dark places.

To help others to see the silver lining.

To find meaning and purpose in life through the lighter side of life—friends, mixing and mingling, happy socializing, small talk.

To express your thoughts—to communicate.

To develop and express your creative talents.

To maintain a good sense of humor.

Your success:

Depends on the help of friends, the way you express yourself, being optimistic.

Anne Frank, Holocaust Victim, June 12, 1929
(6 + 12/3 + 1929/3 = 12/3 Life Path)

"I see the world being slowly transformed into a wilderness, I hear the approaching thunder that, one day, will destroy us too, I feel the suffering of millions. And yet, when I look up at the sky, I somehow feel that everything will change for the better, that this cruelty too shall end, that peace and tranquility will return once more."

These words from *The Diary of Anne Frank* serve to remind us that this 15-year-old girl, who somehow managed to keep her thoughts upbeat despite the impending dangers and horrors hovering around her, did indeed fulfill her 3 destiny to bring light where there was darkness.

Other Celebrated Persons with a 3 Life Path

Carol Burnett, actress   4/26/1935
Hillary Rodham Clinton, U.S. senator   10/26/1947
F. Scott Fitzgerald, writer   9/24/1896
Merv Griffin, talk show host   7/6/1925
John Grisham, writer   2/8/1955
Alec Guinness, actor   4/2/1914
Ann Landers, advice columnist   7/4/1918
Alfred Stieglitz, photographer   1/1/1864
Sir Walter Scott, writer   8/15/1771
John Travolta, actor   2/18/1954

The 4 Life Path

"The price of success is hard work, dedication to the job at hand, and the determination that whether we win or lose, we have applied the best of ourselves to the task at hand."
—**Vince Lombardi,** football coach, June 11, 1913
$$(6 + 2 + 5 = 13 = 4 \text{ life path})$$

If 4 is your life path, you need to:

Learn order and self-discipline.
Be the doer, the one who can be counted on to get the job done.
Learn the joy that comes through accomplishment, and take pride in your work.
Learn to be practical, thorough, and efficient.
Learn to be patient, well organized, and dependable, and know the value of routine.

Your destiny is:

To produce tangible results.

To build for lasting benefit.

To teach those less evolved than yourself.

To be the rock that others can lean on.

To achieve great things through strict application to duty.

Your success:

Depends on hard work, long-range goals, common sense, and being down-to-earth.

Bill Gates, Computer Programmer and Entrepreneur, October 28, 1955 (1 + 1 + 2 = 4 Life Path)

With 1 as his soul urge, Bill Gates wants to be first in what he undertakes, a goal that he has achieved as the world's richest man and CEO of Microsoft, the world's most successful software company. As he's often said, his goal is to put a computer on every desk. With 90-plus percent of PC owners using Microsoft's Internet Explorer, Bill Gates has standardized software. Not having a computer operating system is a liability for most businesses, and not having a PC is a liability for most individuals in today's cyberspace world. Bill Gates, with his 4 life path, has done his part to change the very nature of work in the 21st century.

Other Celebrated Persons with a 4 Life Path

Johnnie Cochran, lawyer   10/2/1936

Le Corbusier, architect	10/6/1887
Laurence Harvey, actor	10/1/1928
Henri Matisse, painter	12/31/1869
Kim Novak, actress	2/13/1933
Dolly Parton, singer	1/19/1946
Leontyne Price, opera diva	2/10/1927
Ariel Sharon, Israeli leader	2/27/1928
Pierre Trudeau, Canadian prime minister	10/19/1919
Oprah Winfrey, talk show host	1/29/1954

The 5 Life Path

"Life is a daring adventure or nothing at all."
—**Helen Keller,** author, June 27, 1880
(6 + 27/9 + 1880/8 = 23/5 life path)

If 5 is your life path, you need to:

Learn the thrill of the new and the unusual.

Learn to be versatile and flexible.

Expect change and the unexpected.

Develop ingenuity and opportunism.

Learn the right use of freedom, when to change, and what to change to.

Learn not to hold on to the past, but seek the new and untried and know when to discard.

Learn to understand people.

Not be a *love 'em and leave 'em* type.

Your destiny is:

To travel, to experience frequent changes.
To experience an adventurous life.
To enjoy the full use of your five senses.
To inject new life into what you touch.
To be progressive.

Your success:

Depends on experiencing life to the fullest, and then learning from your experiences; being resourceful and coping with the unexpected.

Mick Jagger, Rock Star, July 26, 1943
(7 + 8 + 8 = 23/5 Life Path)

As the lead singer of the Rolling Stones, Mick Jagger is one of the most popular and influential front men in the history of rock and roll. With his lascivious lips, his flippant defiance, his charismatic stage presence, and the rebellion implicit in his lyrics, there is no one quite like him. He is also known for his sexual dalliances. In the words of rock groupie Bebe Buell (who had an affair with him), "You can't say he's homosexual, or even bisexual. He's beyond that. Mick Jagger is the world's greatest practitioner of cosmic sex!"

Other Celebrated Persons with a 5 Life Path

Diahann Carroll, actress   7/7/1935
William Faulkner, writer   9/25/1897

B. B. King, singer	9/16/1925
Dean Martin, singer	6/17/1917
Walter Matthau, actor	10/1/1920
Robert Mitchum, actor	8/6/1917
Bettie Page, pinup girl	4/22/1923
Anthony Quinn, actor	4/21/1915
Pierre-Auguste Renoir, painter	2/25/1841
Shelley Winters, actress	8/18/1923

The 6 Life Path

"We're in a fight for our principles and our first responsibility is to live by them."

—**George Walker Bush,** U.S. president, July 6, 1946 (7 + 6 + 1946/2 = 6 life path)

If 6 is your life path, you need to:

Develop a sense of responsibility.

Be willing to lend your support and encouragement to those in need of it.

Learn the difference between helping out and meddling.

Learn to deal with the problems of domesticity.

Teach and set an example for those dependent on you, and develop a social consciousness.

Your destiny is:

To be there for family and friends.

To be kind, responsible, and protective.

To help those who lean on you . . . cheerfully.

To take an active role in a group activity.

To develop and express your creative talents.

To hold fast to your principles, but not impose them on others.

Your success

Depends on your willingness to serve family, community, country, and your code of ethics.

Louis B. Mayer, Film Mogul, July 4, 1885
(7 + 4 + 4 = 15/6 Life Path)

As production chief of MGM from 1924 to 1951, Louis B. Mayer sought to use the power of film to exert the proper moral influence on the American public. Motherhood, God, patriotism, sentimental family fare, and chaste romance were equal parts of a lifetime strategy that would establish MGM as the industry's dominant film factory from the silent era through the talkies. Among Mayer's successes were *Ben Hur, Grand Hotel, Dinner at Eight,* and the *Andy Hardy* series. In Mayer's case, morality did indeed sell at the box office, for by 1936 he was the highest-paid person in the U. S.

Other Celebrated Persons with a 6 Life Path

Michael Caine, actor	3/14/1933
Charles de Gaulle, French president	11/22/1890
T. S. Eliot, poet	9/26/1888
Jane Goodall, scientist	4/3/1934

Francesco Goya, painter	3/30/1746
Deborah Kerr, actress	8/30/1921
Ted Koppel, TV news analyst	2/8/1940
Elizabeth Kubler-Ross, psychiatrist	7/8/1926
Sandra Day O'Connor, U.S. jurist	3/26/1930
Eugene O'Neill, playwright	10/16/1888

The 7 Life Path

"If you have knowledge, let others light their candles with it."
　　—**Winston Churchill,** statesman, November 30, 1874 (11/2 + 30/3 + 1874/2 = 7 life path)

If 7 is your life path, you need to:

Obtain as good an education as possible.
Seek knowledge, think deeply, and develop intuition.
Investigate the unknown in life.
Read between the lines and not judge by superficial appearances.
Cultivate your inner resources.
Learn how to be alone without feeling lonely.
Learn to value silence, solitude, nature.
Learn how to apply spiritual laws to material affairs.

Your destiny is:

To study, meditate, and become wise.
To attain a workable philosophy of life.
To help others gain insight.

Your success:

Depends on intuition, faith, study, and reflection. Opportunity often comes to you rather than through what you seek for yourself.

George Harrison, Rock Star, February 24, 1943
(2 + 6 + 8 = 16/7 Life Path)

At the time of George's death, his family issued a statement: "He left this world as he lived it, conscious of God, fearless of death, and at peace, surrounded by family and friends." He often said, "Everything else can wait, but the search for God cannot wait, and love one another." George's life was a spiritual quest. He led the other Beatles to India to take up meditation with the Maharishi. He communicated his search for inner peace in such songs as the 1971 number-one hit "My Sweet Lord." He also staged the Concert for Bangladesh, the first instance of a charity event in rock music.

Other Celebrated Persons with a 7 Life Path

Ansel Adams, photographer	2/20/1902
Eric Clapton, musician	3/30/1945
Tommy Franks, U.S. general	6/17/1945
Paul Gauguin, painter	6/7/1848
Robert H. Goddard, scientist	10/5/1882
Jennifer Jones, actress	3/2/1919
Ida Lupino, actress-director	2/4/1918
Susan Sarandon, actress	10/4/1946

Teresa of Avila, mystic   3/28/1515
Voltaire, writer   11/21/1694

The 8 Life Path

"I've been rich and I've been poor; Believe me, honey, rich is better."
    —**Sophie Tucker,** singer, January 13, 1884
    (1 + 4 + 3 = 8 life path)

"No man becomes rich unless he enriches others."
    —**Andrew Carnegie,** steel industrialist,
November 25, 1835 (2 + 7 + 8 = 17/8 life path)

If 8 is your life path, you need to:

Develop drive and ambition.

Learn to think big and strive for success.

Learn how to make, save, and accumulate money.

Develop executive talents—the capacity to manage, organize, direct, and lead.

Learn to manage your own affairs—and get results: to be productive, capable, and efficient regardless of struggle.

Your destiny is:

To develop expertise in business.

To take charge, achieve, use power wisely, make the most of your talents.

To learn the true value of money.

Your success:

Depends on good judgment, drive, determination, fortitude, and thinking big.

Douglas MacArthur, U.S. Military Leader, January 26, 1880 (1 + 26/8 + 17/8 = 17/8 Life Path)

General Douglas MacArthur seemed destined from birth to hold positions of power and executive responsibility: as superintendent at West Point, as army chief of staff, as commander in chief of the Pacific Command in World War II, as administrator of postwar Japan, and as commander of the UN forces during the Korean War. After he recovered from measles at age four, his mother would say to him at bedtime, "You must grow up to be a great man . . . like your father and Robert E. Lee." That is exactly what MacArthur did! Most critics agree that he possessed a superior intelligence, rare command ability, and a zealous dedication to duty, honor, and country.

Other Celebrated Persons with an 8 Life Path

Edward Albee, playwright	3/12/1928
Warren Beatty, actor	3/30/1937
Jane Fonda, actress	12/21/1937
Robert Fulton, inventor	11/14/1765
John Galsworthy, writer	8/14/1867
Larry Hagman, actor	9/21/1931
Lyndon Johnson, U.S. president	8/27/1908

Rollo May, psychiatrist	4/21/1909
Michelangelo, sculptor	3/6/1475
Rembrandt, painter	7/15/1606

The 9 Life Path

"I don't know what your destiny will be, but one thing I know, the only ones among you who will be really happy are those who will have sought and found how to serve."

—**Albert Schweitzer,** humanitarian, January 14, 1875 (1 + 14/5 + 1875/3 = 9 life path)

If 9 is your life path, you must:

Learn to love and serve your fellow man.

Learn to be a humanitarian.

Give others your love, sympathy, help, and under-standing without thought of reward.

Learn to put the common good before self.

Cultivate selflessness.

Develop your creative abilities.

Your destiny is:

To meet people from all walks of life and to relate to them—to empathize.

To do your part to eliminate prejudice; to show that despite differences in race, color, or creed, we are all members of the planet earth.

Your success:

Depends on your finding out what you have in common with the greater whole—then you will find yourself and your destiny.

The common humanity we all share was the subject matter of painter **Norman Rockwell** (2/3/1894). Through **Carl Jung** (7/26/1875), we learned that we all share a collective unconscious. **Charles Lindbergh** (2/4/1902) is remembered for the first nonstop solo flight across the Atlantic, but in his later years he was flying around the world again on behalf of endangered species, wild places, and vanishing tribal people. Former U.S. president **Jimmy Carter** (10/1/1924) is revered as a champion of international human rights. Millionaires **Al Kroc** (10/5/1902) and **Brooke Astor** (3/31/1902) shared their wealth with the less fortunate. All these individuals were born with a life path of 9.

Other Celebrated Persons with a 9 Life Path

Johann Sebastian Bach, composer	3/31/1685
Brigitte Bardot, actress	9/28/1934
E. M. Forster, writer	1/1/1879
Shirley MacLaine, actress	4/24/1934
Henry Moore, sculptor	7/30/1898
Jack Nicklaus, golfer	1/21/1940

Camille Paglia, critic	4/2/1947
Gloria Steinem, feminist	3/25/1934
Diego Velázquez, painter	6/6/1599
Frank Lloyd Wright, architect	6/8/1867

The 11/2 Life Path

"All that we see or seem is but a dream within a dream."

—**Edgar Allan Poe,** writer, January 19, 1809
$(1 + 19/1 + 9 = 11$ life path)

If 11 is your life path (also read 2 life path), you need to:

Learn to heed your intuition, and then you'll be at the right place at the right time to meet your destiny.

Develop your talents, as you are capable of new discoveries, inventions, and achievements in the arts, sciences, and social services.

Search for new truths beyond the accepted realities; have faith in a higher guidance.

Realize that you have a mission in life that will be found by listening to your inner voice—that you can be a channel through which the world receives a new revelation.

Your destiny is:

To be the inspired leader.

To hold fast to your ideals.

To "reveal messages from above."

Your success:

Depends on idealism, intuition, inspiration, inventiveness, and spirituality.

In the midst of the Depression, there was a bright note, and that was child star **Shirley Temple (Black)** (4/23/1938), Hollywood's top box-office attraction from 1935 through 1938. Her spirited singing ("On the Good Ship Lollipop") and her dimples and blond ringlets inspired hope and optimism. In later years, Shirley served as U.S. ambassador to both Ghana (1974–75) and Czechoslovakia (1989–92), in keeping with the fact that 11, the number of her life path, reduces to 2, the number of the diplomat. **Rosa Parks** (2/4/1913), whose refusal to give up her seat on a public bus to a white man precipitated the 1955 Montgomery, Alabama, bus boycott, is recognized as the spark that ignited the U.S. civil rights movement.

Other Celebrated Persons with an 11 Life Path

Chet Baker, jazz great	12/23/1929
George Gordon, Lord Byron, poet	1/22/1788
Maria Callas, opera diva	12/2/1923
Bill Clinton, U.S. president	8/19/1946
Jean Paul Getty, entrepreneur	12/15/1892
Martha Graham, choreographer	5/11/1894
Michael Jordan, basketball star	2/17/1963
Norman Mailer, writer	1/31/1923

Wolfgang Amadeus Mozart, composer   1/27/1756
J. M. W. Turner, artist   4/23/1775
Jules Verne, writer   2/8/1828
Antonio Vivaldi, composer   3/4/1678
Prince William, British royalty   6/21/1982

The 22/4 Life Path

"One man's magic is another man's engineering."
   —**Robert A. Heinlein,** writer, July 7, 1907
                  (7 + 7 + 8 = 22 life path)

Many people with a 22/4 life path will operate at the level of 4 rather than 22. With a 4 life path, you will find meaning in life through work. As a 22, though, your work will have an impact on the progress of humanity. For example, biologist **Rachel Carson** (22 life path) wrote *Silent Spring,* the book that sparked the ecology movement.

If 22 is your life path (also read 4 life path), you need to:

Find practical ways to turn your visionary ideas into realities, because you have the potential to create, invent, or implement projects, ideas, and works of art that will benefit, transform, and inspire the human race.

Your destiny is:

To become the practical idealist who builds cities,

plans highways, funds global projects, or in some other enlightened way functions on a universal or even cosmic level.

Your success:

Depends on thinking globally, using power spiritually, being the humanitarian, doing something to contribute to humanity's betterment.

Peter the Great, Russian Emperor, June 9, 1672
(6 + 9+ 1672/7 = 22/4 Life Path)

During Peter's 25-year reign, he began a series of reforms that revamped industry, commerce, culture, technology, and administration. He turned Russia into a great power. Not only was Peter an original thinker, but he also had an enormous capacity for hard work. Peter saw himself as the servant of Russia and dedicated his life to its betterment. He instituted the first Russian newspaper, an academy of sciences, and was the first czar to sponsor education along secular lines. Peter was visionary, exuberant, courageous, industrious, shrewd, and iron-willed—truly "the great"!

Other Celebrated Persons with a 22 Life Path

Abigail Adams, U.S. first lady	11/22/1744
Anne Bancroft	9/17/1931
Barbara Bush, U.S.first lady	6/8/1925
James Fenimore Cooper, writer	9/15/1789

David Duchovny, actor	8/7/1960
Roger Ebert, film critic	6/18/1942
Hugh Hefner, publisher	4/9/1926
Paul McCartney, rock star	6/18/1942
Will Smith, actor	9/25/1968
Barbara Stanwyck, actress	7/16/1907

More About the Life Path

If your life path is the same number as your soul urge: Reincarnation theory teaches that the soul chooses its path in life. From this perspective, you have come back to earth for the express purpose of fulfilling the potentialities of your life path. Since you will receive opportunities to achieve what you want from life, you will have the opportunity to live a life that is indeed rewarding.

The danger here, though, is that life may be too easy for you. As a result, you may settle for only the fringe benefits of your life path and may not embrace the full potentialities of the principles associated with its number.

A belief in reincarnation theory, though, is not a prerequisite for believing in the principles of numerology. To look at what I just said in another way, you were born with a soul urge that is the same number as your destiny number. That fact alone ensures that you'll enthusiastically meet your destiny.

If your life path number is the same as your expression, you are well equipped to meet the challenges and opportunities of your life path. Because the expression indicates natural abilities, life will give you the opportunities to develop and explore your potential to the fullest. In other words, your parents gave you the perfect name to meet and fulfill your destiny.

If your life path number is the same as your quiet self, it will be your intuition that puts you on the right track to fulfilling your destiny. No matter what your life path number, the fact that it is the same as your quiet self indicates a creative turn to your destiny. Again, if you'll listen to your intuition, you'll be at the right place at the right time when destiny calls. On a less positive note, take care that fantasy doesn't keep you from seeing a real opportunity when it does arrive.

If your life path number is the same as one of your missing numbers: You may feel that numerology missed the boat when it comes to figuring you out. Because we tend to shy away from the experiences necessary to understand our missing numbers, you may shy away from confronting the meanings of your life path, your destiny. In fact, you may literally stumble onto the meaning of your life path, and most likely it will occur at a time when you are seemingly moving in the opposite direction of the path that your life number indicates you must take.

CHAPTER 7

CYCLES, PINNACLES, AND CHALLENGE

✿ ✿
✿

People can always change their names, but they can never change their date of birth. For this reason, it is important to learn all you can about your life path. In chapter 1, you learned how to find your life path number by adding up the day, the month, and the year of your birth. Now you're going to look at the numbers that make up that life path number.

The number of the month, the day, and the year—each of these is like a sub-life-path number operating for a span of approximately 28 years. These numbers are called *cycles*. The number of each cycle tells you of the opportunities and the kinds of people you will meet during the span of time the number operates.

The road to an understanding of your life path is seldom a direct one. For example, suppose you were born on March 4, 1963 (3/4/1963). You then have an 8 life path, and your cycle numbers are 3, 4, and 1 (1963 reduced to 10 and then to a single digit). From birth to age 28, the accent is on the development of creative talents (3). From 28 to 56, the accent switches to the development of self-discipline (4). From 56 on, you will need the self-reliance of 1. In short, you must develop the qualities of creativity, self-discipline, and independence in order to achieve an understanding of the 8 life path.

Remember that cycles deal with qualities to be developed, people you will meet, and environmental conditions, but not with events. The lower your cycle number, the easier it is to deal with as a child. The higher your cycle number, the easier it is to deal with as an adult. Go back to chapter 6; read what it says there about the life path numbers that match in digit. For example, if you're concerned about a 3 cycle, read what it says in chapter 6 about the 3 life path.

Pinnacles

What can you expect from the opportunities that come your way as indicated by your cycle numbers? What kinds of events will highlight your life path? For the answers to these questions, you need to find the *pinnacle* numbers.

The pinnacles are derived from the three cycle numbers, and there are four of them:

- The 1st pinnacle is the sum of the 1st and 2nd cycles.

- The 2nd pinnacle is the sum of the 2nd and 3rd cycles.
- The 3rd pinnacle is the sum of the 1st and 2nd pinnacles.
- The 4th pinnacle is the sum of the 1st and 3rd cycles.

All of these sums are reduced to single digits, unless the sum is 11 or 22.

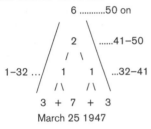

```
              6 ...........50 on

                2      \ ......41–50
              /   \
1–32 .../    1     1    \ ...32–41
         /  / \   / \    \
        3  +  7  +  3
        March 25 1947
```

Once you memorize the rules for finding the pinnacles, it's a simple thing to set up a chart. Just put down the cycle numbers, then write the pinnacle numbers above them as shown. Beside each pinnacle number, write down the numbers for the time span they will be in effect. The sample birth date belongs to Elton John.

To find how long the **1st pinnacle** will be in effect, subtract the number of the life path from 36. (If your life path is 11 or 22, reduce it to a single digit before subtracting from 36.) The remainder gives you the number of years of influence of the 1st pinnacle. For example, Elton John has a life path number of 4. Subtract 4 from 36; the remainder is 32. Elton's 1st pinnacle lasts from birth to age 32.

The **2nd pinnacle** always lasts for a period of nine years and begins when the 1st pinnacle ends. Elton's 2nd pinnacle covers the years from 32 to 41.

The **3rd pinnacle** always lasts for a period of nine years and begins when the 2nd pinnacle ends. Elton's 3rd pinnacle covers the years from 41 to 50.

The **4th pinnacle** always begins when the 3rd pinnacle ends, and is in effect until death.

Pinnacles describe peak experiences. For example, if you have a 3 as a 1st pinnacle, a poem that gets published in a school magazine, parties with friends, or a trip to New York City to see a Broadway play may strike you as highlights. A 3 pinnacle doesn't guarantee all happy events, but what will stand out in life will be the happy experiences. Conversely, 7 as a 1st pinnacle may mean that moments spent alone on a ski trail or doing a biology lab experiment may strike you as important, even though you have your share of dating, parties, and exciting trips. In all probability, the fact that these experiences stand out in your consciousness means that you will accomplish something of the nature of that number during the length of that pinnacle. With 3 as a 1st pinnacle, at 14 it may be a love of writing that turns into a writing career by 28. Sometimes it isn't until the very last year of the pinnacle that its meaning is recognized and understood. Usually this happens as many little peaks culminate in a final acceptance of the period's significance.

These peak experiences come from your interaction with the world. You may have a 4 soul urge that is serious, and yet with a 3 pinnacle, what strikes you about life as it is being lived are the happy experiences. Your soul urge is your natural perspective toward life, but experience—which is signified by the pinnacle as part of the life path—has resulted in you treasuring the lighter moments of life as you find and create them.

A 1 pinnacle means you look at the conditions of your cycle number in terms of your own self-development. You may be a loner, yet 1 is consistent with the growing-up years. This is the time when you should learn self-reliance and be concerned with the growth of your own individuality. Later in life, a 1 pinnacle means a new start.

A 2 pinnacle means peak experiences come in close association with another. You may be impressionable and inclined to follow the example of the person you just met. It is not a time for pushing the self forward. When you are cooperative and helpful, life goes your way. You face life with another, perhaps a partner.

A 3 pinnacle at the start of life delays maturity until this number changes. You should seek opportunities along creative lines, as this number is unfavorable for studying (7) or facing harsh reality (4). No matter how hard life is, you'll come through it with childlike trust in the joys of living.

A **4 pinnacle** at the start of life means early maturity. At a young age, you receive more than your share of the workload, which makes you view experience practically and realistically. You learn to take life seriously, but you may feel deprived of the fun of growing up. At any age, this pinnacle means peak experiences through work and by facing reality.

A **5 pinnacle** at the start of life means you take an adventurous attitude toward life. You'll have your share of unexpected changes. Sometimes you court danger and trouble as well as romantic adventures. Peak experiences are those that differ from the ordinary. Like 3, 5 is not a good number for studying (7), self-discipline (4), or settling down (6).

A **6 pinnacle** at the start of life means a long stay in the parental nest or hometown. You tend to fall in with the group or to hold on to parental standards. You view experience moralistically and idealistically. The times when you help loved ones with their responsibilities may give you a sense of both belonging and accomplishment. 6 is the best marriage vibration.

A **7 pinnacle** at the start of life makes you feel separated, perhaps isolated, from your contemporaries. At times you may feel lonely, as you tend to go off by yourself. At an early age, you're concerned with the meaning of life, and peak experiences center on the insights about life that you gain by observing it from the sidelines. Later in life, this signifies intellectual accomplishment and investigation of occult subjects.

An 8 pinnacle at the start of life means you look at experience with the attitude of one who wants to get ahead, earn money, and become an important person. This you'll achieve, but when the pinnacle number changes, it may be hard to follow up on your early success. In later life, 8 always brings with it a chance for money and recognition.

A 9 pinnacle at the start of life is difficult. Your interest in the whole world makes you seem old before your time. You learn to place everyone's interests ahead of your own. Often there is a sense of loss with this pinnacle. It signifies disappointment in personal matters, but reward in larger matters. Later in life, you bring a vision of the whole to the particular, which leads to artistic success or involvement with humanitarian concerns.

An 11 pinnacle at the start of life puts you on a different wavelength, and many people find your viewpoint either strange or inspiring. You may be bewildered by the real world and live a life of fantasy. There is fame for those who hold on to their ideals. This is a time for inspiration, spiritual insight, and inventive ability. Most people, though, experience this vibration as a 2.

A **22 pinnacle** brings opportunity for magnificent humanitarian accomplishment through the practical implementation of ideals. Most people, though, experience this vibration as a 4.

More About the Pinnacles

If a pinnacle is the same number as your life path, opportunities will come now to meet your destiny—or at the very least you will come to a greater awareness of what the meaning and purpose of your life are.

If a pinnacle is the same number as your birthday number, you can expect major career developments during the duration of this pinnacle.

If a pinnacle is the same number as your soul urge, you will find opportunities to get what you want from life. It should be a very fulfilling time and one in which you'll attain a great degree of personal happiness.

If a pinnacle is the same number as your quiet self, it will be a time when dreams come true or a time when fantasies may take hold. You'll need the ability to distinguish between fact and wishful thinking during this period.

If a pinnacle is the same number as your expression, you'll meet with opportunities to showcase your talents.

If a pinnacle is the same number as a karmic lack, it will be a very significant period of personal development and growth. Though you may meet with some obstacles, challenges, or even setbacks during this period, these will serve as catalysts to give you a better understanding of the principles that lie behind your missing number. Life now is giving you the opportunity to pick up the qualities of your missing number, to make them an integral part of your being. After this pinnacle is finished, your missing number should no longer be considered as missing. The qualities and abilities associated with your missing number should now be a part of your nature, never again to trip you up as they did in the years before. Before this pinnacle, you may have known something was wrong, but you may not have had a clue about how to go about correcting it.

Challenges

Life has it low points as well as its peak experiences. To find out about potential obstacles that could throw us off the course of the life path, we need to learn the numbers of the *challenges*.

```
            March   25   1947
              3      7    3
               \    / \   /
(Ages 1–32)    4       4   (Ages 32–41)
                 \   /
The Challenge >>>  0       always (strongest ages 41–50)
                   0       (age 51 on)
```

Like the pinnacles, the numbers of the challenges are derived from the cycles. Instead of adding, as we do to obtain the pinnacles, we subtract.

- To find the number of the 1st subchallenge, subtract the smaller number of the 1st cycle and the 2nd cycle from the larger. The 1st subchallenge lasts the same length of the time as the 1st pinnacle.
- Do the same with 2nd and 3rd cycle numbers, and your remainder is the 2nd subchallenge. The 2nd subchallenge is in effect the same length of time as the 2nd pinnacle.
- Repeat the formula with the 1st and 2nd subchallenges, and the remainder is the challenge. The challenge is in effect always, but is felt most intensely while the 3rd pinnacle is in effect.
- To find the 4th subchallenge, subtract the smaller number of the year and the month from the larger. The 4th subchallenge is in effect the same length of time as the 4th pinnacle.

1

With 1 as a challenge, people with stronger wills may try to control your life, telling you what to do and what not to. Often you don't know what's owed the self. At times, you can be vacillating, and at other times you may be pigheaded. When you insist on having your own way, you usually butt heads with others, arousing opposition and maybe even enmity. On the other hand, when you try to please everybody, you end up not pleasing anybody, including yourself.

In order not to be a bully or a pushover, you need a greater awareness of your uniqueness and true worth as an individual. Then you will neither step on others nor be stepped upon. And you will gain respect for being the person you are, which after all is what you wanted in the first place. Meanwhile, your behavior may fluctuate from being too accommodating to being overly self-insistent.

An essential food supplement for you is vitamin A.

2

With 2 as a challenge, you take life's problems too personally. You're easily hurt and often think people are being unkind to you when they're simply going about their business. You find it hard to forgive others when they are thoughtless or inconsiderate. Somebody doesn't return your phone call and you let it ruin your whole day.

An essential food supplement for you is vitamin B.

3

With 3 as a challenge, social contact scares you. You either become reclusive or overplay your hand with offensive and outlandish behavior. You share this challenge with Howard Hughes and Greta Garbo, both of whom wanted to be left alone—and were! The tide goes against you when you don't take care of your physical appearance, and when you forget to smile.

An essential food supplement for you is vitamin C.

4

With 4 as a challenge, you may be straitlaced, too conservative, and a square. You may be a person who doesn't like to work or, conversely, a workaholic. Your challenge is self-discipline. If you make schedules and stick to them, most of your problems will disappear. If you're too conservative, however, loosen up a bit.

An essential food supplement for you is vitamin D.

5

With 5 as a challenge, you either hold on too long or let go too soon. You have to learn when to change and what to change. You shouldn't stay in a rut; nor should you change just because you're restless. The impulse to satisfy an urge as soon as it arises can get you into trouble. You may be the person who's tried everything once and has nothing to show for it. Your challenge is the five senses.

An essential food supplement for you is vitamin E.

6

With 6 as a challenge, you may be overpositive about right and wrong, and can be smug and self-righteous. You cannot expect others to live up to your moral standards. In some cases, this challenge means domestic and marital problems that interfere with the main objectives of the life path.

An essential food supplement for you is vitamin E.

7

With 7 as a challenge, you are your own worst enemy. At war with yourself, you find yourself in constant rebellion against existing conditions. Yet you do nothing to better them, and you choose to remain aloof and indifferent. Fear, loneliness, depression, and skepticism must give way to a more optimistic view of life.

Multiple vitamins and minerals are important food supplements for you.

8

With 8 as a challenge, you either disregard material affairs or are overly concerned about money and power. You may think all your problems would disappear with more money, yet an attitude that places financial considerations before all else has a problem with values, not finances.

Guard against overweight, high cholesterol, and high blood pressure. You need physical exercise.

9

There is no 9 challenge, as no single digit can be subtracted from another single digit leaving a result of 9.

0

With 0 as a challenge, if you'll trust your intuition to guide you, there is no challenge for you.

Subchallenges

For definitions of the subchallenges, read definitions for the challenges that match the number of the subchallenge.

Example: Elton John

To understand what Elton's 1st subchallenge of 4 means, read what is written about the 4 challenge, but apply its meanings to the shorter time span of the subchallenge.

```
            Elton John
          March   25   1947
              3     7    3
               \   / \  /
 (Ages 1–32)    4     4      (Ages 32–41)
                 \   /
The Challenge >>>  0      always (strongest ages 41–50)
           0   (Age 51 on)
```

For interpretation, *always interpret the pinnacle number in conjunction with the challenge that is in effect during the same time span.* For example, from birth to age 32, Elton was under the combined influences of a 1 pinnacle and a 4 subchallenge.

Suggested Interpretation

With 1 as a first pinnacle, Elton's peak experiences centered on establishing his identity, finding and doing his own thing—but with 4 as a first subchallenge he had to be careful not to become a workaholic or to go to the other extreme of becoming lazy.

We know from Elton's track record of success in the music industry that work (4) became a vehicle for him to express his individuality (1). If it had gone the other way, no doubt he would have been working at a dreary job (4) that could have stamped out his individuality (1) because it offered him no hope to be his own person. If that had been the case, we probably never would have heard of Elton John.

The challenge itself (not the subchallenges) should also be compared to the number of the life path. A look at the challenge number can give us insights into possible obstacles that could interfere with achieving the main goals of the life path. For example, a person with a 2 challenge and an 8 life path might find oversensitivity a drawback in getting ahead in a 8-type business world.

CHAPTER 8

THE DAY YOU WERE BORN

If You Were Born on the 1st

Behavior and Personality Traits

You are self-reliant, strong-willed, and independent.

You are a better planner than doer.

You are both practical and idealistic.

You are inclined to refer most things to your head rather than your heart.

You are capable of great devotion, but may not always be demonstrative.

You have leadership qualities, creativity, drive, and the courage of your convictions; you are pioneering.

You love to shine, to stand out as number one.

Who stands supreme among the goddesses of Hollywood? None other than actress **Marilyn Monroe** (6/1/1926). Other women born on the 1st who have distinguished themselves as unique individuals are:

Mother Jones, labor union agitator	5/1/1830
George Sand, writer	7/1/1804
Mary Martin, actress	12/1/1913
Alanis Morrisette, singer	6/1/1974
Dinah Shore, singer	3/1/1917
Betsy Ross, flag maker	1/1/1752
Hildegarde, singer	2/1/1905
Olivia de Havilland, actress	7/1/1916
Julie Andrews, actress	10/1/1935

Vocational Indicators

No matter what field you are in, you will always be an individualist, someone who puts your personal stamp on what you do. *Main principles to be utilized in career:* initiative, originality, the ability to go it alone. You will always have many irons in the fire, but you should focus on one main interest. You will prosper in a job that keeps you active and allows you the freedom to be creative.

Independent filmmaker extraordinaire **Woody Allen** (12/1/1931) always puts his personal stamp on whatever he undertakes in film. Writer **J. D. Salinger** (1/1/1931), author of *The Catcher in the Rye*, celebrates the uniqueness of the individual in his fiction. 1 as the male principle is best epitomized by film star **Clark Gable** (2/1/1901), known in Hollywood as a "man's man." Heroism and courage are associated with 1, traits that are the subject matter of **Stephen Crane's** (11/1/1871) novel *The Red Badge of Courage*. It should come as no surprise that the creator of Tarzan the ape-man, **Edgar Rice Burroughs**, was born on September 1, 1875.

If You Were Born on the 2nd

Behavior and Personality Traits

You are cooperative, courteous, and diplomatic.

You would rather make love than war.

You like to be cuddled, petted, and fussed over.

You are sensitive, imaginative, and intuitive.

You have good taste and love to collect nice things.

You love poetry, moonlight, candlelight, and places with a romantic atmosphere.

You have strong maternal or paternal instincts; you are a wonderful homemaker.

You work well in partnerships; sometimes you're a leaner.

You are a good peacemaker and go-between.

You may be a good dancer.

Myrna Loy (8/2/1905) first captured the public's fancy with her femininity and easy charm in 1934's *The Thin Man*, in which she and William Powell played the husband-and-wife detective team of Nick and Nora Charles. Soon after that film, Men Must Marry Myrna Loy clubs sprung up all across the United States; by 1936, she had become Hollywood's top female box-office attraction. Five sequels to *The Thin Man* followed, in which Myrna continued her portrayal of Nora as one of the most likable, cooperative, fun-loving spouses ever to hit the Hollywood screen. It's not surprising that from 1934 on, Myrna Loy was known as "the perfect wife."

Vocational Indicators

Art, music, writing poetry or fiction, and dancing are likely to be avocations and possibly vocations. *Main principles to be utilized in career:* cooperation, diplomacy, attention to details. Attract what you want through friendliness rather than aggressively pursuing your goals. You work better in partnership or as someone's guy or gal Friday than on your own.

It was *The Common Sense Book of Baby and Child Care,* first published in 1946 by Dr. Benjamin Spock (5/2/1903) and in print ever since, that took the principles of number 2—love, cuddling, and nurturing—and made them into the standard for raising children. In addition, in keeping with the peace-loving qualities of number 2, Spock was an antiwar activist and a renowned pacifist. He also had strong thoughts about partnerships another number 2 keyword: "The surest measure of a man's or woman's maturity is the harmony, style, joy, and dignity he creates in his marriage, and the pleasure and inspiration he provides for his spouse."

If You Were Born on the 3rd

Behavior and Personality Traits

You are versatile with a variety of interests.
You are quite a talker and good raconteur.
You love to mix and mingle; to gad about.
You are cheerful, optimistic, and spontaneous.
You are talented, sociable, and imaginative.
You have vitality and bounce back quickly from illness.
You are easily satisfied and always make the best of
  whatever conditions you find yourself in.
You are at your best before an audience.
You need hobbies to offset a tendency to be restless.

3 is carefree, relaxed, easygoing, and laid-back. And don't those words aptly describe the singing style of crooners **Bing Crosby, Andy Williams,** and **Tony Bennett**—all of whom were born on the 3rd? The job of 3 is to entertain, to help us see the silver lining, as Bing Crosby (5/3/1903) has successfully done with his rendition of "White Christmas"; Andy Williams (12/3/1928) with his "Moon River"; and Tony Bennett (8/3/1926) with his always heartrending "I Left My Heart in San Francisco." On the distaff side, cabaret singer **Mabel Mercer** (2/3/1900) was known for the intimacy of her phrasings. Just before her death in 1984, Frank Sinatra said, "She taught me everything I know."

Vocational Indicators

Any field involving communications is your natural milieu. *Main principles to be utilized in career:* Charm will open many important doors for you. Friends will be helpful to you in business. A cheerful, optimistic attitude helps.

Success often comes to 3 with the written or spoken word. Talk show hosts **Dennis Miller** (11/3/1953), **Joey Bishop** (2/3/1918), and **Montel Williams** (7/3/1956) were born on the 3rd, as were newspaper columnists **Dorothy Kilgallen** (7/3/1913), **Dave Barry** (7/3/1947), and **Emily Post** (10/3/1872). Novelists **Gore Vidal** (10/3/1925), **James Michener** (2/3/1907), and **Joseph Conrad** (12/3/1857) were also born on the 3rd. The film *Catch Me If You Can* is about onetime con man **Frank Abagnale** (3/3/1948), who used his verbal skills to successfully impersonate an airline pilot, doctor, lawyer, and teacher all before the age of 18. Frank now lectures at the FBI's Financial Crimes Unit.

If You Were Born on the 4th

Behavior and Personality Traits

You love home, family, and country and often espouse conservative values.

You are hardworking, thorough, and dutiful.

You are responsible, practical, serious, and a realist.

You are conscientious, a careful planner, and may be a stickler for duty.

You are cautious and unlikely to take a chance unless you're sure of the outcome.

You may be set in your opinions and inclined to force them on others.

You may be inarticulate or inhibited in expressing your feelings, especially regarding romance.

"You can spend a lifetime, and if you're honest with yourself, never once was your work perfect."
　　—**Charlton Heston,** actor, October 4, 1923

"One thing I never want to be accused of is not working."
　　—**Don Shula,** football coach, January 4, 1930

"It is the first of all problems for a man to find out what kind of work he is to do in the universe."
　　—**Thomas Carlyle,** historian, December 4, 1795

"The soul's joy lies in doing."
　　—**Percy Bysshe Shelley,** poet, August 4, 1792

Vocational Indicators

Music, painting, and sculpture may be avocations, if not vocations; you are usually at home in the business world and work well in the corporate structure. *Main principles to be utilized in career:* patience, self-discipline, attention to duty and details, technical expertise.

People born on the 4th excel as teachers. **Horace Mann** (5/4/1776), the great American advocate of public education, was president of Antioch College (1852–59); **Nathan Pusey** (4/3/1907) revitalized the teaching of humanities while president of Harvard University (1953–71); and **A. Bartlett Giamatti** (4/4/1938) was president of Yale (1978–87). On the football field, **Knute Rockne** (3/4/1888) led Notre Dame to national prominence during his 13-year tenure as coach; **Al Davis** (7/4/1929) transformed the Oakland Raiders into pro football's top team as head coach and then owner; and **Don Shula** (1/4/1930), as coach of the Baltimore Colts (1963–69) and the Miami Dolphins (1970–95), is the winningest NFL head coach ever, with a career mark of 347–173–6 (.665).

If You Were Born on the 5th

Behavior and Personality Traits

You love change, travel, and adventure.

You probably would agree with this quote from playwright **Sam Shepard** (11/5/1943): "The road's what counts. Don't worry about where it's going."

You are freedom loving, versatile, progressive, active, adaptable, imaginative, and impulsive.

You are happy-go-lucky and a "people person."

You are independent and do not like to be tied down.

You may be inclined to many romantic attachments.

You tend to go from one thing to another—with great rapidity; you're opportunistic and resourceful. You are multifaceted, outgoing, entertaining.

Actress **Raquel Welch** (9/5/1940) once said, "Being a sex symbol was rather like being a convict." Be that as it may, sex or a sexual image often plays a pivotal role in the lives of those born on the 5th. **Rex Harrison** (3/5/1908) in his younger days obtained the moniker sexy Rexy. And most of us have seen actor-model **Mark Wahlberg** (5/5/1971) in his Calvin Klein underwear in various print and billboard ads. **Jennifer Jason Leigh** (2/5/1962) was nominated for two Critics Circle Awards for playing prostitutes in both *Miami Blues* and *Last Exit to Brooklyn* in 1990. She also played a phone sex operator in Robert Altman's *Short Cuts*. As she once said, "I could never play the ingénue, the girl next door. That would be a bore."

Vocational Indicators

Main principles to be utilized in career: Any field involving travel, speculation, and constant change is your natural milieu. You do not like to be tied down by a desk job; have natural sales ability and promotional skills; are at ease with others and will do well in fields where the personal touch is a factor.

People born on the 5th often experiment before settling on a career. This was certainly true for legendary film director **John Huston** (8/5/1906), who began his career as a Hollywood scriptwriter in 1931. Prior to that, he had been a pro boxer, a soldier in the Mexican cavalry, a reporter, an editor of a magazine, an author of short stories and plays, and an actor. **P(hineas) T(aylor) Barnum** (7/5/1810), who popularized such amusements as the public museum, the music concert, and the three-ring circus, held a variety of sales jobs, managed a boardinghouse, and ran a newspaper before finding his true calling as the world's greatest showman.

If You Were Born on the 6th

Behavior and Personality Traits

You have a need to love and be loved; you will lavish your affection on your chosen one.

You have a love of home and children, but children of your own are not necessary for your happiness.

You need to feel appreciated and can feel miserable when criticized.

You may have a fear of poverty.

You are mental, but not necessarily intellectual.

You may have a tendency to exaggerate.

You must have people around you.

You must live in an atmosphere of harmony.

Loretta Young (1/6/1913) appeared in nearly 100

films. Invariably she played the strong-willed heroine with firm principles. She refused to play what she called "unsavory" roles, and a Loretta Young movie usually had a happy ending. She achieved her greatest popularity, however, as the first lady of dramatic television with *The Loretta Young Show*. The story lines on her TV shows were based on moral themes. In addition, she would end each episode with an uplifting quotation, usually from the Bible. Though critics derided the moralistic melodrama as "Sunday night soap opera," the series became one of the most popular on television. Loretta Young's career indeed reflected the principles of 6, her birthday number.

Vocational Indicators

You have strong artistic and literary inclinations. Many successful actors and film directors are born on the 6th. You work well with others and groups. You have a social consciousness. *Main principles to be utilized in career:* Fields that cater to the needs of people are your milieu. You do best if given a free rein and do not function well in an unfriendly working environment. Usually you are successful in getting financial backing for your endeavors.

Social worker and political activist **Jane Addams** (9/6/1860) founded Hull House in Chicago in 1896 to serve the needs of the immigrant poor. Within a few years, Hull House offered medical care, child care, and legal aid, as well as classes teaching immigrants English and vocational skills. Addams was also active in the suffragist movement, worked hard on the behalf of economic reforms, and advocated research aimed at determining the causes of poverty and crime. She was involved in the founding of the American Civil Liberties Union in 1920. In 1931, she became the first American woman to be awarded the Nobel Peace Prize. Jane Addams epitomized the principles of 6.

If You Were Born on the 7th

Behavior and Personality Traits

You do not wear your heart on your sleeve.

You are a private and reserved person; you can be the silent type; sometimes you're aloof or secretive.

You are analytical and discriminating, but may not always see the other person's point of view.

You need to spend a part of each day alone to meditate, reflect, rest, study, and tune in.

You often have good judgment in money matters.

You may be psychic and should follow your hunches.

You need as good an education as possible.

You are introspective, unobtrusive, and tend to think before you act.

You are a perfectionist.

"I'm kind of private, but not aloof. I just like being by myself. I don't open up to a lot of people."
　　　　　—**Toni Braxton,** singer, October 7, 1967

"Privacy is something that I've come to respect."
　　　　　—**David Duchovny,** actor, August 7, 1960

"Sit still and watch, look, be aware, and you will learn many things."
　　　　　—**Gary Cooper,** actor, May 7, 1901

"I shut my eyes in order to see."
　　　　　—**Paul Gauguin,** painter, June 7, 1848

"Truth is within ourselves."
　　　　　—**Robert Browning,** poet, May 7, 1812

Vocational Indicators

Main principles to be utilized in career: You work best in fields requiring mental analysis and in-depth thinking; usually you do better on your own than in partnership; you're often a specialist in your field. You are at home in scientific, academic, philosophical, and spiritual fields, and talented as a researcher. You have an ability to read between the lines—to get to the heart of the matter.

Introspection and soul searching are associated with 7—qualities reflected in the music of **Joni Mitchell** (11/7/1943), who taught us how to look at life from "both sides now." Country singer **Garth Brooks** (2/7/1962) bade us to look deeply at the meanings of life, love, and death in such hit songs as "If Tomorrow Never Comes" and "The Dance."

Nothing, though, quite compares to the incredible heartfelt vocalizations of the Lady of the Blues, **Billie Holiday** (4/7/1915). As singer **Sylvia Syms** noted about Billie, "Her education was her search for the truth within her. She used all the things that happened in her life and made them work for her in her music."

If You Were Born on the 8th

Behavior and Personality Traits

You have terrific drive; you can organize and direct.

You have a flair for moneymaking.

You are inclined to large gestures; you may be fond of display, of showing off.

You are practical and dependable.

You have good business sense and can manage large concerns.

You are ambitious for achievement, money, power, authority, influence, and recognition.

You don't mind the struggle involved in getting ahead.

You thrive on challenges.

You can overdo on red meat and rich foods.

People born on the 8th often meet with situations

involving the use of power. Such was the case with U.S. president **Harry S Truman** (5/8/1884), upon whose shoulders it fell to decide whether or not to employ the atomic bomb. But Truman was not one to shirk responsibilities. As the sign of his desk read, THE BUCK STOPS HERE. Another favorite quote of Truman that exemplifies his grit and fortitude is IF YOU CAN'T STAND THE HEAT, GET OUT OF THE KITCHEN. Truman once read an epitaph on a tombstone that impressed him deeply—it read HE DONE HIS DAMNEDESS. Many in this world believe that Harry Truman also did "his damnedess."

Vocational Indicators

Main principles to be utilized in career: You do best in positions of responsibility and authority. You're right at home in the nine-to-five business world, are often drawn to large enterprises, and do well as head of your own business and in management.

> *"God gave me my money. I believe the power to make money is a gift from God, to be developed and used to the best of our ability for the good of mankind. Having been endowed with the gift I possess, I believe it is my duty to make money and still more money and to use the money I make for the good of my fellow man according to the dictates of my conscience."*
> —**John D. Rockefeller,** U.S. industrialist, born

July 8, 1839, whose 8 birthday number helped make him a millionaire and whose 9 life path number guided him to become one of the world's greatest philanthropists

If You Were Born on the 9th

Behavior and Personality Traits

You are compassionate, tolerant, sympathetic, and forgiving.

You are magnetic, metaphysical, and dramatic.

You are broad-minded and can see the larger picture.

You are concerned with the welfare of others and have a natural interest in world problems.

You are emotional and strong-willed.

You may not like to give an account of yourself and cannot be dictated to.

You are universal and humanitarian in thought and spirit.

You are willing to sacrifice yourself for a cause.

You belong in the world and to it and can rarely lead a strictly personal life with success.

9s often have an interest in politics and reform, and this was certainly true of **Samuel J. Tilden** (2/9/1814), who was elected governor of New York in 1874 on a reform platform and won national recognition for exposing the Canal Ring, a conspiracy of corrupt contractors and politicians engaged in defrauding the state. Tilden also gained acclaim for his role in overthrowing the notorious Tweed Ring, another group of corrupt politicians. Tilden's law practice and investments brought him great wealth; he left the bulk of his estate in trust to establish a free public library for New York City. He was a true humanitarian.

Vocational Indicators

You are a valuable public servant—in any capacity—and do best in a position of leadership. *Main principles to be utilized in career:* need outlets for your sympathy, understanding of human needs, and willingness to give service.

People born on the 9th are often drawn to acting and have an interest in social and political causes. **Candice Bergen** (5/9/1946), who starred in TV's popular series *Murphy Brown*, also enjoyed a second career as a photojournalist. A political activist, Candice slept in at Alcatraz to protest the plight of the American Indians, campaigned for antiwar candidates, protested restrictive abortion laws, and became a board member of Friends of the Earth.

Oscar winner **Glenda Jackson** (5/9/1936) often gave benefit performances for humanitarian causes. In 1992, Glenda retired from her successful acting career to devote her time to politics and was elected a member of the British Parliament.

If You Were Born on the 10th

Behavior and Personality Traits

You are hospitable, but not very domestic.
You are healthier than you look.
You can handle a variety of interests at once.
You are sometimes jealous and possessive.
You have a strong will and a fine mind.
You are direct, honest, and determined.
You have the courage of your convictions.
You can stand on your own two feet.
You are ambitious.
You are creative.

Helen Hayes (10/10/1900) was commonly known as the First Lady of the American Theater, an epithet that became hers after she performed her most celebrated stage role, Queen Victoria. Helen Hayes was the first person ever to win an Oscar, an Emmy, a Tony, and a Grammy in competitive categories. She won Oscars in 1932 and 1971; Tonys in 1947, 1958, and 1970; Emmys in 1953 and 1978; and a Grammy in 1976. In 1920, she was the first actress ever to have her name in lights on Broadway. However, her name will always be in lights, as a Broadway theater was renamed for her in 1983. Helen Hayes was also feted for a life dedicated to humanitarian causes and she received the Presidential Medal of Freedom in 1986.

Vocational Indicators

You belong in a vocation where you can utilize your intellectual qualities. You have much creative ability. *Main principles to be utilized in career:* You do well in positions of authority; you have leadership abilities, especially for a fine cause; you are inventive and idealistic.

People born on the 10th are often original thinkers whose accomplishments benefit humanity. **Joseph Pulitzer** (4/10/1847), American publisher, introduced the comics, sports coverage, women's fashion, and illustrations into his newspapers, thus making them vehicles of entertainment as well as of the news. In the theater, German playwright **Bertolt Brecht** (2/10/1898) departed from the conventions of theatrical illusion and developed the drama as an ideological forum for left-wing causes. Another spokesman for a cause was **William Lloyd Garrison** (12/10/1805), who contributed to the movement against slavery in the United States by publishing the newspaper *The Liberator*.

If You Were Born on the 11th

Behavior and Personality Traits

You are visionary, imaginative, intuitive, psychic, high-strung, and possibly eccentric.

You are zealous about your beliefs.

You are charismatic, magnetic, futuristic, and capable of inspired leadership for a cause.

You enjoy being in the limelight.

You are dramatic in thought and action.

You may be philanthropic and humanitarian in outlook, but are also given to going to extremes.

You need money to feel important, but should think of the greater glory of cultivating your creative gifts.

You can love or hate without reason.

11s can inspire others. Here are some words of inspiration from **Eleanor Roosevelt** (10/11/1884):

"Many people will walk in and out of your life, but only true friends will leave footprints in your heart."

"To handle yourself, use your head; to handle others, use your heart."

"Anger is only one letter short of danger."

"If someone betrays you once, it's his fault; if he betrays you twice, it is your fault."

"Yesterday is history. Tomorrow is mystery. Today is a gift."

Vocational Indicators

You often have a mission in life and march to the

beat of your own drummer. *Main principles to be utilized in career:* inspiration, idealism, and inventiveness.

People born on the 11th are crusaders and sometimes eccentric. **Anne Royall** (6/11/1769) was one of the very first American newspaperwomen. She gained widespread notoriety for her outspoken and often controversial views. From 1831 until her death in 1854, she crusaded against government corruption and incompetence and promoted states' rights, Sunday mail service, and tolerance for Roman Catholics and Masons. President John Quincy Adams called her "a virago errant in enchanted armor." Once when Adams was taking his daily nude swim in the Potomac, Royall took his clothes and wouldn't give them back until the president gave her the interview she wanted.

If You Were Born on the 12th

Behavior and Personality Traits

You are magnetic, imaginative, and upbeat.
You have high ideals with many artistic tendencies.
You are inclined to flirtations and affairs.
You have writing and public speaking skills.
You are persuasive, sociable, and convincing.
You are inclined to spend freely.
You are fond of life and action; you may be charming.
You need to keep intellectually active to avoid ups
    and downs in mood.

In keeping with the meanings of his 12 birthday number, lyricist **Oscar Hammerstein II** (7/12/1896), in collaboration with composer Richard Rodgers, showed us in *The King and I* and other Broadway shows that if we whistle a happy tune, the happiness in the tune will keep us from feeling afraid. Rodgers and Hammerstein songs of hope and joy include:

"A Cockeyed Optimist"	*South Pacific*
"Climb Every Mountain"	*The Sound of Music*
"Do Re Mi"	*The Sound of Music*
"Happy Talk"	*South Pacific*
"I Have Confidence"	*The Sound of Music*
"I Whistle a Happy Tune"	*The King and I*
"June Is Bustin' Out All Over"	*Carousel*
"Oh What a Beautiful Mornin'"	*Oklahoma!*
"You'll Never Walk Alone"	*Carousel*

Vocational Indicators

Work for public benefit and you'll reach the top. *Main principles to be utilized in career:* You can organize, promote, and sell; should seek a mission in life; are mechanically inclined.

Showmanship comes naturally to those born on the 12th. Circus performer **Gunther Gebel-Williams** (9/12/1934) is universally known as the greatest wild animal trainer of all time. Film director **Cecil B. DeMille** (8/12/1881) is often credited with making

Hollywood the film capital of the world. DeMille was first and foremost a showman. *The Ten Commandments, Samson and Delilah, Cleopatra,* and *The Greatest Show on Earth* are some of his best-known films. Singer-actress-dancer **Liza Minnelli** (3/12/1946) has a knack for captivating audiences with sheer exuberance. And Ol' Blue Eyes, **Frank Sinatra** (12/12/1915), redefined the popular song in the 20th century with his charming manner, impeccable phrasing, and exquisite timing.

If You Were Born on the 13th

Behavior and Personality Traits

You often are spiritual, intuitive, and psychic—though others may think you a bit strange.

You have a good mind and a strong will, but can be stubborn and fixed in your views.

You have a strong need for love, but seldom show your feelings—consequently, you suffer.

You need a home to be happy, but are not always easy to live with; you may be dictatorial.

You are creative and practical, but sometimes have difficulty reconciling these qualities.

You may be centered on self, home, and loved ones, but need a more universal outlook to rise above self-imposed limitations.

You are dutiful and loyal.

Many people born on the 13th have a liking for mysteries, suspense, and the paranormal. This was certainly true of **Daphne du Maurier** (5/13/1907), who wrote many successful gothic romances. It's not surprising that the master of mystery and the macabre, **Alfred Hitchcock** (8/13/1899), adapted du Maurier's *The Birds, Rebecca,* and *Jamaica Inn* to film—he, too, was born on the 13th. *Unsolved Mysteries,* the reality-based TV series that reenacts real-life mysteries, was hosted by actor **Robert Stack** (1/13/1913) from 1987 until his death in 2003. **Chris Carter**, creator of the hit TV series *The X-Files* (1993–2002) and *Millennium* (1996–1999), was born on October 13, 1956.

Vocational Indicators

Main principles to be utilized in career: You may be inclined to lay down the law, but are an excellent manager; you are a good organizer and do well as the head of your own business; usually you're blessed with some artistic talent, which should be cultivated—if not as a career, then as a hobby.

Many great physicians were born on the 13th. **Thomas Young** (6/13/1773), English physician and physicist, discovered the cause of astigmatism in 1801. **Walter Reed** (9/13/1851), U.S. Army bacteriologist, led the experiments that proved that yellow fever is transmitted by the bite of a mosquito. The Walter Reed Hospital in Washington, DC, was named in his honor.

British bacteriologist **Ronald Ross** (5/13/1857) received the Nobel Prize for Physiology or Medicine in 1902 for his work on malaria. **Albert Flexner** (11/13/1866) played a major role in the introduction of modern medical education to American colleges and universities, and **Joycelyn Elders** (8/13/1933) served as U.S. surgeon general.

If You Were Born on the 14th

Behavior and Personality Traits

You have a logical mind.

You are practical and innovative.

You are prophetic, versatile, and, at times, the rebel.

You are more mature and responsible than those born on the 5th, yet you have 5's love of adventure, experimentation, freedom, and new thrills.

You can usually extricate yourself from emergency situations, which are often of your own making.

You are usually fortunate in accumulating money.

You may abuse the physical appetites—your destiny is often affected by your attitude toward sex.

You can get away with murder, but need to learn from experience and not repeat your mistakes.

You can be appealed to through your feelings, emotions, and sympathies.

You are lucky at taking chances—and usually have a knack for gambling.

Many rebels and revolutionaries were born on the 14th:

Jawaharlal Nehru, Indian patriot   11/14/1889
Che Guevara, Cuban revolutionary   6/14/1928
Frederick Douglass, abolitionist   2/14/1817
Emmeline Pankhurst, English suffragist   7/14/1858
Margaret Sanger, feminist   9/14/1879
Kate Millet, writer and feminist   9/14/1934
Jerry Rubin, activist   7/14/1938
Maulana Karenga, black activist   7/14/1941
Woody Guthrie, folksinger   7/14/1912

Vocational Indicators

You can shine in acting, brokerage, or law; do well as the head of your own business; can handle big operations, especially involving commodities; need an artistic outlet as a safety valve. *Main principles to be utilized in career:* Innovation—you can inject new life into things that come from the past. You are lucky and will do well in fields that require taking a chance or risk.

People born on the 14th have the ability to extricate themselves from emergency situations. After accumulating a multibillion-dollar fortune, high roller **Donald Trump** (6/14/1946) saw most of it wiped away under massive loan payments, only to regain it after making some very clever business moves. His greatest talent as a businessman is turning bad real estate properties into gold mines. He has amassed a fortune through owning key New York properties and Atlantic City casinos. He's also the owner of the Miss Universe, Miss Teen USA, and Miss USA pageants. His propensity for dating supermodels is well known, as are his divorces from Marla Maples and Ivana Trump.

If You Were Born on the 15th

Behavior and Personality Traits

You have excellent financial judgment and are a good moneymaker.

You have a love of home, comfort, and luxury.

You are generous, but more inclined to help out friends and family rather than to give to philanthropy in general.

You will serve a just cause or friend unselfishly, but won't become subservient to another's will; you're a natural-born counselor.

You are usually youthful in manner and give the impression of abounding good health.

You have leadership qualities and do not belong in a subordinate position.

People born on the 15th have a talent for making money and a need to live in beautiful surroundings. Oil magnate **J. Paul Getty** (12/15/1893) ran his business empire from his castle, Sutton Place, formerly the home of Anne Boleyn. Greek shipping magnate **Aristotle**

Onassis (1/15/1906) built his own palatial Shangri-la on his privately owned island, Skorpios. British mystery writer **Agatha Christie** (9/15/1890) had two magnificent homes, Greenway House and Winter Brook House. Cereal heiress **Marjorie Merriweather Post** (3/15/1887) owned several estates. Her favorite was Hillwood, which she bought in 1955 to serve both as a residence and as a future museum.

Vocational Indicators

Main principles to be utilized in career: You have inventive genius; can bring new life to old businesses; can rejuvenate lost causes; are able to commercialize any form of art to which you are attracted; can preach and teach; may have scientific gifts.

Many people born on the 15th are discoverers and inventors. **Cyrus McCormick** (2/15/1809) invented the mechanical reaper, **Lewis Terman** (1/15/1877), the IQ test, and **Christopher Sholes** (2/15/1819), the typewriter. Perhaps history's most celebrated inventor, though, is Italian painter, draftsman, sculptor, architect, and engineer **Leonardo da Vinci** (4/15/1452), whose notebooks reveal a spirit of scientific inquiry and a mechanical inventiveness that were centuries ahead of their time. Another genius born on the 15th was the scientist **Galileo** (2/15/1564), whose discoveries with the telescope revolutionized astronomy and paved the way for the acceptance of the Copernican heliocentric system.

If You Were Born on the 16th

Behavior and Personality Traits

You are a deep thinker, a good observer, and always a
leader, teacher, and philosopher.

You are inclined to live too much within yourself,
and though you want affection, you do not always
make the effort to earn it.

You will need a fine education, in both books and
travel, for your greatest success.

You are not satisfied with less than the best you can
do.

You feel at home with animals and nature.

You can be irritable at times with others and need
periods of solitude to renew your spirit.

You are somewhat practical, but live on the subjective
plane and in mental realms.

Many people born on the 16th excel as critics and
commentators on society and its values. Novelist **Jane
Austen** (12/16/1775) and playwrights **Oscar Wilde**
(10/16/1854) and **Noël Coward** (12/16/1899) all were
keen observers of their social milieu and the times in
which they lived. Noted intellectual and writer **Susan
Sontag** (1/16/1933) is known for her essays on modern
culture. **Margaret Mead** (12/16/1901) is best known for
her anthropological studies of the culture of the nonlit-
erate peoples of Oceania. Rap star **Ice-T** (2/16/1958)

and U.S. associate Supreme Court justice **William O. Douglas** (10/16/1898) are both known for their outspoken defense of civil liberties.

Vocational Indicators

A professional career is apt to appeal to you more than business, most notably writing, science, law, and teaching; you have a talent for music, painting, acting, or research. *Main principles to be utilized in career:* You'll thrive in fields where you can utilize your originality and your fine powers of reason and analysis; any mental field is your natural milieu; you'll often choose a job where ethics and morals are factors.

16s do well in careers that involve making ethical choices. **Katherine Graham** (6/16/1917), publisher of the *Washington Post,* sided in 1971 with her editors against the advice of the paper's lawyers and published the Pentagon Papers, secret documents about U.S. involvement in Vietnam. A year later, *Post* reporters Bob Woodward and Carl Bernstein began investigating a break-in at the Democratic National Committee's headquarters. Their stories linked the Watergate break-in to top officials in Richard Nixon's White House. Despite pressure from the Nixon administration not to pursue the story, Graham stood by her reporters. The scandal ultimately led to Nixon's resignation in 1974.

If You Were Born on the 17th

Behavior and Personality Traits

You have a thirst for knowledge and love to explore.

You can manage the interests and affairs of others with great success.

You are often erratic in the handling of your own financial affairs, at times being penurious, and at others times overly generous.

You are capable of scrimping and saving for a long time, and then blowing it all in a fit of extravagance.

You may be more economical at home than in public.

You may be very set in your ways and seldom give in to others; you're quite self-sufficient.

You are more at home with large affairs than details.

You may find the adages listed below of special significance, as they were penned by one who shares your birthday number: **Benjamin Franklin**, statesman (1/17/1726).

"Remember that time is money."

"A penny saved is a penny earned."

"Early to bed and early to rise, makes a man healthy, wealthy, and wise."

"If you'd know the power of money, go and borrow some."

"Necessity never made a good bargain."

"In this world nothing is certain but death and taxes."

Vocational Indicators

Main principles to be utilized in career: You do best as your own boss. Choose business associates carefully. You have excellent executive, organizing, and management skills. Think big and deal with large affairs.

Financier **J. P. Morgan** (4/17/1837) single-handedly bailed the U.S. government out of many financial crises. The company he founded in 1895 became one of the most powerful banking houses in the world. In 1891, he arranged the merger of Edison General Electric and Thompson-Houston Electric to form General Electric. Soon after, he merged several steel companies to form U.S. Steel Corporation, the world's first billion-dollar corporation. In 1902, he organized International Harvester, and later the International Merchant Marine, an amalgamation of many transatlantic shipping lines. These industrial consolidations reshaped the structure of American manufacturing.

If You Were Born on the 18th

Behavior and Personality Traits

You can expect an eventful life, one filled with change, activity, and travel.

You are strong-willed; you dislike taking advice and are seldom in need of it.

You belong in a position of leadership, but take care not to be dictatorial.

You are highly emotional, but will shine in intellectual fields.

You have good judgment and are responsible where financial matters are concerned.

You may be ultraconservative, with a need to learn to think big.

You have a fine understanding of human nature.

The 8 in your 18 gives you opportunities to attain financial successes and a certain measure of power. However, because 18 adds up to 9, that power must be utilized for the benefit of others. To achieve a Union of South Africa in which the power would be invested in the people was the lifelong goal of **Nelson Mandela** (7/18/1918). However, to achieve this end, Mandela needed the cooperation of South African president **F. W. de Klerk**, also born on the 18th (3/18/1936). In recognition of their efforts to rid that nation of apartheid and create a truly free South Africa, President Nelson Mandela and his predecessor, President F. W. de Klerk, were jointly awarded the Nobel Peace Prize in 1993.

Vocational Indicators

Main principles to be utilized in career: Don't let conservatism and overcaution cause you to sell yourself short—enlarge your horizons and go after the big things. You'll do well in any large field requiring efficient administration. You would make a good business head or consultant.

Many people born on the 18th achieve prominence as political leaders:

Willy Brandt, German politician	12/18/1913
Leonid Brezhnev, Soviet president	12/18/1906
Grover Cleveland, U.S. president	3/18/1837
John Glenn, U.S. senator	7/18/1921
Jacob Javits, U.S. senator	5/18/1904
Wilma Mankiller, Cherokee Indian chief	11/18/1945
John D. Rockefeller IV, U.S. senator	6/18/1937
Pierre Trudeau, Canadian prime minister	10/18/1919
Mary Tudor, Queen of England	2/19/1576
Daniel Webster, U.S. senator	1/18/1872
Wendell Wilkie, U.S. politician	2/18/1892

If You Were Born on the 19th

Behavior and Personality Traits

You are a composite of all the numbers from 1 through 9, and your emotions will run the gamut from love to hate to everything in between.

You can rise to great heights or fall to great depths, both in actions and emotions.

You have leadership abilities with the desire to make the world a better place to live.

You are unconventional in your private life, but will never give offense in public.

You will be called upon to make many adjustments in your personal life, and your life will be filled with a series of endings (9) and new starts (1).

To be an individual who is both unique (1) and universal (9) in outlook is the mission of those born on the 19th. Brash maverick entrepreneur **Ted Turner** (11/19/1938) is known for speaking his mind, going his own way, and pioneering the Cable News Network. Often forgotten is the fact that he was the skipper of the boat *Courageous,* which won the America's Cup in 1977. A visionary, a billionaire, and a rugged individualist, he runs his own ranch. He epitomizes 19—always remaining true to himself (1), yet never forgetting to be a humanitarian (9). He started (1) a foundation to support environmental (9) causes; pioneered the Goodwill Games; and donated $1 billon to the United Nations.

Vocational Indicators

You are independent, persevering, tenacious, and logical, with a strong will, a fine mind, and a progressive outlook. As symbolized by 19, you stand for progress in a new era. *Main principles to be utilized in career:* You have an innate understanding of financial matters and know how to make things pay. You are versatile, but more inclined to the arts (especially music) and professions than business.

19s are good promoters of culture and have a natural interest in politics and current events. This is especially true of talk show hosts born on the 19th. **Dick Cavett** (11/19/1936) received renown during the '70s for his insightful and in-depth interviews with film director Orson Welles, playwright Tennessee Williams, rock star Jimi Hendrix, and novelist Gore Vidal. **David Susskind** (12/19/1920) produced some of TV's finest cultural fare during TV's golden age in the '50s and also hosted a talk show. PBS newscasters **Robert MacNeil** (1/19/1931) and **Jim Lehrer** (5/19/1934) were both born on the 19th. **Larry King** (11/19/1933) has achieved a global audience of over 200 million viewers with his syndicated interview show.

If You Were Born on the 20th

Behavior and Personality Traits

You are friendly and affectionate.

You are cooperative and a peacemaker.

You have a need and desire for partnership.

You are sympathetic and would make a fine physician.

You would rather work with others than be in charge.

You may not wish to take on too much responsibility.

You are efficient in handling details.

You may meet with extremes in poverty and wealth.

You are a master of diplomacy.

You may listen politely to advice, but seldom take it.

You may have healing powers in your hands.

The number 20 is associated with partnerships. **John Goodman** (6/20/1952) is best known for his portrayal of Dan Conner—the husband of Roseanne on the TV hit sitcom *Roseanne*—for which he earned six Emmy nominations. The forever young **George Burns** (1/20/1896) for almost 20 years played sidekick to his wife, Gracie Allen, on the popular hit sitcom *The George Burns and Gracie Allen Show,* which first aired in 1950. Another popular TV show from the '50s was *The Adventures of Ozzie and Harriet,* costarring **Ozzie Nelson** (3/20/1906) and his wife, Harriet Nelson. During the early '70s, the always popular **Cher** (5/20/1945) costarred with her husband, Sonny Bono, on TV's *The Sonny and Cher Show.*

Vocational Indicators

You are most comfortable in a small business. A pressure-charged, unfriendly environment is not for you. Symbolically, 20 indicates that you must do your part to establish the unity of religions, the brotherhood of man, and the amalgamation of interests between East and West. *Main principles to be utilized in career:* attention to detail, diplomacy, and cooperation.

Although **Gordon Paul Getty** (12/20/1933) was ranked in *Forbes* magazine as the wealthiest man in the United States in both 1983 and 1984, he is more identified with the arts and sciences than business. In keeping with the principles associated with his 20 birthday number, he would rather compose music, write poetry, or fulfill his role as a patron of the arts and sciences and keep a low profile in business. He has been variously described as a "shy and reserved man," "a preoccupied absentminded professor type," and an "exceptionally modest and trusting man"—traits associated with his birthday number of 20.

If You Were Born on the 21st

Behavior and Personality Traits

You usually have a good speaking or singing voice.

You are clever, artistic, sensitive, imaginative, and
    have a good sense of humor.
You are magnetic, charming, and musical.
You have a love of beauty, art, and dancing.
You learn much through travel and extensive reading.
You are somewhat nervous and need to control some
    of your unaccountable aversions to things.
You are a better friend than lover, for you're easily
    inclined to be unduly suspicious.
You are more receptive than active in your expres-
    sions of love, but enjoy putting your loved ones on
    a pedestal.

People born on the 21st often have a good sense of
humor:

Al Franken, writer-actor	5/21/1951
Andy Dick, actor	12/21/1965
Benny Hill, comedian	1/21/1924
Bill Murray, actor	9/21/1950
Dizzie Gillespie, jazz great	10/21/1917
Elaine May, actress-writer	4/21/1932
Garry Trudeau, cartoonist	7/21/1928
Harpo Marx, actor	11/21/1888
Kelsey Grammer, actor	2/21/1955
Robin Williams, actor	7/21/1962
Rosie O'Donnell, actress	3/21/1962
Voltaire, writer	4/21/1694

Vocational Indicators

Main principles to be utilized in career: You need a job where you can put your fine writing, speaking, artistic, social, and communication skills to good use.

Quotes from humorist writer **Erma Bombeck** (2/21/1927) to make you laugh:

"Marriage has no guarantees. If that's what you're looking for, go live with a car battery."

"There's nothing more miserable in the world than to arrive in paradise and look like your passport photo."

"Onion rings in the car cushion do not improve with time."

"Sometimes, I can't figure designers out. It's as if they flunked human anatomy."

"I never leaf through National Geographic *without realizing how lucky we are to live in a society where it's traditional to wear clothes."*

If You Were Born on the 22nd

Behavior and Personality Traits

You are intuitive, but skeptical—and need to learn to rely on your first impressions.

You are a good organizer, with a superb intellect, a

philosophical outlook, a generous heart, and great sympathy for the underdog.

You can start movements for civic and national betterment, run a large corporation, or lead a crusade.

You have the ability to take ideals and make them practical realities—you're the master builder!

You need periodic times by yourself to replenish your energy and spirit.

Actors born on the 22nd are often considered geniuses. **Sarah Bernhardt** (10/22/1844) was the greatest actress of the 19th century. **Laurence Olivier** (5/22/1907) was acclaimed in his lifetime as the greatest English-speaking actor of the 20th century. **Catherine Deneuve** (10/22/1943) is one of France's top stars, and **Derek Jacobi** (10/22/1938), one of England's greatest actors. **Jack Nicholson** (4/22/1937) has received 12 Oscar nominations, and **Meryl Streep** (6/22/1949) an incredible 13! As Sandra Bullock once said, "The Academy Awards shouldn't even nominate Meryl Streep anymore. She should be just given an award every year. There should just be the Meryl Streep category."

Vocational Indicators

You can succeed in any line that interests you. In general, 22s who have made a name for themselves have made contributions that have benefited all humanity.

You would feel stifled in a job that has no place for your visionary thinking. Actually, you have a mission in life rather than a profession. *Main principles to be utilized in career: Intuition, inventiveness,* and *idealism* are your keywords. You're capable of highly original work in both the arts and sciences and would be a fine leader of a cause or humanitarian endeavor.

The number 22 has an affinity with the piano and musical genius. Note the following gifted composers and musicians who were born on the 22nd:

Tori Amos	8/22/1963
Benjamin Britten	11/22/1913
Glen Campbell	4/22/1936
Frédéric Chopin	2/22/1810
Sam Cooke	1/22/1935
Claude Debussy	8/22/1862
Peter Framptom	4/22/1952
Maurice Gibb	12/22/1949
Robin Gibb	12/22/1949
John Lee Hooker	8/22/1917
Franz Liszt	10/22/1811
Charles Mingus	4/22/1922
Puccini	12/22/1858
Stephen Sondheim	3/22/1930
Richard Wagner	5/22/1813
Andrew Lloyd Webber	3/22/1949

If You Were Born on the 23rd

Behavior and Personality Traits

You have a good intuition that is often better than your reason, so follow your hunches.

You are not only progressive in outlook, but also very practical—a winning combination!

You make the best of life wherever you find yourself and are a wonderful friend and comrade.

You are self-sufficient, yet also sympathetic, understanding, and able to lift others' spirits.

You are versatile with a facility for languages and chemistry, but seldom become a specialist.

You are independent and may not always adhere to the accepted codes of society.

Many 23s have numerous love affairs. Italian-born model **Carla Bruni** (12/23/1967) has been an item in the tabloids for her high-profile affairs with Mick Jagger, Eric Clapton, and tycoon Donald Trump. **Joseph Smith** (12/23/1805), the founder of the Mormon religion, may have had as many as 50 wives. Listed below are some 23s who have wed several times:

Johnny Carson, talk show host	four wives
Joan Collins, actress	four husbands
Joan Crawford, actress	five husbands

Douglas Fairbanks, actor	five wives
Boris Karloff, actor	five wives
Mickey Rooney, actor	nine wives
Artie Shaw, bandleader	eight wives

Vocational Indicators

Main principles to be utilized in career: You have the ability to inject original and progressive ideas into your work. You have people skills, are a fine host, and would be good at managing a restaurant, hotel, health spa, or the like. Your skill at diagnosing ailments, combined with your sympathetic and understanding nature, makes you a natural for nursing and doctoring.

It was **Albert Kinsey** (6/23/1894) who gave us comprehensive statistics about human sexual behavior in his Kinsey Reports, but it was **Erich Fromm** (3/23/1900) who gave us *The Art of Loving,* a book that has helped hundreds of thousands of readers develop their hidden capacities for love. People born on the 23rd have a good understanding of human nature, as can be seen in the lyrics of rock sensation **Bruce Springsteen** (10/23/1949). Nowhere, though, do we obtain a greater insight into human beings and their complete range of emotions and conflicts than in the writings of playwright and poet **William Shakespeare**, who was born on April 23, 1564.

If You Were Born on the 24th

Behavior and Personality Traits

You have an excellent sense of responsibility.

You will learn much through your fine powers of observation.

You are practical (4), but a little inclined to dream (2).

You may not have much appreciation of the value of time and money.

You are dramatic by nature, with a highly developed ego and a good imagination.

You are decidedly domestic.

You are an asset in public affairs—arranging charities, working on committees, engaging in welfare work, and supporting large interests.

Many fine journalists and editors were born on the 24th. **Sarah Josepha Hale** (10/24/1788), author of "Mary Had a Little Lamb," was the first woman magazine editor in the United States. Satirist **Ambrose Bierce** (6/24/1842) was known for his critical newspaper attacks on dishonest politicians and other frauds. **Margaret Anderson** (11/24/1896) edited *The Little Review* (1914–29), which gave avant-garde writers a voice. Noted critic **Malcolm Cowley** (8/24/1898) was literary editor of *The New Republic* for many years. **Pete Hamill** (6/24/1935) wrote a column for the *New York*

Daily News. **Norman Cousins** (6/24/1912) was a long-time editor of the *Saturday Review*. **William F. Buckley** (1/24/1925) founded the *National Review*.

Vocational Indicators

You require action and should never retire from productive work. Without something meaningful to do, you can become lethargic and listless. You are smart enough to get by on your wits. *Main principles to be utilized in career:* You have management abilities and promotional talents; any form of public service is your milieu; you shine in art, music, sculpture, literature, and acting.

People born on the 24th are good observers of their own social milieu. **Anthony Trollope** (4/24/1815) aptly portrayed the social structures of Victorian England in his Barsetshire novels (such as *Barchester Towers*). **Edith Wharton** (1/24/1862) is best known for her stories and novels (including *Age of Innocence*) about the upper-class New York society of the late 19th century into which she was born. Short-story writer and novelist **F. Scott Fitzgerald** (9/24/1896) became famous for his depictions of the Jazz Age (such as *The Great Gatsby*). He and his wife, **Zelda Fitzgerald** (7/24/1900), in their private lives symbolized the Roaring '20s with its high living, big spending, and partygoing.

If You Were Born on the 25th

Behavior and Personality Traits

You should always listen to your inner voice, as you're naturally prophetic, intuitive, and inclined to mysticism.

You are progressive in outlook, yet have a fondness for old things, such as antiques and the artwork of the Old Masters.

You are discriminating and a perfectionist, though at times you may procrastinate.

You can succeed not only in creative areas, but also in technical and mechanical fields.

You may conceal your thoughts and feelings.

You need to watch your morals, as you're better at preaching them than practicing them.

Many people born on the 25th have an exceptional talent for painting, and many are also mediumistic. This was certainly true of **Pablo Picasso** (10/25/1881), the most dominant figure in Western art in the 20th century. Picasso himself thought his work was mediumistic. As he once said, *"Painting is stronger than me, it makes me do what it wants."* Other great painters born on the 25th:

Thomas Eakins	7/25/1844
Robert Henri	6/25/1865

Maxfield Parrish	7/25/1870
Pierre-Auguste Renoir	2/25/1841
Mark Rothko	9/25/1903
George Stubbs	8/25/1784

Vocational Indicators

A good education is essential; you should become an expert at something—a specialist, a connoisseur! *Main principles to be utilized in career:* Painting, sculpture, acting, writing, and music are fields that you can successfully commercialize. You are often extremely talented at the same. You'd make a fine art dealer or seller of antiques.

Many celebrated writers were born on the 25th:

Anthony Burgess	2/25/1917
Robert Burns	1/25/1759
Carlos Castaneda	12/25/1931
Ralph Waldo Emerson	5/25/1803
Bret Harte	8/25/1836
William Somerset Maugham	1/25/1874
Flannery O'Connor	3/25/1925
Robert Ludlum	5/25/1927
Edward Bulwer-Lytton	5/25/1803
William Faulkner	9/25/1897
George Orwell	6/25/1903
Anne Tyler	10/25/1941
Virginia Woolf	1/25/1882

If You Were Born on the 26th

Behavior and Personality Traits

You are inclined to introspection and reminiscence.

You are intellectual, creative, inventive, and practical, but spend a great deal of time in your own dream world.

You are warmhearted and generous to others.

You are domestic by nature, with a strong love for home, family, and children.

You do not insist on physical comforts.

You are likely to be fastidious about your personal belongings and are fond of show and color—you know how to look your best.

Nothing is too small for your practical use.

You do best with a good education.

People born on the 26th have a love of animals. **Paul Gallico** (7/26/1897) and **T. S. Eliot** (9/26/1888) both wrote books of poetry about cats. **John Audubon** (4/26/1785) devoted his life to drawing birds; and cartoonist **Charles M. Schulz** (11/26/1922) in his *Peanuts* gave us the dog Snoopy and the bird Woodstock. American frontier nurseryman **John Chapman**, aka Johnny Appleseed (9/26/1774), was known for his kindness to animals. Singer **Olivia Newton-John** (9/26/1948) once wanted to be a veterinarian. In 1978, she canceled a concert tour of Japan as a protest against the slaughter of dolphins by the fishermen of Iki Island. She has been the owner of numerous pets since childhood.

Vocational Indicators

Main principles to be utilized in career: You are an idealist—no matter what form your work takes. You have executive talents combined with creative skills.

26s have the ability to commercialize their artistic talents in a big way. **Macaulay Culkin** (8/26/1980) is the richest child star there ever was. *Home Alone* was one of the top-grossing movies of all time. Forever young **Tina Turner** (11/26/1939) has sold more concert tickets than any other female performer in history. **Mick Jagger** (7/26/1943) truly is the Rolling Stone who gathers no moss. At age 60, Mick and the Rolling Stones performed for over 500,000 people on July 30, 2003, at Downsview Park in Toronto. This was the biggest crowd the Rolling Stones have ever played for. In 1994, their Voodoo Lounge tour was the biggest tour in rock history, raising more than $300 million.

If You Were Born on the 27th

Behavior and Personality Traits

You are quiet, self-assured, and determined.
You have a strong will and leadership abilities.

You are a law unto yourself; you won't be told what to do; you may not like to give an account of yourself.

You are ardent in your affections and may overdo family ties; you will sacrifice for loved ones.

You have philosophic and literary interests; you're spiritual, but not orthodox in your views.

You are resilient in crisis situations and can bounce back from setbacks; you are persistent.

You do not suffer defeat gladly, and—like the celebrated persons listed below—you never know when you're beaten.

"I propose to fight it out on this line, if it takes all summer."

—**Ulysses S. Grant,** U.S.
general and president (4/27/1822)

*"Do not go gentle into the night . . .
rage, rage against the dying of the light."*
—**Dylan Thomas,** poet (10/27/1914)

"I've been through it all, baby, I'm Mother Courage."
—**Elizabeth Taylor,** actress (2/27/1932)

"There is no reason to ever give up when you know you can find reasons to believe and hope."
—**Mother Teresa,** humanitarian (8/27/1910)

Vocational Indicators

Main principles to be utilized in career: You are a born leader and need a job that makes good use of your executive talents; are skilled in argument, yet diplomatic; would thrive in an artistic or literary career; enjoy challenges; excel as an abstract thinker.

Many people born on the 27th are concerned about the environment. **Theodore Roosevelt** (10/27/1858) was the first American president to take seriously the concept of the protection of nature. He increased the size of the national forest by 400 percent, took steps to protect the Grand Canyon as a natural resource, and pressed Congress to pass the Pure Food and Drug and Meat Inspection acts, which created agencies to protect consumers. Biologist **Rachel Carson**'s (5/27/1907) 1962 book *Silent Spring* is credited with creating a worldwide awareness of the dangers of environmental pollution. Another friend of the environment is consumer advocate **Ralph Nader** (2/27/1934), who was instrumental in the creation of the Environmental Protection Agency in 1970.

If You Were Born on the 28th

Behavior and Personality Traits

You have a keen imagination and are capable of carrying out great responsibilities.

You are practical in the material world, but happiest when detached from it.

You are tenacious and strong-willed, yet also loving, warmhearted, and affectionate.

You love freedom and wilt if restrained or cooped up in a cage; are a breaker of traditions—an iconoclast, proud to be unique and independent.

You are inclined to magnify your joys and sorrows and thus subject yourself to disappointments.

You may not like to work with your hands.

Many people born on the 28th have unconventional unions. Eyebrows were raised when **Jackie Kennedy** (7/28/1929) married Aristotle Onassis; likewise when actress **Julia Roberts** (10/28/1967) married singer Lyle Lovett, and ditto, when 26-year-old ex-*Playboy* playmate **Anna Nicole Smith** (11/28/1967) married 89-year-old billionaire J. Howard Mitchell. People were also perplexed when the poet **William Blake** (11/28/1757) married an illiterate girl, Catherine Boucher, in 1792. **Elsa Lanchester** (10/28/1902), who achieved fame as the star of the 1935 film *The Bride of Frankenstein*, shared an open marriage with hugely talented (but gay) actor Charles Laughton for 33 years until his death.

Vocational Indicators

You are not always cut out for business—you'll fare better in a professional, intellectual, or artistic career; you may be fitful in performance, periods of productivity alternating with bouts of inactivity. You want to excel, however, and will sacrifice to further your ambitions. *Main principles to be utilized in career:* You are better at inventing, creating, and planning than running the shop; you may be a trailblazer.

People born on the 28th are often iconoclasts. French artist **Marcel Duchamp** (7/28/1877) broke down the boundaries between works of art and everyday objects. In 1912, his *Nude Descending a Staircase,* No. 2 created a sensation. His lack of reverence for conventional aesthetic standards led him to devise his famous readymades and heralded an artistic revolution. Around 1947, abstract expressionist **Jackson Pollock** (1/28/1912) developed the radical "drip painting" technique that became his hallmark. Pop artist **Andy Warhol** (10/28/1930) received notoriety in 1962 when he exhibited paintings of Campbell's soup cans, Coca-Cola bottles, and wooden replicas of Brillo soap pad boxes.

If You Were Born on the 29th

Behavior and Personality Traits

You have great psychic power and your intuition, if heeded, will help you triumph over all problems.

You are able to achieve a good balance between personal affection (2) and universal love (9).

You are democratic in outlook, but prefer to keep a distance between yourself and the masses.

You are both idealistic and practical, but may have difficulty reconciling these qualities.

You are an extremist in all things, with great mood swings (manic-depressive?); you're highly nervous.

You need a home to be happy, but often live in your own dream world; you are resourceful and magnetic.

People born on the 29th are futuristic and often patriotic. It was political theorist **Thomas Paine** (1/29/1737) who said, *"We have the power to begin the world over again."* This hope for the future was echoed by American orator and statesman **Patrick Henry** (5/29/1736): *"I like dreams of the future better than the history of the past,"* and then again in the words of U.S. president **John F. Kennedy** (5/29/1918): *"Those who look only to the past or present are certain to miss the future. We stand today on the edge of a new frontier."* To Polish patriot **Lech Walesa** (9/29/1943), *"The thing that lies at the foundation of positive change is service to a fellow human being."*

Vocational Indicators

Main principles to be utilized in career: You are an inspired and innovative leader, especially as an instigator of social and political reforms. You work best when inspired, and your contributions in artistic and scientific areas are often ahead of the times. Humanitarian and philanthropic, you are a good fund-raiser and spokesperson for the causes that you espouse.

People born on the 29th are innovative. Film director and choreographer **Busby Berkeley** (11/29/1895) was noted for the elaborate dance-girl extravaganzas he created on film. Utilizing innovative camera techniques, he revolutionized the genre of the musical in the Depression era. Jazz was forever changed by the improvisations of **Charlie "Bird" Parker** (8/29/1920) and the musical compositions of fellow genius **Duke Ellington** (4/29/1899). With *Baseball, The Civil War,* and other projects, filmmaker **Ken Burns** (7/29/1953) revolutionized the documentary. And Spanish author **Miguel de Cervantes** (9/29/1547) taught us how to believe in the impossible dream with his *Don Quixote*.

If You Were Born on the 30th

Behavior and Personality Traits

You are a born orator; you can speak and write with eloquence and conviction.

You have a good memory, imagination, and intuition.

You can be unyielding in argument; fixed in ideas, will, and opinions; can stubbornly adhere to extreme viewpoints; are often too outspoken.

You are loyal and faithful to those in your circle, but inclined to force your will on others.

You are high-minded, dutiful, conscientious, and
   responsible, but insist on having your own way.
You are basically faithful, but inclined to be
   flirtatious; can be overly suspicious and lacking in
   trust in others; can be obsessive.
You think you know a lot, but need to know more.

Since 30 reduces to 3, the number of childhood, it
should not come as a surprise that **Anna Sewell**, author
of the children's classic *Black Beauty*—the "autobiography" of a horse—was born on March 30, 1820.
Nowhere do we get a better picture of the carefree days
of childhood than in **Mark Twain**'s (11/30/1835) *Tom
Sawyer* and *Huckleberry Finn*. Another writer whose
children's books will endure for all time is **Rudyard
Kipling** (12/30/1869), author of *Just So Stories, Kim,*
and *The Jungle Book*. **Jonathan Swift**'s (11/30/1667)
Gulliver's Travels has fascinated both children and
adults since it was first published in 1726.

Vocational Indicators

Teaching, writing, law, medicine, painting, acting,
and singing are your best fields. *Main principles to be
utilized in career:* In business, you can sell, advertise,
gamble, and promote, but fare better in intellectual
fields. You are an excellent manager, but are not overly
fond of work and can be indolent. You can excel at diagnosing problems.

Many people born on the 30th have made their mark in the world as singers. Note the following:

Tracy Chapman	3/30/1964
Eric Clapton	3/30/1945
Phil Collins	1/30/1951
Celine Dion	3/30/1968
Bo Diddley	12/30/1928
MC Hammer	3/30/1962
Lena Horne	6/30/1917
Norah Jones	3/30/1979
Wynonna Judd	5/30/1964
Johnny Mathis	9/30/1935
Willie Nelson	4/30/1933
Grace Slick	10/30/1939

If You Were Born on the 31st

Behavior and Personality Traits

You are fair, honest, spiritual, and intuitive.

You are practical, but often lack ambition; you need to cultivate the self-discipline and application of 4 to make a success of your life.

You may not be overfond of work—in the words of numerologist Florence Campbell, "It's hard work to get you up in the morning."

You are not one to forget a kindness—or an injury.

You love travel and do not like to live alone.

You may have aspirations that are unrealistic and likely to bring you disappointments.

Some people born on the 31st are macho types, like actors **Clint Eastwood** (5/31/1930), **James Coburn** (8/31/1928), and **Tom Berenger** (5/31/1949), while others seem stone-faced, like TV news analyst **Dan Rather** (10/31/1931), actor **Christopher Walken** (3/31/1943), and politician **Al Gore** (3/31/1948). And then there are those 31s who greet the world with a smile, like banjo-eyed comedian **Eddie Cantor** (1/31/1892) and *Hello, Dolly!* star **Carol Channing** (1/31/1921). Comics **Buddy Hackett** (8/31/1924) and **John Candy** (10/31/1950) were born on the 31st, as was genial ukulele-playing TV host **Arthur Godfrey**, who was born on August 31, 1903.

Vocational Indicators

31s often have an outstanding talent for music, writing, or teaching. *Main principles to be utilized in career:* You are a fine promoter and organizer with leadership and executive talents; your great diagnostic skills serve you well in research, science, and medicine. Your uncanny sense of smell is an asset to you in such fields as perfumes, wine tasting, cooking, and dietetics.

Your birthday number is made up of the number 3 of communication, followed by 1, the number of the self.

This combination translates as an ability to advertise (3) and promote (3) yourself (1). It's not surprising that **Norman Mailer** (1/31/1923) wrote a book titled *Advertisements for Myself,* and that the opening poem in **Walt Whitman's** (5/31/1803) first collection of poems, *Leaves of Grass,* was called "Song of Myself." A person who was never at a loss of words, especially when the subject was herself, was inimitable actress **Tallulah Bankhead** (1/31/1903). Note also how the symbolism of 31 is reflected in the philosopher **Descartes**'s (3/31/1596) most famous tenet: *"I think [3], therefore I am [1]."*

CHAPTER 9

YOUR SUCCESS NUMBER

A re there differences between someone born on February 1 and one born on March 1? Yes, there are, and these are revealed by the *Success Number*, which is found by adding the numbers of the day and month. For February 1, the Success Number is 3 (2 + 1 = 3); for March 1, the Success Number is 4 (3 + 1 = 4). In this section, the Success Number for all 365 birthdays will be given and interpreted along with other valuable information about your birthday.

Your birthday number is your chief vocational indicator, your calling in life. Your Success Number, however, indicates your method of attack—your "mundane ego," in the words of the great numerologist Florence Campbell. In the principles of your Success Number will be found the best approach, the best method, for realizing the potential of your birthday number.

The Success Number is the same as your 1st pinnacle, already discussed in chapter 7. There you learned that the 1st pinnacle signifies your peak experiences during the first part of your life, the types of events that will stand out in consciousness as significant during that period of time. When you found your pinnacle number, you reduced it to a single digit.

However, in viewing the sum of the month and day as the Success Number, we keep in mind that the Success Number of 8 for March 23 (3 + 23 = 26 or 8) is derived from the number 26. If you were born on March 23, then an understanding of the principles associated with both 8 and 26 will help you achieve greater insights as to the best way to realize the potential of 23, your birthday number.

Accordingly, if you were born on March 23, you should read what is written in chapter 8, "The Day You Were Born," for both those born on the 8th and those born on the 26th, to attain additional insights about how to realize the potential of your birthday number. Realize, however, that people born on the 26th have as part of their nature the principles of the number 26, whereas you have to develop them, so to speak. Still, in some cases, the Success Number rather than the birthday number will indicate the choice of vocation.

For example, 6 is the number of morality, but 7 is the number of the inner life. Many people born on January 6 found their career direction through the Success Number of 7. The martyr **Joan of Arc** was guided by her inner voices to lead the French armies, whereas philosopher **Alan Watts** gave Buddhist teachings a modern relevance. The mystic Lebanese poet **Kahlil Gibran** inspired millions of readers throughout the world with *The Prophet* and other books of poetry. American poet **Carl Sandburg** taught us that "the fog comes in with little cat feet." For film star **Loretta Young,** it was prayer and faith that sustained her through life's crises.

If your Success Number adds up to a number between 1 and 31, read what is written in chapter 8 about the corresponding birth date. If your Success Number is 22, for instance, the section "If You Were Born on the 22nd" will apply to you.

If your Success Number adds up to a number greater than 31, such as 41, which equals 5, first read the material written for "If You Were Born on the 5th." Since there is no birthday number for the 41, you will have to read what is written for both "If You Were Born on the 4th" and "If You Were Born on the 1st," and then combine their meanings to gain further insights about your 41/5 Success Number. If these additional steps to fully comprehend your Success Number seem time consuming or complicated, you can simply read what is written below about your Success Number.

JANUARY

January 1   Success Number 2 (1 + 1 = 2)

You are independent with leadership abilities. Original and highly creative, you not only come up with great ideas, but can also execute them. Your executive talents ensure that you will attain a position at the top. With 2 as your Success Number, however, your path in life will be made smoother if you'll place an accent on friendliness and cooperation. Then you become the iron hand in the velvet glove. You can succeed in creative fields and may also have an interest in government service. *Birthday of J. Edgar Hoover, FBI director; E. M. Forster, writer; and Barry Goldwater, U.S. senator.*

January 2   Success Number 3 (1 + 2 = 3)

You are sensitive and imaginative, with a strong need for financial and emotional security. You're good at boosting other people's interests, but perhaps you need to spend more time in making your own dreams come true. With a Success Number of 3, you're often creatively talented and will have success at writing, acting, or art. You may have an interest in politics and religion; are an excellent teacher; and may have a love for antiques and art objects. A sense of humor (3) will keep you from becoming overly sensitive (2). *Birthday of Isaac Asimov, writer; Cuba Gooding, actor; and Renata Tebaldi, opera diva.*

January 3 Success Number 4 (1 + 3 = 4)

Your sense of humor (3) keeps you from becoming overly serious, while your practicality (4) will keep you from being too lighthearted. With 4 as your Success Number, being self-disciplined and well organized will enable you to make the most of your creative talents. Otherwise you may tend to scatter your energies. Though you're a hard worker, you must avoid having your fingers in too many pies. Writing, acting, science, publishing, teaching, and medicine are some of the fields in which you'll enjoy success. *Birthday of Victor Borge, pianist; J. R. R.Tolkien, writer; and Ray Milland, actor.*

January 4 Success Number 5 (1 + 4 = 5)

You are ambitious and a hard worker. You could easily become a workaholic and need to check yourself every once in a while to make sure you're not getting into a rut. With 5 as your Success Number, a willingness to experiment and broaden your horizons will enable you to enjoy your greatest success. At your best, you inject new life into the tried-and-true. If in a scientific field, you're capable of making new discoveries. Real estate, government, brokerage, teaching, acting, and sculpture are some of the fields that promise you success. *Birthday of Jane Wyman, actress; Isaac Newton, scientist; and Floyd Patterson, boxer.*

January 5   Success Number 6   (1 + 5 = 6)

You are a free spirit who's likely to experiment before settling on a career. You thrive on action and will do well in fields that involve taking a chance. Acting, writing, sales, and brokerage are fields for which you may have a special aptitude. With 6 as your Success Number, you do best when you quell your restlessness, settle down, and assume a willingness to shoulder responsibility. You often put your energies in the service of the community and would make a fine politician or government leader. *Birthday of Konrad Adenauer, German statesman; Umberto Eco, Italian novelist; and Robert Duvall, actor.*

January 6   Success Number 7   (1 + 6 = 7)

You are community-minded and work well with groups. You also have a reflective side and may be interested in philosophy, religion, teaching, law, and psychology. Though you work well with others, a part of you remains aloof. You need privacy every once in a while to replenish your energies. You are not keen on handling details, but usually have good management skills. You have strong moral principles, and home and family are important to you. With 7 as your Success Number, you must keep trying to better yourself and resist an inclination to become complacent when your goals are attained. *Birthday of E. L. Doctorow, novelist; Danny Thomas, comedian; and Samuel Rayburn, U.S. politician.*

January 7   Success Number 8   (1 + 7 = 8)

You often work better on your own than in partnership. You are apt to be drawn to a career where you can put your intellect to good use. If you did not have 8 for a Success Number, you might find yourself isolated in an ivory tower of your own making. But your 8 Success Number directs your attention outward and enables you to commercialize your talents. *Think big* should be your motto, for you have the necessary ambition to do a good job. Law, education, science, engineering, and writing are some of the fields that promise you success. *Birthday of Nicolas Cage, actor; Terry Moore, actress; and Charles Addams, cartoonist.*

January 8   Success Number 9   (1 + 8 = 9)

If you're not in a business career (your 8 birth date), your Success Number of 9 may lead you into public service. Ambitious for leadership and prominence, you have a dramatic, if not flamboyant, flair and a good sense of what the public wants. You'd be a crass materialist except for the fact that your 9 Success Number is apt to draw you to higher mind pursuits, such as art, music, and writing. Your 9 is the key to developing a universal consciousness. When you work for public benefit, there's no stopping you. Then you are generous, public-spirited, and genuinely concerned about the welfare of others. *Birthday of Elvis Presley, rock star; David Bowie, rock star; and Simone de Beauvior, writer.*

January 9　Success Number 10/1　(1 + 9 = 10/1)

You have an interest in world affairs and may be drawn to politics. More than most individuals, you like to be on top and dislike being in a subordinate position. With 10/1 as a Success Number, you are a person meant to do your own thing. Personal ambition can lead you astray, however, if you sacrifice your individuality to get ahead. The combination of a 10/1 Success Number with a 9 birth date makes you well qualified to be a leader (10/1) of the people (9). At times, though, you are given to discouragement. *Birthday of Richard Nixon, U.S. president; George Balanchine, choreographer; and Dave Matthews, musician.*

January 10　Success Number 11/2　(1 + 10 = 11/2)

You are innately practical, but with 11/2 as your Success Number, it's your visionary qualities that will ensure your success. Highly ambitious, you will work hard to achieve your goals. You have a genuine desire to better yourself and to be of service to others. Making money and obtaining recognition for your talents are important to you; however, these should not be attained at the sacrifice of your more idealistic yearnings. Though you can succeed in business, you'll find greater fulfillment in such fields as art, music, the stage, and poetry. *Birthday of Rod Stewart, rock star; Jim Croce, rock star; and George Foreman, boxer.*

January 11   Success Number 12/3 (1 + 11 = 12/3)

You often have unusual ideas that are difficult to get across to others. If you'll cultivate the charm and a sense of humor of your 12/3 Success Number, however, others will be amenable and responsive to what you have to say. Though you can succeed in business, you are usually happier in an artistic or professional career. You have a talent for self-expression and often choose a creative medium through which to express your individuality. Your work is likely to be ahead of its time, but you're often nervous, temperamental, and high-strung. *Birthday of William James, philosopher; Naomi Judd, singer; and Alexander Hamilton, American patriot.*

January 12   Success Number 13/4 (1 + 12 = 13/4)

Both creative and practical, you sometimes have difficulty reconciling these qualities. You are quite ambitious and have a flair for communicating your ideas. In business, you would succeed in advertising, banking, and promotional work. With 13/4 as your Success Number, you have the practicality and necessary self-discipline to make good use of your creative talents. It is important, though, to find work that you like—otherwise you may tend to drift. You may have a special talent for writing or painting. Making things pay is important to you, but don't let financial priorities dominate your outlook on life. *Birthday of Jack London, novelist; Kirstie Alley, actress; and John Hancock, American patriot.*

January 13   Success Number 14/5   (1 + 13 = 14/5)

With 14/5 as your Success Number, you should welcome change and variety into your life. A willingness to explore the new and to learn more about your fellow man (14/5) will keep you from becoming rigid (13/4). Though ambitious, you're inclined to be expedient. You'll find that there's no shortcut for hard work, however, and that when you apply yourself, you make progress. You must base your career on what truly interests you and not settle for what chance throws your way. Develop your creative talents and you will go far. *Birthday of Robert Stack, actor; Gwen Verdon, dancer; and Patrick Dempsey, actor.*

January 14   Success Number 15/6   (1 + 14 = 15/6)

Both adventurous and ambitious, you're likely to experiment before settling on a career. Somewhat restless, you like things to move quickly and at times can make needless changes in your life. It's when you develop a sense of responsibility (Success Number 15/6) and a willingness to see things through to completion that you come into your own. Not afraid of taking risks, you can be a pioneer in your field. With 15/6 as your Success Number, you can succeed in large enterprises and are a good moneymaker. However, you may need to learn that money isn't everything. Your 15/6 will attract you to such fields as acting, writing, art, and music. *Birthday of Joseph Losey, filmmaker; Faye Dunaway, actress; and Yukio Mishima, writer.*

January 15   Success Number 16/7 (1 + 15 = 16/7)

In business, you gravitate to large enterprises, and you may have an interest in politics and government service. Dramatic by nature, you can write, act, lecture, teach, and preach. Sometimes you're found in businesses allied to the arts. With a 16/7 Success Number, you'll develop a workable philosophy of life that will enable you to overcome a tendency to be obstinate and overly meticulous. 16/7 may also draw you to a career in law, science, religion, or literature. *Birthday of Molière, French playwright; Lloyd Bridges, actor; and Edward Teller, nuclear physicist.*

January 16   Success Number 17/8 (1 + 16 = 17/8)

You often serve the community in some advisory capacity and may also have an interest in the arts. Cultivate the ambition of your 17/8 Success Number and keep your sights set high, for you have the abilities to make your mark on the world. Your 17/8 will help you develop management and organizational skills, which will be helpful to you in business or government service. A tendency to keep things to yourself, however, can work against you in personal relationships. Be sure to let others know how you feel toward them. *Birthday of Sade, singer; Ethel Merman, actress; and Dian Fossey, zoologist.*

January 17 Success Number 18/9 (1 + 17 = 18/9)

You have administrative talents and often are drawn to politics and government service. You can succeed in business for yourself and often have financial skills. Your reasoning mind may draw you to academic pursuits, especially writing and teaching. Your 18/9 Success Number invites you to develop a global consciousness, a love and empathy for your fellow man. Then you will overcome an occasional tendency to be aloof. 18/9 is also favorable for a career involving theater—as an actor, playwright, or director. *Birthday of Jim Carrey, actor; James Earl Jones, actor; and Anton Chekhov, Russian playwright.*

January 18 Success Number 19/10/1 (1 + 18 = 19/10/1)

You are industrious and ambitious. You have a good head for business and can succeed as a consultant or head of a corporation. You also have strong intellectual leanings and may be drawn to writing or a teaching career. Your 19/10/1 Success Number puts an added emphasis on getting ahead in life. Though you are versatile, 19/10/1 indicates that you should focus on one primary goal to enjoy your greatest success. Your Success Number encourages you to cultivate your originality, be independent, and do your own thing. You are a good money-maker and are often drawn to an artistic or professional career. *Birthday of Cary Grant, actor; Kevin Costner, actor; and Muhammad Ali, boxer.*

January 19   Success Number 20/2 (1 + 19 = 20/2)

You have natural leadership abilities and can succeed in business for yourself. Your 20/2 Success Number indicates that being tactful and diplomatic will help you to achieve your ends. 20/2 also indicates that you have a mystical, poetic side and will have success in creative areas. Often you are reform-minded and may be drawn to politics and government service. You work well in partnership and are apt to have a strong need for financial and emotional security. Although you're basically conventional, there's a part of you that's not. *Birthday of Robert E. Lee, army officer; Paul Cézanne, painter; and Janis Joplin, rock star.*

January 20   Success Number 21/3 (1 + 20 = 21/3)

You work well with others and are partnership-oriented. Your innate diplomacy qualifies you for success in both politics and business. With 21/3 as your Success Number, you'll find that friendliness and charm will ease your path your life. Maintaining a good sense of humor and an optimistic outlook will help you ward off an occasional inclination toward moods of depression. Though you have an outgoing personality, you may be slow to take others into your confidence. Develop the communication skills of your 21/3 and you will have success in creative areas. *Birthday of Federico Fellini, film director; David Lynch, film director; and Patricia Neal, actress.*

January 21   Success Number 22/4 (1 + 21 = 22/4)

You are clever and artistic. At times, though, you can scatter your energies and need the self-discipline of your 22/4 Success Number to make the most of your talents. By placing the accent on practicality (4) and hard work (4), you can succeed in any field that measures up to your ideals (22). You're often found in business for yourself and are likely to be drawn to both the arts and sciences. Writing, banking, merchandising, publishing, architecture, and design are some of the fields in which your inventive genius will flourish. *Birthday of Jack Nicklaus, golfer; Geena Davis, actress; and Placido Domingo, opera star.*

January 22   Success Number 23/5 (1 + 22 = 23/5)

First of all, you are a unique individual. You're likely to march to the beat of your own drummer and are creative and inventive. Though you're a hard worker, you dislike routine. You're very intuitive, but inclined to be skeptical. You have much nervous energy and need time by yourself to keep your life on an even keel. Your 23/5 Success Number will help you gain a greater understanding of your fellow man. At times, you may be detached and impersonal, but 23/5 will warm you up and give you a spirit of adventure. You're capable of outstanding achievement in both the arts and sciences. *Birthday of Lord Byron, poet; Piper Laurie, actress; and August Strindberg, playwright.*

January 23   Success Number 24/6   (1 + 23 = 24/6)

You have a good understanding of human nature and are both progressive and practical in outlook. You have the ability to make friends easily, but sometimes you can be a bit aloof and overly insistent on maintaining your freedom and independence. Your 24/6 Success Number, though, will help you quell your restlessness and add more warmth to your nature. Cultivate the stability of 24/6 and you'll be less likely to flit from one thing to another. Your 24/6 will also assure you success in such fields as acting, writing, journalism, and medicine. *Birthday of Jeanne Moreau, actress; Randolph Scott, actor; and Stendhal, writer.*

January 24   Success Number 25/7   (1 + 24 = 25/7)

You belong in public affairs—politics, civic reform, social betterment. Visionary and idealistic, you are a natural-born leader who has the ability to inspire others. It is important, though, that you like your work. Otherwise you may not put in the effort to succeed. 25/7 as your Success Number indicates the need for you to develop a workable philosophy of life to offset restlessness, rashness, and a tendency to scatter your energies. Dramatic by nature, you can succeed in creative areas, especially art, acting, music, and writing. *Birthday of Frederick the Great, Prussian king; Robert Motherwell, painter; and John Belushi, actor.*

January 25   Success Number 26/8 (1 + 25 = 26/8)

You are naturally prophetic and intuitive. You have intellectual gifts as well, and with 26/8 as your Success Number, you have the ability to commercialize them successfully. Though you can succeed in business, you would be unhappy in work that does not reflect your ideals. You are something of a dreamer and need the practicality and organizational skills of your 26/8 Success Number to help you keep your feet on the ground. You have a talent for invention and a love of music. An interest in what makes others tick may draw you to writing or counseling. Don't let your strong principles cause you to become intolerant. *Birthday of Virginia Woolf, writer; W. Somerset Maugham, writer; and Etta James, singer.*

January 26   Success Number 27/9 (1 + 26 = 27/9)

You can succeed in business, but you may find the arts and politics more to your liking. With 27/9 as your Success Number, you may be especially drawn to literature, religion, and philosophy. Your 27/9 Success Number also gives you humanitarian leanings and indicates that you'd be quite successful in social service. The combination of your birthday and Success Numbers indicates that you would be a good fund-raiser for a cause. If you'll accent the 27/9 love for humanity, you'll overcome a tendency to withdraw into yourself and suffer periodic bouts of loneliness. *Birthday of Douglas MacArthur; U.S. general; Paul Newman, actor; and Wayne Gretzky, hockey star.*

January 27   Success Number 28/10/1 (1 + 27 = 28/10/1)

You have an interest in the general welfare and may be drawn to politics and social service. You do not like taking orders and are inclined to do your own thing. Often you are very gifted in music, acting, writing, and art. With a 28/10/1 Success Number and a 27/9 birthday, you are an individual who is both unique (1) and universal (9). Cultivate the courage of your 28/10/1 Success Number and you will become a leader of the people, a leader in thought and action—a person able to impress the minds and hearts of humanity at large. *Birthday of Wolfgang Amadeus Mozart, composer; Lewis Carroll, writer; and Bridget Fonda, actress.*

January 28   Success Number 29/11/2 (1 + 28 = 29/11/2)

You may not be well suited for business, as you are high-strung, emotional, and unconventional. However, you are also ambitious and do want to excel. With 29/11/2 as your Success Number, you should let your idealism—rather than a desire for material success—be your prime motivator. Listen to your inner voice and you may create work that's ahead of its time, especially in such fields as music, art, science, and writing. You also may be inventive and an inspired leader. Your greatest task is with yourself. Be at peace with yourself and don't let nerves or temperament undermine accomplishment. *Birthday of Elijah Wood, actor; Arthur Rubenstein, pianist; and Mikhail Baryshnikov, dancer.*

January 29 Success Number 30/3 (1 + 29 = 30/3)

You are a lover of freedom for yourself and for others. Though you can succeed in business, you're usually happier in the arts and professions. You have unusual ideas, but often they are ahead of their time. If you'll cultivate the charm, friendliness, and good humor of your 30/3 Success Number, you'll overcome a tendency to let nerves get the best of you. Your 30/3 often leads you into a creative field, such as acting, writing, journalism, and art. You'll do best in vocations that you truly like—you would be very unhappy in an uncongenial profession. *Birthday of Oprah Winfrey, actress; Germaine Greer, writer; and W. C. Fields, actor.*

January 30 Success Number 31/4 (1 + 30 = 31/4)

You have leadership qualities and are humanitarian in outlook. Sometimes, though, you can be fixed in your views and need to pay more attention to ideas that differ from your own. Still, you're good at promoting yourself, and this quality will help you in business, politics, and creative fields. With 31/4 as your Success Number, self-discipline, concentration, and hard work will be your chief allies in making progress—otherwise you may tend to scatter your energies and fail to realize your potential. You can excel in any line of work you choose. *Birthday of Dick Cheney, U.S. vice president; Vanessa Redgrave, actress; and Gene Hackman, actor.*

January 31   Success Number 32/5 (1 + 31 = 32/5)

You can be a bit unorthodox and are not always inclined to go along with established customs. You have much creative ability, but need to be self-disciplined to make the most of your potential. Some of the fields that promise you success are acting, writing, music, teaching, journalism, art, science, and publishing. Your 32/5 Success Number is an invitation to explore the new and to cultivate your originality. Then you'll avoid falling into a comfortable, but nonprogressive, rut. Always be willing to expand your horizons. Dare to take a chance on yourself. *Birthday of Jackie Robinson, baseball star; Minnie Driver, actress; and Justin Timberlake, singer.*

FEBRUARY

February 1   Success Number 3 (2 + 1 = 3)

You are a person intent on doing your thing. You have natural leadership abilities and can succeed in business for yourself. Blessed with an abundance of creative energy, you are often drawn to the theater, writing, and art. With 3 as your Success Number, you'll excel in any field where communication skills and a pleasing personality are factors. At times, though, you can have your fingers in too many pies—and you don't always finish what you start. *Birthday of John Ford, film director; Boris Yeltsin, Soviet leader; and Sherman Hemsley, actor.*

February 2   Success Number 4   (2 + 2 = 4)

You would make a fine teacher, psychologist, or adviser. You work well in partnership and are usually quite imaginative. Financial security is important to you, but you also have strong artistic leanings. Music, dance, poetry, and art are areas that offer you fulfillment, and your innate diplomacy makes you a natural for government service. With 4 as your Success Number, hard work, self-discipline, and practicality are the keys to making the most of your potential. Then you'll overcome a tendency to be indecisive, overly sensitive, lazy, or fearful. *Birthday of Jascha Heifetz, violinist; James Joyce, writer; and James Dickey, poet.*

February 3   Success Number 5   (2 + 3 = 5)

You are versatile, but must curb a tendency to scatter your energies. With 5 as your Success Number, you'll do well in fields where the personal touch is a factor. A born communicator, you like people and often have an outstanding gift for writing. Cultivate the showmanship and the spirit of adventure of your 5 Success Number and you'll succeed in show business, sales, and occupations involving travel. Other fields that promise you fulfillment are public relations, politics, hotel management, editing, journalism, and teaching. *Birthday of James Michener, writer; Gertrude Stein, writer; and Horace Greeley, newspaper editor.*

February 4   Success Number 6 (2 + 4 = 6)

You have progressive ideas and strong ideals, but you are also practical and down-to-earth. With 6 as your Success Number, you would make a fine public servant, for you have a genuine interest in the welfare of the community. You work well with groups and can achieve a position of leadership in that capacity. Both science and the arts are likely to appeal to you. Dramatic by nature, you can acquit yourself well in theatrical pursuits. Music, sculpture, and floriculture are also possible avocations or vocations. *Birthday of Charles Lindbergh, aviator; Ida Lupino, actress-film director; and Betty Friedan, feminist writer.*

February 5   Success Number 7 (2 + 5 = 7)

Born on the 5th, you are restless, adventurous, and experimental. Left unchecked, your 5 may cause you to flit from one thing to another. With 7—the number of reflection and specialization—as your Success Number, however, you will make progress in life when you learn to focus on one thing. Your 7 will give you a philosophical bent and the ability to learn and profit from your experiences. Law, religion, politics, writing, and the academic life are likely to appeal to you. Though you work well with people, a part of you may remain aloof. You are an innovator who loves to take a risk now and then. *Birthday of Hank Aaron, baseball star; William Burroughs, writer; and Zsa Zsa Gabor, actress.*

February 6 Success Number 8 (2 + 6 = 8)

You have an engaging personality and work well with groups. With 8 as your Success Number, you are ambitious and a good moneymaker. You must resist the tendency of 6 to get into a rut of complacency, though your 8 Success Number will goad you to strive to keep bettering yourself. Intuitive by nature, you're capable of progressive thought. Enthusiastic about the causes you espouse, you are often magnetic and charismatic, qualities that will serve you well in show business, politics, and public life. You need congenial surroundings to do your best work. *Birthday of Ronald Reagan, U.S. president; François Truffault, film director; and Axl Rose, rock star.*

February 7 Success Number 9 (2 + 7 = 9)

Your 7 birthday number directs your attention inward, inclining you toward introspection and sometimes discouragement. With a Success Number of 9, however, you have an interest in world problems and a desire to solve social ills. The acute powers of observation of your 7 combined with the love and compassion of 9 makes you a good student of human nature and a person who has a genuine interest in the greater welfare. You would make a fine writer or critic, social worker, counselor, or psychologist. Research, science, and music may also appeal to you. *Birthday of Charles Dickens, writer; Sinclair Lewis, writer; and James Spader, actor.*

February 8   Success Number 10/1 (2 + 8 = 10/1)

You have executive talents and can succeed in the business world, especially in large enterprises. Ambitious to make something of yourself, you are often found in an artistic or professional career. With 10/1 as your Success Number, you will rise to the top when you learn to do your own thing. Cultivate the idealism, the courage, and the creativity of number 10, and you can succeed in any vocation that reflects your ideals. You have a desire to be great, but you also want others to profit from the magnitude of your achievement. Take care not to become self-righteous. *Birthday of Nick Nolte, actor; Lana Turner, actress; and Jules Verne, writer.*

February 9   Success Number 11/2 (2 + 9 = 11/2)

You have a natural interest in public service and may be drawn to a career in politics or government. With 11/2 as your Success Number, you work best when inspired, but are sometimes nervous and high-strung. Independent and unconventional, you march to the beat of your own drummer. You are more suited for the arts than business and are capable of unique accomplishments in your chosen field, especially music, acting, and writing. You have the best interests of everyone at heart, but you dislike being told what to do. You are a born lecturer, teacher, or preacher. Take care not to spread yourself too thin. *Birthday of Carole King, singer; Alice Walker, writer; and Joe Pesci, actor.*

February 10   Success Number 12/3 (2 + 10 = 12/3)

You are independent, highly original, and usually stand out from the crowd as a person who does your own thing. With 12/3 as your Success Number, a sense of humor and a positive outlook will ease your path in life. Your 12/3 Success Number gives you communication skills and promises you success in both business and the arts, especially writing, music, and acting. You are versatile but must take care not to scatter your energies. You have natural leadership abilities and excel at promoting yourself and your ideas. You love an audience and enjoy being in the public eye. *Birthday of Boris Pasternak, writer; Donovan, singer; and Jimmy Durante, comedian.*

February 11   Success Number 13/4 (2 + 11 = 13/4)

You are independent, inventive, and unconventional. Though you're usually willing to experiment and take risks, you'll need the self-discipline of your 13/4 Success Number to turn your dreams into realties. Both creative and practical, you seem to know how to combine these qualities to your advantage. Though you often rely on your intuition, genius, and hunches, you also realize the value of work. In the words of Thomas Edison, born on February 11, "Genius is 1 percent inspiration and 99 percent perspiration." You are at home in both the arts and sciences and are likely to have strong humanitarian leanings. *Birthday of Eva Gabor, actress; Burt Reynolds, actor; and Mary Quant, fashion designer.*

February 12 Success Number 14/5 (2 + 12 = 14/5)

Your 14/5 Success Number makes you a trailblazer, a person willing to explore the new and to experience life to the fullest. These qualities combine with the natural friendliness and communication skills of your 12 birthday number to make you an individual who has people skills, warmth, and a keen understanding of human nature. You have a fine legal mind, a brilliant imagination, and a genuine concern for the well-being of your fellow man. You are multitalented and versatile, but do take care not to scatter your energies. *Birthday of Charles Darwin, scientist; Christina Ricci, actress; and Judy Blume, writer.*

February 13 Success Number 15/6 (2 + 13 = 15/6)

You have a natural interest in the unusual in experience. The practical and the here-and-now are your milieu, but at times you're given to escapism. Your 15/6 Success Number, though, will point you in the right direction, for it gives you the ability to accept responsibility and enables you to successfully commercialize your creative talents. However, if you keep your feelings hidden, your path in personal relationships will not be easy. When you think of the greater good, you are at your best. Real estate, writing, medicine, and music are fields that promise you fulfillment. *Birthday of Grant Wood, painter; Chuck Yeager, U.S. test pilot; and Jerry Springer, TV talk show host.*

February 14   Success Number 16/7 (2 + 14 = 16/7)

You are a people person—your personality enables you to win the support of others. Dramatic by nature, you can be successful in theatrical pursuits. Naturally experimental and adventurous, you may be inclined to take unwise risks and to be expedient. Your 16/7 Success Number, however, will incline you to perfect your talents, obtain a good education, develop a workable philosophy of life, and refrain from scattering your energies. Then you will become a person fully aware of your mission in life. You're capable of handling large responsibilities. *Birthday of Hugh Downs, TV journalist; Thelma Ritter, actress; and Jack Benny, comedian.*

February 15   Success Number 17/8 (2 + 15 = 17/8)

You are a good moneymaker, but may tend to become complacent once success is achieved. Let your 17/8 Success Number spur you on to greater heights. With the organizational skills of your 17/8, you can succeed in large enterprises that will have an impact on the world at large. You have a taste for luxury and are not always given to making sacrifices. Still, you are inclined toward humanitarianism and are tolerant, generous, inventive, and optimistic in outlook. A home of your own is important to you. Writing, acting, law, medicine, music, and design are fields in which you'll excel. *Birthday of Harvey Korman, actor; Melissa Manchester, singer; and Susan Brownmiller, feminist.*

February 16   Success Number 18/9 (2 + 16 = 18/9)

You have an interest in social problems and are a natural critic of society and its values. More inclined to academic fields than business, you work better on your own than with groups. A bit detached and impersonal, you need to cultivate the warmth and compassion of your 9 Success Number to reach a greater audience (if in a creative field) and a better rapport with personal ties. You will go all-out for any cause you espouse and may find government service, politics, science, teaching, writing, theater, and music to be congenial and fulfilling vocations. *Birthday of Henry Adams, historian; John McEnroe, tennis star; and Sonny Bono, singer.*

February 17   Success Number 19/10/1 (2 + 17 = 19/10/1)

You have moneymaking talents, but your approach to business is likely to be unorthodox. Usually you're more at home in an artistic or professional field, especially one that will allow you to fully employ your fine intuition and inventive skills. With 19/10/1 as your Success Number, you will rise to the top when you find and then do your own thing. 19/10/1 gives you leadership abilities and points you in the direction of politics, public service, and reform movements. Writing, music, painting, and acting may also be fields in which you are exceptionally talented. *Birthday of Alan Bates, actor; Marian Anderson, opera star; and Yasser Arafat, PLO leader.*

February 18   Success Number 20/2 (2 + 18 = 20/2)

You often have an interest in social service and administrative work. Well suited for business, you usually are a good moneymaker. You have strong humanitarian leanings as well and will do your part to help the underdog. However, you dislike taking orders and treasure your personal freedom. Still, you're not averse to making sacrifices for those you care for. With a 20/2 Success Number, your path in life will be made easier if you'll place a special accent on being tactful, cooperative, and diplomatic. Your 20/2 Success Number attracts you to such fields as literature, acting, and medicine. *Birthday of Jack Palance, actor; Cybill Shepherd, actress; and Matt Dillon, actor.*

February 19   Success Number 21/3 (2 + 19 = 21/3)

With 21/3 as your Success Number, be sure to cultivate an optimistic attitude toward life, for at times your temperament can cause you to despair of getting ahead. You are reform-minded and naturally drawn to politics and social service. Though you have a good capacity for making money, you are more inclined to the arts and professions than business. Your inner feelings are likely to be intense, but your 3 Success Number gives you charm, aplomb, and communication skills. Take care, though, not to scatter your energies and not to make mountains out of molehills. *Birthday of Amy Tan, writer; Carson McCullers, writer; and Smokey Robinson, singer-songwriter.*

February 20   Success Number 22/4   (2 + 20 = 22/4)

You are sensitive, mystical, and poetic. With a 22/4 Success Number, you often have a visionary outlook on life and will do best in work that measures up to your ideals. You usually fare better in an artistic or professional field than in business, especially acting, writing, music, dance, and photography. Naturally empathetic and compassionate, you may be drawn to such fields as psychology, medicine, social work, and nursing. Cultivate the self-discipline of your 22/4 Success Number to offset an inclination to be indolent. Learn the value of discipline and order. *Birthday of Jackie Gleason, actor; Kelsey Grammer, actor; and Cindy Crawford, model.*

February 21   Success Number 23/5   (2 + 21 = 23/5)

You have marked creative talents and are gifted in self-expression, but you must avoid scattering your energies. With a 23/5 Success Number, you're adventurous and inclined to experiment before settling on a career. It is important that you clarify your goals and not simply settle for what chance throws your way. Your 23/5 Success Number will get you out into the world and offset your tendency to withdraw or to become overly introspective. Because you like to help others, you may be drawn to social service or medicine. You're most at home, though, in the arts and show business. *Birthday of Nina Simone, singer; W. H. Auden, poet; and David Geffen, record producer.*

February 22   Success Number 24/6 (2 + 22 = 24/6)

You have a genuine concern for human suffering and are often active in humanitarian service. You enjoy public life and would make a good spokesperson for a cause. Sensitive and poetic, you would succeed in acting, art, and writing. You may be drawn to the sciences as well. With 24/6 as your Success Number, responsibility seems to bring out the best in you. You need to keep busy, to be involved—otherwise you become listless and, perhaps, inclined to self-indulgence and lethargy. At times, you need periods by yourself to replenish your energies. *Birthday of Edna St. Vincent Millay, poet; Drew Barrymore, actress; and Ted Kennedy, U.S. senator.*

February 23   Success Number 25/7 (2 + 23 = 25/7)

You have an adventurous approach to life, yet you're also introspective. Progressive in thought, you are also practical. You enjoy travel and may be drawn to the field of education. You're willing to try anything once, but with a 25/7 Success Number you will eventually learn to specialize. An interest in helping others sometimes draws you to a medical or counseling career. You get along well with people, but there may be a part of you that remains aloof. Take care not to place too much emphasis on money and success. You may have an uncanny affinity for flowers, perfumes, plants, and herbs that hold curative powers. *Birthday of George Frideric Handel, composer; Peter Fonda, actor; and Elston Howard, baseball star.*

February 24   Success Number 26/8   (2 + 24 = 26/8)

You work well with groups and often achieve a position of leadership in that capacity. Though you're anxious for material success, you're basically an idealist at heart. You are intellectual and practical, but you also have a good imagination. You need to keep busy to be happy. Otherwise you seem to wilt. With a 26/8 Success Number, you have a good business sense and also know how to turn your artistic potential into profit-making activities. Your 26/8 invites you to think big and helps you offset a tendency to worry too much. *Birthday of Winslow Homer, painter; Steven Jobs, CEO, Apple Computer; and Zachary Scott, actor.*

February 25   Success Number 27/9   (2 + 25 = 27/9)

You are contemplative, intuitive, and mystical. You may have a great talent for music and are often drawn to a theatrical career, often preferring to work in some behind-the-scenes capacity. With 27/9 as your Success Number, you are resilient in crisis situations and can bounce back from setbacks. Your 27/9 promises you fulfillment in humanitarian work. When you lose yourself in service to others, you also find yourself. Then you overcome a tendency to be self-deprecating or melancholy. The religious life, painting, writing, and teaching are other likely vocations. *Birthday of Anthony Burgess, writer; Enrico Caruso, opera star; and Pierre-Auguste Renoir, painter.*

February 26   Success Number 28/10/1 (2 + 26 = 28/10/1)

You are introspective and are inclined to live in the past. You work well from behind the scenes, are generous, and are a good spender. With 28/l0/1 as your Success Number, try to develop your originality. Find and then do your own thing, but take care not to be eccentric and too unconventional. You understand human nature and will have success as a writer, psychologist, or actor. You need an artistic outlet through which to express your sensitive feelings. Otherwise you'll need to periodically overcome a tendency toward fits of melancholy and negativity. *Birthday of Tony Randall, actor; Johnny Cash, singer; and Victor Hugo, writer.*

February 27   Success Number 29/11/2 (2 + 27 = 29/11/2)

You have a knack for overcoming adversity. You are strong-willed, and do not suffer defeat gladly. You are philosophical and inclined to a mental career, such as writing, journalism, or poetry. With a 29/11/2 Success Number, you work best when inspired, and you are capable of being a visionary leader in your field. You also love art, music, and the theater, but must not let temperament and nerves sap your energies and spirit. Universal in outlook, you are a humanitarian and inclined to public service. You insist on freedom in your personal life, but will sacrifice anything else for those you love. *Birthday of John Steinbeck, writer; Lawrence Durrell, writer; and Joanne Woodward, actress.*

February 28   Success Number 30/3 (2 + 28 = 30/3)

With 30/3 as your Success Number, you often choose a creative medium through which to express your individuality. You can achieve fame in acting, music, and art —that is, if you'll learn to apply yourself and to overcome an inclination to scatter your energies. You are both independent and cooperative, but may have trouble reconciling these qualities. And you also have an unconventional side. If you cultivate the cheerfulness, optimism, and sense of humor of your 30/3 Success Number, you'll overcome a tendency to magnify small setbacks. *Birthday of Linus Pauling, chemist; Stephen Spender, poet; and John Turturro, actor.*

February 29   Success Number 31/4 (2 + 29 = 31/4)

You have the temperament of genius, and perhaps the talent as well! Subject to mood swings, you tend to be an extremist in all things. To make the most of your great potential, you need to cultivate the self-discipline of your 31/4 Success Number. Let your 31/4 teach you the value of organization and order in all your activities. You are capable of creating work that's ahead of its time, and with 31/4 on your side, you have the practicality to make your dreams and visions come true. Public service, work of a humanitarian nature, and artistic pursuits are your milieu. *Birthday of Balthus, painter; Rossini, composer; and Antonio Sabato Jr., actor.*

MARCH

March 1   Success Number 4 (3 + 1 = 4)

You can succeed in business for yourself and are a person meant to do your thing. Your 4 Success Number gives you the ability to work hard for results and ensures that you will make constructive use of your potential. You can easily become buried in your job, however, and must be careful not to get in a rut. Often you have an outstanding talent for music and writing, but sometimes you're given to bouts of depression. Multitalented, you often have your fingers in many pies. *Birthday of Harry Belafonte, singer; Glenn Miller, musician; and Ron Howard, film director.*

March 2   Success Number 5 (3 + 2 = 5)

You are incredibly sensitive, perhaps even psychic, and naturally empathetic and diplomatic. Your Success Number of 5 gives you a good understanding of human nature and a progressive outlook—talents that will serve you well in such fields as writing, teaching, psychology, politics, religion, and the arts. If you'll capitalize on the adventurousness and originality of your Success Number, you'll overcome a tendency toward lethargy and insecurity. With action and assertion, your dreams of a better tomorrow for your loved ones and the human race at large will come true. *Birthday of Tom Wolfe, writer; Mikhail Gorbachev, Soviet leader; and Lou Reed, rock star.*

March 3   Success Number 6 (3 + 3 = 6)

You're a gifted communicator and versatile, but you may have a tendency to scatter your energies. With 6 as your Success Number, you will do best when settled down in a position of responsibility. Your 6 Success Number makes you community-minded, with an ability to work well with groups. You'll succeed in such fields as banking, advertising, acting, public relations, and writing. You have a flair for fashion and would make a fine decorator or designer. An innovative person, you're capable of work that's ahead of its time. You also work well with those who are less fortunate. *Birthday of Jean Harlow, actress; Alexander Graham Bell, inventor; and Matthew Ridgway, U.S. general.*

March 4   Success Number 7 (3 + 4 = 7)

You are a blend of practicality and idealism. Your 4 birthday number keeps your feet on the ground, whereas your 7 Success Number makes you introspective and spiritually inclined. With 7 as your guide, you'll develop a workable philosophy of life that will help offset your 4 inclination to worry too much. You can succeed in real estate, art, literature, music, writing, sculpture, and acting. You'll also do well in the caring professions and may be drawn to the religious or academic life. A good education will help you make the most of your considerable potential. *Birthday of Mary Wilson, singer; Miriam Makeba, singer; and Antonio Vivaldi, composer.*

March 5   Success Number 8   (3 + 5 = 8)

You need excitement in your work and the freedom to be creative. Versatile and adventurous, you may change your mind more than once before settling on a vocation. Cultivate the ambition and the organizational skills of your 8 Success Number and you will make your mark on the world. You may have special talents for acting and for brokerage, though you're likely to be happier in an artistic career than business. You have an engaging personality and usually get along very well with others. A tendency, though, to burn the candle at both ends can work against getting ahead. *Birthday of Dean Stockwell, actor; Samantha Eggar, actress; and Frank Norris, writer.*

March 6   Success Number 9   (3 + 6 = 9)

You have an ability to work well with groups and are willing to assume responsibility. Family life and a home of your own are important to you. With 9 as your Success Number, you are naturally sympathetic and have a genuine interest in public service. Your greatest talent, though, lies in the arts. Often you excel as a writer, painter, dancer, composer, or actor. Be sure to develop your creative talents, for your 9 Success Number will enable you to touch the minds and hearts of a global audience. Naturally caring and empathetic, you'll also succeed in the healing professions. *Birthday of Michelangelo, painter; Shaquille O'Neal, basketball star; and Lou Costello, actor.*

March 7   Success Number 10/1 (3 + 7 = 10/1)

You enjoy exploring the mysteries of life and may be drawn to a research occupation. You can achieve recognition in academic fields, and with a Success Number of 10/1 you usually stand out from the crowd as an individual who does your own thing. If you're not in a healing profession, you would find fulfillment in art, music, writing, or acting. Your 7 birthday number inclines you to be reflective, whereas your 10/1 Success Number encourages you to be original and independent. Your 7 gives you a keen and inquiring mind, and your 10/1 Success Number gives you the courage to voice your convictions. *Birthday of Anna Magnani, actress; Luther Burbank, botanist; and Maurice Ravel, composer.*

March 8   Success Number 11/2 (3 + 8 = 11/2)

Your 8 birthday number gives you a good head for business, but your 11/2 Success Number may incline you to a career in the arts or public service. With 11/2, you work best when inspired, but be careful not to let temperament undermine your efficiency. You are visionary and capable of work that's highly original. Your concern for human rights and the betterment of humankind may incline you to such fields as law, medicine, philanthropy, and education. Your love of the sea may attract you to maritime commerce. *Birthday of Oliver Wendell Holmes Jr., Supreme Court justice; Cyd Charisse, dancer; and Freddie Prinze Jr., actor.*

March 9   Success Number 12/3   (3 + 9 = 12/3)

Your 9 birthday number makes you keenly aware of the sufferings of others and desirous of making a contribution to improve world conditions. With 12/3 as your Success Number, you have the urge to bring light to dark places, to bring hope to the downtrodden. A true servant of the people, you may devote your life to service. With the number of communication as your Success Number, you often choose a creative medium through which to express your concern for others. You would make a good spokesperson for a cause. Cultivate the cheerfulness of 3 to offset a tendency to take life's woes too personally. *Birthday of Juliette Binoche, actress; Mickey Spillane, writer; and Yuri Gagarin, Soviet cosmonaut.*

March 10   Success Number 13/4   (3 + 10 = 13/4)

Being born on the 10th, you are very much the individualist, but you'll need the self-discipline of your 13/4 Success Number to make the most of your talents. Take care, though, not to give in to the discouragement that sometimes accompanies the number 4. Both creative and practical, you may at times have difficulty reconciling these qualities. You work best when interested in your work, and you require a creative outlet for your feeling nature. You can succeed in business for yourself, but you're more likely to be drawn to an artistic or professional career. *Birthday of Chuck Norris, actor; David Rabe, playwright; Clare Boothe Luce, playwright-diplomat.*

March 11   Success Number 14/5 (3 + 11 = 14/5)

Born on the 11th, you are intuitive, idealistic, and, perhaps, psychic. With a 14/5 Success Number, however, you may be something of an opportunist. You are quick to see the main chance, yet you can get discouraged if results aren't immediately forthcoming. Restless and adventurous, you're liable to experiment before settling on a career. Music and acting are two of the fields for which you may have an outstanding talent. Your interest in reform could draw you to a political career. You're good at extricating yourself from emergency situations. *Birthday of Lawrence Welk, bandleader; Rupert Murdoch, publisher; and Sam Donaldson, TV journalist.*

March 12   Success Number 15/6 (3 + 12 = 15/6)

Dramatic and self-expressive, you have promotional skills and strong artistic leanings (especially the theater). Your 15/6 Success Number will help you gain a sense of responsibility to offset a tendency to spread yourself too thin. In business, your 15/6 will draw you to large enterprises. No matter what field you choose, you're usually a good moneymaker. Your talent with the written and spoken word makes you a good writer and a fine teacher. Advertising, publishing, and sales are other promising vocations. A home is important to your happiness, and you enjoy beautiful surroundings. *Birthday of Edward Albee, playwright; James Taylor, singer; and Jack Kerouac, writer.*

March 13   Success Number 16/7 (3 + 13 = 16/7)

Your home, family, and immediate circle of friends are likely to be very important to you. However, you may need to curb a tendency to be dictatorial with others. You have intense feelings and need a creative outlet for them. Music, writing, design, sculpture, and writing are some of the fields that promise you fulfillment. With 16/7 as a Success Number, you need to develop a workable philosophy of life in order to overcome a tendency to dwell on worries too much. With that achieved, you'll have success in such fields as religion, science, law, teaching, real estate, and counseling. *Birthday of L. Ron Hubbard, scientologist; Neil Sedaka, songwriter; and William H. Macy, actor.*

March 14   Success Number 17/8 (3 + 14 = 17/8)

You have an adventurous approach to life and are an idealist, a humanitarian, and an innovator. Your 17/8 Success Number gives you management skills, but your monetary fortunes may tend to fluctuate. If you capitalize on the ambition and organizational talents of your 17/8 Success Number, you will offset a tendency to drift or to burn the candle at both ends. Both the arts and sciences are likely to be areas in which you will succeed. You may be very talented in dancing, music, acting, and art. You are often lucky, but take care not to push your luck too far. *Birthday of Michael Caine, actor; Quincy Jones, composer; and Albert Einstein, scientist.*

March 15   Success Number 18/9 (3 + 15 = 18/9)

You have a flair for the dramatic and for large enterprises. Whether in business or the arts, you're usually a good moneymaker. You have a keen sense of responsibility and are protective toward others. With 18/9 as your Success Number, you're likely to have administrative talents. Politics, social service, law, medicine, and religion are some of the fields that promise you fulfillment. Your 18/9 Success Number inclines you to community service and humanitarian endeavors. You would make a good spokesperson for a cause. *Birthday of Andrew Jackson, U.S. president; David Cronenberg, film director, Ruth Bader Ginsburg, U.S. Supreme Court justice.*

March 16   Success Number 19/10/1 (3 + 16 = 19/10/1)

You have a natural interest in community affairs and may have a philosophical, introspective, or religious bent as well. Money and power are important to you, but you must take care not to become dictatorial with success. A good education is a must for you—you do best in vocations that allow you to utilize your intellectual gifts. Writing, teaching, law, business, and religion are some of the fields in which you'll succeed. With 19/10/1 as your Success Number, your rise to the top begins when you find and then do your own thing. Be original! *Birthday of Jerry Lewis, actor; Pat Nixon, U.S. first lady; and Bernardo Bertolucci, film director.*

March 17   Success Number 20/2 (3 + 17 = 20/2)

You can succeed in business and are not afraid of taking a financial risk now and then. Kindly and humanitarian in outlook, you would do a world of good for others as a lawyer, physician, religious cleric, or counselor. An interest in investigating the unknown may attract you to scientific research, though you are equally at home in the arts. With a 20/2 Success Number, you value financial and emotional security. You dislike disharmony and do not fare well when criticized. With encouragement and praise, you blossom! Cultivate the cooperative spirit and friendliness of 20/2, and you'll go far. *Birthday of Rudolf Nureyev, ballet star; Danny DeVito, actor; and Nat King Cole, singer.*

March 18   Success Number 21/3 (3 + 18 = 21/3)

You may be drawn to politics and public service. With 21/3 as your Success Number, your talent for communicating your ideas will serve you well in both business and the arts. Though you have a friendly manner, it may take a while for others to get to know you. You're quite versatile, but you may be inclined to scatter your energies. Intellectual and dramatic, you can excel in creative areas. If you cultivate the optimism of your 21/3 Success Number, you'll overcome an inclination to get discouraged. *Birthday of John Updike, writer; Queen Latifah, actress-singer; and Nikolay Rimsky-Korsakov, composer.*

March 19   Success Number 22/4 (3 + 19 = 22/4)

You often have an interest in politics and reform and would make a fine public servant. With 22/4 as your Success Number, you are visionary in outlook and capable of work that's ahead of its time. However, your 22/4 also makes you subject to nervous tension and bouts of depression. It's by holding on to your ideals that you'll rise above life's rough spots to make your mark on the world. You have leadership qualities and can succeed in business for yourself, though you are more likely to seek a professional or artistic career. Usually you're good at making money. *Birthday of Earl Warren, U.S. Supreme Court justice; Glenn Close, actress; and Bruce Willis, actor.*

March 20   Success Number 23/5 (3 + 20 = 23/5)

You are sensitive and diplomatic. Politics and religion are two fields for which you may have a special affinity. Interested in reform, you'll do your part to establish universal brotherhood. You also have healing abilities and would succeed in medicine. With 23/5 as your Success Number, you may experiment before settling on a career. 23/5 will get you out into the world, despite your tendency to withdraw into yourself now and then. Through your Success Number, you'll gain an understanding of human nature that will be especially valuable to those of you in creative or counseling fields. *Birthday of Henrik Ibsen, playwright; Holly Hunter, actress; and Spike Lee, film director.*

March 21 Success Number 24/6 (3 + 21 = 24/6)

You are a person who needs to keep busy to be happy. You have promotional skills and will have success in such fields as advertising, publishing, and public relations. Dramatic by nature, you may be drawn to journalism and acting. A person of quick enthusiasm, you may not always finish what you start. To make the most of your potential, cultivate the sense of responsibility that comes with your 24/6 Success Number. Once you do, you'll find your proper niche in this world. Still, if you ever do lose your job, you're capable of getting by on your wits. *Birthday of Matthew Broderick, actor: Rosie O'Donnell, actress; and Gary Oldman, actor.*

March 22 Success Number 25/7 (3 + 22 = 25/7)

You are visionary in outlook, but inclined to be impatient. An original thinker, you're capable of work that's ahead of its time. Both the arts and sciences are likely to appeal to you. Often you have outstanding musical and writing abilities. You are at your best when you believe in what you do. With 25/7 as your Success Number, you need a good education to help you develop your gifts. 25/7 will enable you to attain a workable philosophy of life, important to one who has a mission to accomplish. At times, you need periods of quiet to quell your sometimes restless spirit. *Birthday of Marcel Marceau, mime; William Shatner, actor; and Reese Witherspoon, actress.*

266

March 23   Success Number 26/8 (3 + 23 = 26/8)

You are versatility-plus and can succeed in almost any line you choose. Progressive in outlook, you're capable of making innovations in your field that will lead to a better tomorrow. With 26/8 as your Success Number, you are ambitious and a seeker of material wealth. 26/8 gives you the will to make something of yourself and inclines you to large ventures. You will have success in business, but you also may be drawn to artistic and scientific fields. You're not one to sit on the sidelines and can be counted on to take an active role in whatever you undertake. *Birthday of Wernher von Braun, scientist; Joan Crawford, actress; and Roger Bannister, British runner.*

March 24   Success Number 27/9 (3 + 24 = 27/9)

You have promotional skills and are a person who needs to keep busy to be happy. You'll do well in fields involving finances and real estate. 27/9 as your Success Number gives you philosophical and literary tendencies, an interest in politics, and a desire to help others. Dramatic by nature, you can succeed in the theatrical world and may be drawn to music and sculpture as well. Resilient in spirit, you have the ability to bounce back from setbacks. Your views on religious subjects are apt to be unorthodox, and you do not like to be told what to do. *Birthday of Steve McQueen, actor; Wilhelm Reich, psychiatrist; and Lawrence Ferlinghetti, poet.*

March 25 Success Number 28/10/1 (3 + 25 = 28/10/1)

You are independent in thought and likely to speak your own mind. You have a powerful personality, but may at times be touchy and argumentative. Having the courage of your convictions, you are often a skilled debater, orator, or writer. Often you are blessed with exceptional musical talent. With a 28/10/1 Success Number, you come into your own when you find and do your own thing. With 28, you will learn how to be cooperative without losing your independence and individuality. You're more likely to be found in the arts and professions than in business. *Birthday of Gloria Steinem, feminist; Arturo Toscanini, conductor; and Simone Signoret, actress.*

March 26 Success Number 29/11/2 (3 + 26 = 29/11/2)

You are an active person who wants quick results. You need to develop patience, lest you abandon worthwhile projects too soon. Though you're a good moneymaker, with 29/11/2 as your Success Number, you are happiest in work that reflects your ideals. You may have an outstanding talent in the arts and are capable of work that's ahead of its time. You also are able to commercialize your creative gifts in a big way. With 29/11/2, you may be high-strung and inclined to get depressed. You are an accurate observer of human nature and enjoy public life. You may have philanthropic interests. *Birthday of Sandra Day O'Connor, U.S. Supreme Court justice; Diana Ross, singer; and Leonard Nimoy, actor.*

March 27   Success Number 30/3 (3 + 27 = 30/3)

You are independent with a strong personality. You thrive on challenges and do not know the meaning of the word *defeat*. You have executive talents and leadership abilities. With 30/3 as your Success Number, you often choose a creative medium through which to express your individuality. With 30/3, you have a friendly manner, but you also know how to look out for number one. Cultivate the warmth and good humor of 30/3 to offset your tendency to push too hard and to be overly self-involved. Being born on the 27th, you must rise beyond self-glorification and make a contribution that benefits the world at large. *Birthday of Mariah Carey, singer-actress; David Janssen, actor; and Michael York, actor.*

March 28   Success Number 31/4 (3 + 28 = 31/4)

You are independent and self-reliant. At times, you can be both impulsive and argumentative; however, you have the capacity to love deeply. You'll have success in business, but you also may have a talent for art and music. Writing, teaching, and medicine may also appeal to you. With 31/4 as your Success Number, the cultivation of self-discipline will help you make the most of your talents. Your 31/4 indicates that you would enjoy work that allows you to travel and that you have promotional skills. Politics and law are other possible vocations. *Birthday of Reba McEntire, singer; Nelson Algren, writer; and Dirk Bogarde, actor.*

March 29 Success Number 32/5 (3 + 29 = 32/5)

Your genuine concern for the rights of the underdog may draw you to a vocation in politics or social service. Fiery, you would make an excellent spokesperson for a cause. You will also excel in creative areas and work best when inspired. You're visionary in outlook and capable of highly original thought. An extremist at times, you need to keep a check on your temperament. Your 32/5 Success Number will give you a good understanding of human nature. Really getting to know others in the flesh is your best way to keep your ideas from being too abstract or theoretical. *Birthday of Pearl Bailey, singer; John Major, British statesman; and Jennifer Capriati, tennis star.*

March 30 Success Number 33/6 (3 + 30 = 33/6)

You have a pioneering spirit and a progressive outlook. A gift for self-expression is an asset to you in both business and the arts. Though you have an engaging personality, it may take a while before others get to know you well. With a 33/6 Success Number, you're capable of assuming great responsibilities and can be a driving force in the community. You would make an excellent teacher, writer, or social worker. The law, theater, and painting are other areas in which you can excel. Take care, though, to finish what you start and refrain from being overly fixed in your ideas. *Birthday of Francisco Goya, painter; Warren Beatty, actor; and Vincent van Gogh, painter.*

March 31   Success Number 34/7 (3 + 31 = 34/7)

You have a talent for self-promotion, but usually manage to keep part of yourself hidden from public view. You often have progressive ideas, which you tend to act on impulsively. With a 34/7 Success Number, you will learn to think before you act. Your 34/7 may draw you to literature, music, philosophy, and art, fields in which you can excel. You would also make a fine teacher. Though multitalented, you should specialize to achieve your greatest success. Sometimes you are prone to spend extravagantly. *Birthday of Al Gore, U.S. vice president; Shirley Jones, actress; and Richard Chamberlain, actor.*

APRIL

April 1   Success Number 5 (4 + 1 = 5)

You are inspired leader. You do not hide your lamp under a bushel—others will always know where you stand. You can succeed in business for yourself and also have creative leanings. Never one to sit still for long, you are constantly on the go. Your 5 Success Number only adds to your spirit of adventure and may cause you to experiment before settling on a vocation. Your 5 almost guarantees success in the field of show business, but it may also tempt you to go overboard in pleasure seeking. *Birthday of Debbie Reynolds, actress; Lon Chaney, actor; and Sergey Rachmaninoff, composer.*

April 2   Success Number 6 (4 + 2 = 6)

Sensitive and imaginative, you often make your mark in creative fields. Writing, music, art, poetry, acting, and dance are likely interests. Though at times restless, you work well in partnerships and are capable of doing your fair share. You may not always take kindly to routine, but with your 6 Success Number you will not shirk your duties. You would make an excellent teacher and a good promoter of the causes that you espouse. Not especially ambitious, you nonetheless often find yourself at the forefront of your field. *Birthday of Alec Guinness, actor; Émile Zola, writer; and Buddy Ebsen, actor.*

April 3   Success Number 7 (4 + 3 = 7)

With 3 as your birthday number, you're self-expressive; with 7 as your Success Number, you are also reflective. Your 3 gives you a friendly manner and an engaging personality, but your 7 indicates that you have a need for privacy and at times can be aloof and a bit closemouthed. With its emphasis on mental analysis, discrimination, and specialization, 7 will help you overcome your 3 tendencies to scatter your energies. With a good education (7), you'll make the most of your 3-type creative potential. You have promotional skills and can succeed in sales, publishing, acting, advertising, public relations, and writing. *Birthday of Eddie Murphy, actor; Doris Day, actress; and Marlon Brando, actor.*

272

April 4   Success Number 8   (4 + 4 = 8)

When you want something, you'll work very hard to obtain it. With 8 as your Success Number, you have your eye out for the main chance. 8 gives you ambition, executive talents, and an ability to succeed in the corporate world. You can also succeed in both the business and creative sides of show business. Art, music, sculpture, teaching, real estate, acting, and interior design are other fields that promise you fulfillment. If you will let go of any tendency to be rigid, controlling, or selfish, you will attract more love into your life. *Birthday of Maya Angelou, writer; Anthony Perkins, actor; and Craig T. Nelson, actor.*

April 5   Success Number 9   (4 + 5 = 9)

You're a dynamic person with progressive ideas who is eager to try new things. Restless by nature, you like to be constantly on the go. You dislike taking orders and belong in a leadership position. Always willing to take a chance, you can achieve notable success in such fields as acting and brokerage. Your 9 Success Number widens your scope and vision and keeps you from being overly self-involved. With 9, you'll reach out to help others and may engage in humanitarian endeavors. Take care, though, not to let your 5 pleasure-seeking qualities get the upper hand. *Birthday of Gregory Peck, actor; Bette Davis, actress; and Spencer Tracy, actor.*

April 6   Success Number 10/1   (4 + 6 = 10/1)

You work well with groups and often achieve a position of leadership in that capacity. You have a strong sense of responsibility and are willing to help others with their burdens. Enterprising and daring, you know how to make your own way in life. You can succeed in creative areas and often make your mark as an actor, musician, or journalist. With 10/1 as your Success Number, you're at your best when you find and do your own thing. Cultivate the originality of 1 to offset a 6 inclination to rest on your oars when comfort in life is achieved. *Birthday of Gerry Mulligan, jazz great; Michelle Phillips, singer-actress; and Bob Marley, reggae musician.*

April 7   Success Number 11/2   (4 + 7 = 11/2)

You are a dynamic person, but you need periods of peace and quiet to be at your best. You're likely to have philosophical and scientific interests. Often you're blessed with musical talent. With a 11/2 Success Number, you're intuitive and work best when inspired. You can succeed in business, but you're more suited by temperament for creative work. Your 11/2 makes you capable of highly innovative achievements and inclines you to social work and humanitarian endeavors. You often have an outstanding talent for expressing yourself with the written and spoken word. *Birthday of James Garner, actor; Jackie Chan, actor; and William Wordsworth, poet.*

April 8   Success Number 12/3   (4 + 8 = 12/3)

You are ambitious, with a good head for business. You can succeed in such fields as banking, public relations, real estate, and advertising. With 12/3 as your Success Number, your charm often paves your way to success. Your 3 fluency with the written and spoken word is also an asset to you in both business and the arts. Quite simply, you can sell yourself and your product. In creative fields, your work will be original and distinctive. However, you must be careful not to slacken your efforts after a modicum of success is achieved. You may have a tendency to rest on your laurels. *Birthday of Mary Pickford, actress; Patricia Arquette, actress; and Gerald McRaney, actor.*

April 9   Success Number 13/4   (4 + 9 = 13/4)

You are universal in outlook and may be drawn to politics and public service. You dislike taking orders and belong in an executive position. Your 13/4 Success Number gives you the practical know-how to make your sometimes visionary ideas workable. It is important, though, for you to find work that you can put your heart and soul into. Otherwise you may drift or easily become disheartened. The arts, especially music and acting, are likely to promise you success. You sometimes have an outstanding gift for writing. *Birthday of Jean-Paul Belmondo, actor; Hugh Hefner, publisher; and Charles Baudelaire, writer.*

April 10 Success Number 14/5 (4 + 10 = 14/5)

You have an enterprising spirit and, with 14/5 as your Success Number, are willing to take risks in your attack on life. Your 14/5 gives you a way with people, but take care not to be manipulative. You have executive talents and would be happy in a professional career. You have a strong interest in reform and may be attracted to politics and public service. An effective writer and speaker, you are zealous about the causes you espouse. Acting and art are other areas in which you can excel. Take care that your 14/5 doesn't make you too hasty, impulsive, or overly intent on pleasure seeking. *Birthday of Steven Seagal, actor; Omar Sharif, actor; and Max von Sydow, actor.*

April 11 Success Number 15/6 (4 + 11 = 15/6)

You are sensitive, dynamic, imaginative, and high-strung. Though you can succeed in business, you're usually happier in an artistic or professional career. You can be outspoken and may need to cultivate friendliness and diplomacy. With a 15/6 Success Number, you are a good moneymaker and have a keen sense of responsibility. Your 15/6 is a mandate to help others with their problems. As you give, you shall receive. Sometimes you're drawn to government service, and you usually have outstanding creative abilities. You are capable of being a true innovator in your chosen field. *Birthday of Oleg Cassini, designer; Joel Grey, actor; and Ethel Kennedy, political matriarch.*

April 12   Success Number 16/7 (4 + 12 = 16/7)

You are a good talker and very sure of yourself. Skilled at getting your ideas across to others, you know how to promote yourself. With your 16/7 Success Number, the more you work for public benefit, civic reform, and progress in general, the greater will be your success. Your 16/7 gives you a reflective and introspective side. Through its influence you will learn to think before you act. You may have a special talent for sales, publishing, show business, law, and politics. You are likely to have philosophical or religious interests as well. *Birthday of Shannen Doherty, actress; Claire Danes, actress; and Tom Clancy, writer.*

April 13   Success Number 17/8 (4 + 13 = 17/8)

You usually have keen insights into the motivations of others, a quality that will serve you well in such fields as writing, teaching, and counseling. You can also succeed in your own business, though you may be inclined to be bossy. With 17/8 as your Success Number, you are highly motivated to succeed. Your 17/8 gives you management skills, though at times your own financial fortunes may fluctuate. You have leadership abilities and a strong affinity for music. For your greatest success, it is important that you like your work. You are both creative and practical. *Birthday of Samuel Beckett, playwright; Thomas Jefferson, U.S. president; and Eudora Welty, writer.*

April 14 Success Number 18/9 (4 + 14 = 18/9)

You are adventurous, dramatic, and always willing to take a chance. Often you have a special talent for acting or brokerage. You are somewhat lucky in business, but take care not to push your luck too far. Your 18/9 Success Number invites you to see the larger picture, one that is bigger than self-interest. Develop your love for humanity at large and you can become a person of influence and scope. Politics, social service, education, law, and the arts are some of the fields in which you'll find success and fulfillment. Take care not to let pleasure seeking and restlessness get the upper hand. *Birthday of Julie Christie, actress; Arnold Toynbee, historian; and John Gielgud, actor.*

April 15 Success Number 19/10/1 (4 + 15 = 19/10/1)

You are at home in large enterprises and are a good moneymaker. You're progressive in outlook and, with 19/10/1 as your Success Number, are strongly motivated to do your own thing. If you'll cultivate the originality of your Success Number, you will go to the forefront of your field—and may even become famous! Though you can succeed in business, you'd be happier in an artistic or professional field. Law, acting, music, medicine, literature, promotional work, politics, and social reform are some of the vocations that promise you fame, fortune, and fulfillment. *Birthday of Emma Thompson, actress; Henry James, writer; and Bessie Smith, blues great.*

April 16   Success Number 20/2   (4 + 16 = 20/2)

Proud and courageous, you are eager for self-improvement. Take care, though, not to let financial concerns dominate your outlook when choosing a vocation. You can succeed in business, but you'll find a professional or artistic career to be more fulfilling. Cultivate the tact of your 20/2 Success Number to offset a tendency to be impulsive and too self-involved. Stress the 20/2 spirit of cooperation and you'll find your relationships with others to be more rewarding. A desire to shine may attract you to a theatrical career, but you can also succeed in art, literature, music, and law. *Birthday of Kareem Abdul-Jabbar, basketball star; Herbie Mann, jazz great; and Lucas Haas, actor.*

April 17   Success Number 21/3   (4 + 17 = 21/3)

You usually know how to get your money's worth, and you're willing to work hard to succeed. With 21/3 as your Success Number, you have excellent communication skills. Law, writing, teaching, advertising, banking, and sales are some of the fields in which you'll succeed. You like large-scale projects, but you do not always finish what you start. Sometimes you can be the free spender, yet at other times you're unduly conservative and cautious with your funds. You usually are sure of yourself and your beliefs. *Birthday of William Holden, actor; Thornton Wilder, writer; and Nikita Khrushchev, Soviet leader.*

April 18   Success Number 22/4 (4 + 18 = 22/4)

You often have business skills and humanitarian interests as well. Interested in reform, you would be a good spokesperson for a cause. To achieve your greatest success, cultivate the force, application, and self-discipline of your 22/4 Success Number. You are often visionary, but you can also be impulsive, temperamental, and high-strung. Periodically you need time by yourself to recharge your energies. You will have success in any line that measures up to your ideals. Both the sciences and the arts are likely to appeal to you. At some point in your life, you may be drawn to metaphysics. *Birthday of James Woods, actor; Melissa Joan Hart, actress; and Clarence Darrow, lawyer.*

April 19   Success Number 23/5 (4 + 19 = 23/5)

You are independent and inclined to do your own thing. Often you have an interest in politics and reform and can achieve a position of leadership in that capacity. Your 23/5 Success Number calls upon you to explore, expand your horizons, and to get to know your fellow man. Your 5 Success Number gives you the ability to advertise and sell, but it also may incline you to impulsiveness and displays of temperament. Though you can succeed in business and have a gift for making money, you may be more inclined to an artistic or professional career. *Birthday of Jayne Mansfield, actress; Dudley Moore, actor; and Ashley Judd, actress.*

April 20   Success Number 24/6 (4 + 20 = 24/6)

You are a progressive thinker with strong creative skills. With a 24/6 Success Number, you do well in service fields and in businesses allied to the arts. Your 20 birthday number gives you tact and diplomacy, and your 24/6 Success Number gives you a sense of responsibility. Cultivate the 6 ability to help others out with their problems and you'll overcome the tendency of 20 to be overly sensitive and emotional. Keeping busy will keep you from becoming lethargic. Law, religion, and theater are some of the areas that promise you fulfillment. *Birthday of Luther Vandross, singer; Lionel Hampton, jazz great; and Jessica Lange, actress.*

April 21   Success Number 25/7 (4 + 21 = 25/7)

You are both literary and artistic. Often you have an exceptional talent for painting, though you can acquit yourself in scientific areas as well. With 25/7 as your Success Number, learn to specialize to offset the inclination of your 21 birthday to scatter energies and talents. You like a nice home and enjoy living comfortably. You must avoid any inclination to laziness. Let your 25/7 Success Number motivate you to excel, to perfect your natural talents. Don't let yourself become complacent—you have the capabilities to be tops in your field if you keep yourself motivated. *Birthday of Rollo May, psychologist; Anthony Quinn, actor; and Charlotte Brontë, writer.*

April 22   Success Number 26/8 (4 + 22 = 26/8)

You can succeed in both the arts and sciences. You're inventive, rebellious, and sometimes high-strung. You often need periods of time by yourself to maintain calmness and serenity. If you cultivate the organizational skills and the drive for success of your 26/8 Success Number, you will turn your ideals into practical realities that will be of benefit to all humankind. At times, you can be stubborn and need to learn how to turn *won't* power into *will* power. A job that matches your ideals is the one meant for you. Try not to let temperament impede your overall progress. *Birthday of Aaron Spelling, entertainment mogul; Immanuel Kant, philosopher; and J. Robert Oppenheimer, physicist.*

April 23   Success Number 27/9 (4 + 23 = 27/9)

You are adventurous and like the good things of life. Be careful that self-indulgence doesn't undermine your prospects for success. You are progressive and are willing to work hard to achieve your ends. With a 27/9 Success Number, you're often drawn to politics and humanitarian endeavors. Your 27/9 makes you an individual who thrives on challenges. It also inclines you to literature, philosophy, law, and teaching. Your 23 birthday number gives you a love of travel in a physical sense, whereas your 27/9 Success Number makes you a traveler in mental realms. *Birthday of Max Planck, physicist; William Shakespeare, playwright; and Lee Majors, actor.*

April 24   Success Number 28/10/1 (4 + 24 = 28/10/1)

You work well with groups and, with 28/10/1 as your Success Number, often achieve a leadership position in that capacity. You are responsible and community-minded and will do your fair share to help others. Dramatic by nature, you're at home in the theater and often have exceptional writing or musical talents. Cultivate the originality of your Success Number and you will certainly be a trailblazer in your field. In business, you like large enterprises and have a flair for making money. A person who needs to keep busy to be happy, you usually have more than one iron in the fire. *Birthday of Barbra Streisand, actress-singer; Willem de Kooning, painter; and Shirley MacLaine, actress.*

April 25   Success Number 29/11/2 (4 + 25 = 29/11/2)

You are blessed with creativity and much inventive ability. With 29/11/2 as your Success Number, you may be drawn to humanitarian pursuits. Your 29 makes you ideal-istic, but it may take you a while to realize that you must follow your dream to be happy in a career. When you do, the world often finds that your work is often ahead of its time. You may write, but are best suited for artistic work, such as singing, acting, painting, design, interior deco-rating, and architecture. Law, engineering, science, religion, and teaching are others fields that promise you fulfillment. *Birthday of Al Pacino, actor; Renée Zellweger, actress; and Guglielmo Marconi, inventor.*

April 26 Success Number 30/3 (4 + 26 = 30/3)

You have a good head for business and are usually drawn to large enterprises. With 30/3 as your Success Number, you have a gift for self-expression and will be successful in promoting yourself and your ideas. Your 30/3 also attracts you to writing and creative pursuits. Sometimes you're found in businesses allied to the arts as well. Stubbornness and fixed ideas can get in your way, so you'd do well to become flexible. You're conscientious and will succeed in medicine, education, and welfare. At times, you may be exacting with others. A sense of humor, though, usually rescues the day for you. *Birthday of Carol Burnett, actress; John Audubon, painter; and I. M. Pei, architect.*

April 27 Success Number 31/4 (4 + 27 = 31/4)

You have leadership qualities and are something of a law unto yourself. You have a natural interest in social reform and may be drawn to a political career. Both literary and philosophical, you'll have success in educational lines. Blessed with a good intuition, you're capable of making original contributions to your field of expertise. You are versatile and artistic, but you need the self-discipline of your 31/4 Success Number to make the most of your talents. You do well in crisis situations, but you do not always handle your finances wisely. *Birthday of Coretta Scott King, U.S. civil rights activist; Jack Klugman, actor; and Sandy Dennis, actress.*

April 28   Success Number 32/5 (4 + 28 = 32/5)

You are executive by nature and will make great sacrifices to further your ambitions. However, your energy is liable to come in fits and starts, so that periods of productivity may alternate with bouts of laziness. You can be very stubborn, so it would be wise to cultivate the adaptability and flexibility of your 32/5 Success Number. Your 5 will give you the spirit of adventure and a willingness to explore the new—qualities that will enable you to become less fixed in your views. Law, teaching, architecture, music, design, and teaching are some of the fields that will bring you fulfillment. *Birthday of Jay Leno, talk show host; Ann-Margret, actress; and James Monroe, U.S. president.*

April 29   Success Number 33/6 (4 + 29 = 33/6)

You are idealistic, inventive, and inclined to march to the beat of your own drummer. You have decided humanitarian qualities and would make a fine leader of a cause. In creative areas, you're capable of producing work that's futuristic and ahead of its time. Somewhat nervous and high-strung, you need the stabilizing influence of your 33/6 Success Number to make your dreams a reality. Your 33/6 gives you a sense of responsibility and a social consciousness. Keep your temperament in line and you'll be capable of making a contribution to the betterment of humankind. *Birthday of Uma Thurman, actress; Andre Aggasi, tennis star; and Daniel Day-Lewis, actor.*

April 30 Success Number 34/7 (4 + 30 = 34/7)

You're usually good at getting your ideas across to others and are creatively talented. Art, music, writing, teaching, and acting are your natural milieu. Still, you can be fixed in your ideas and must be careful not to force others to your way of thinking—arousing their wrath in the process. You are loyal and conscientious, but you too often insist on your own way. Though you are sociable, your 34/7 Success Number makes you introspective and a bit of a loner. Your 7 urges you to specialize and to be discriminating to offset your inclination to scatter your energies. *Birthday of Cloris Leachman, actress; Eve Arden, actress; and Alice. B. Toklas, writer.*

MAY

May 1 Success Number 6 (5 + 1 = 6)

You can succeed in business for yourself and are a person meant to do your own thing. A home is important to your happiness, but take care not to be bossy with family members. Your 6 Success Number gives you a sense of responsibility. Often you achieve a position of leadership in connection with a group activity. You are at home in creative areas and can succeed in any artistic profession. Your strong will and determination are qualities that will help you overcome obstacles. *Birthday of John Woo, film director; Joseph Heller, writer; and Kate Smith, singer.*

May 2 Success Number 7 (5 + 2 = 7)

You have a strong need for financial and emotional security. Cooperative by nature, you work well in partnership, though with 7 as your Success Number you're a bit of a loner and are not likely to wear your heart on your sleeve. Your 2 birthday number gives you natural artistic gifts, but your 7 will make you strive to perfect those gifts. With a good education (7) in your field, you will rise to the heights. However, your 7 increases the sensitivity of your 2 birthday, so you'll need to guard against depression. You have a natural "bedside manner." *Birthday of Lorenz Hart, lyricist; Lesley Gore, singer; and Theodore Bikel, folksinger.*

May 3 Success Number 8 (5 + 3 = 8)

You're really good at selling yourself and your ideas. You're great at getting a project off the ground and have natural promotional abilities. Versatile, you're likely to have many irons in the fire. Your 8 Success Number gives you ambition and the ability to successfully commercialize your creative talents, which are likely to be numerous. Writing especially, as well as acting, painting, design, journalism, sales, teaching, engineering, banking, and religion, are some of the fields in which you will make your mark. Businesses allied to the arts may also appeal to you. *Birthday of Sugar Ray Robinson, boxer; James Brown, rock star; and Niccolò Machiavelli, writer.*

May 4 Success Number 9 (5 + 4 = 9)

You have organizational skills and can succeed in business. However, you are also artistically inclined and will enjoy success in such fields as acting, painting, writing, and music. With 9 as your Success Number, you are public-spirited and are drawn to politics and humanitarian endeavors. Your 4 birthday number makes you a hard worker, but your 9 Success Number makes you a hard worker with a heart. You are both practical and mystical. You would make a fine fund-raiser for a cause. *Birthday of Hosni Mubarak, Egyptian president; Randy Travis, country singer; and Roberta Peters, opera star.*

May 5 Success Number 10/1 (5 + 5 = 10/1)

You are a physical person who delights in the exercise of your five senses. You have a love of variety, change, and personal freedom, but you must conquer a tendency to overindulgence—and you must be willing to work hard. Versatile, you can succeed in business, law, politics, show business, science, art, and philosophy. With 10/1 as your Success Number, cultivate originality and you will reach the top of your profession. Your 10/1 gives leadership abilities and much creativity. You do well in positions of authority and often make your mark on the world as an independent thinker or as a leader of a cause. *Birthday of Søren Kierkegaard, philosopher; Alice Faye, actress; and Tyrone Power, actor.*

May 6   Success Number 11/2 (5 + 6 = 11/2)

You have a strong love of home and family. You work well with groups and often achieve a position of leadership in that capacity. With 11/2 as your Success Number, you work best when inspired and you are capable of original contributions in the arts and sciences. You do not fare well when criticized. However, since you often explore the uncharted and the new in experience, you cannot expect everyone to understand where you're coming from. You have much charm and personal magnetism, qualities that will serve you well in politics and theatrical pursuits. *Birthday of Rudolph Valentino, actor; Willie Mays, baseball star; and Orson Welles, actor.*

May 7   Success Number 12/3 (5 + 7 = 12/3)

You have an analytical mentality and a philosophical bent. You usually work better on your own than in partnership. With 12/3 as your Success Number, you will do well in creative areas and may have a special talent for writing, music, or acting. You do best in mental fields and will enjoy success in law, education, and science. Your 7 makes you a bit of a loner, a person with a private side, but your 12/3 makes you sociable, friendly, and self-expressive. Thus, you're a curious mixture of extroversion and introversion. A sense of humor (3) helps you to get over those periods when you feel down (7). *Birthday of Eva Perón, Argentine political leader; Robert Browning, poet; and Pyotr Tchaikovsky, composer.*

May 8   Success Number 13/4 (5 + 8 = 13/4)

You are ambitious and usually a good moneymaker. In business, you have executive strengths and are drawn to large ventures. With 13/4 as your Success Number, you are at your best in work that you like to do; you can easily drift when not interested. Businesses allied to the arts often appeal to you, though you may be creatively talented yourself as well, most notably in music, art, acting, and writing. A home is important to your happiness, but you need to guard against an inclination to be dictatorial with others. Sometimes you have a metaphysical bent. *Birthday of Rick Nelson, singer; Fulton J. Sheen, clergyman; and Edward Gibbon, British historian.*

May 9   Success Number 14/5 (5 + 9 = 14/5)

You are universal in thought and spirit and may be drawn to politics and public service. Though you are a sincere humanitarian, at times you can lay down the law, and you won't be dictated to. Your 14/5 Success Number will give you an understanding of your fellow man and keep your ideals from being too abstract. Often you are creatively talented and capable of achieving notable success as an actor, writer, painter, or musician. Take care, though, to guard against expediency and a tendency to accept what chance throws your way. Make your own talents the foundation of your success. *Birthday of Albert Finney, actor; Billy Joel, singer; and Tony Gwynn, baseball star.*

May 10   Success Number 15/6 (5 + 10 = 15/6)

You can succeed in business for yourself and are some-times found in a professional career. With 15/6 as your Success Number, you work well with groups and often achieve a position of leadership in that capacity. Your 15/6 will attract some of you to the theater, and you will have success as an actor, director, or playwright. Usually you are a good moneymaker. You can reach the heights in your field if you apply yourself. Guard against both complacency and laziness. Music, publishing, writing, teaching, science, and businesses allied to the arts also promise you fulfillment. *Birthday of Barbara Taylor Bradford, writer; Fred Astaire, actor; and Arthur Kopit, playwright.*

May 11   Success Number 16/7 (5 + 11 = 16/7)

You work best when inspired and are often an inno-vator in your field. Dynamic and somewhat high-strung, you need to be careful that temperament doesn't under-mine your accomplishments. Financial and emotional security are important to you, yet usually you're happiest when working for the benefit of the public. Often you have outstanding talent in artistic areas. With 16/7 as your Success Number, a good education in your field will allow you to hone your natural creative gifts to perfec-tion. Your 16/7 may draw you to law, literature, science, and metaphysics. *Birthday of Irving Berlin, composer; Martha Graham, dancer; and Salvador Dalí, painter.*

May 12   Success Number 17/8 (5 + 12 = 17/8)

You appreciate beauty and can succeed in creative areas. You have good communication skills and are usually quite adept at getting your ideas across to others. A pleasing personality helps to ease your path in life. With 17/8 as your Success Number, you have ambition and the capability to commercialize your creative talents successfully. Often you reach the heights in such fields as poetry, art, music, acting, interior design, and businesses allied to the arts. Your 8 helps you to organize and manage your talents, whereas your 12 birthday may incline you to scatter your energies. *Birthday of George Carlin, comedian; Yogi Berra, baseball star; and Katharine Hepburn, actress.*

May 13   Success Number 18/9 (5 + 13 = 18/9)

You are creative and practical but sometimes have difficulty reconciling these qualities. You'll work very hard if interested, but you don't fare so well if you dislike your job. With an 18/9 Success Number, you would make a fine worker (13) for a cause (18/9). Your Success Number may draw you to politics, administrative work, law, and reform, areas for which you have a special aptitude. You would also be highly successful in real estate, building, contracting, and businesses allied to the arts. You have a natural interest in the mysteries of life and would make a fine writer of the macabre. *Birthday of Harvey Keitel, actor; Stevie Wonder, singer; and Beatrice Arthur, actress.*

May 14   Success Number 19/10/1 (5 + 14 = 19/10/1)

You crave change and variety and are adventurous. You are somewhat lucky in business and a bit of an opportunist. With a 19/10/1 Success Number, you are happiest when in charge of your own affairs. Your 19/10/1 may give you an interest in politics and social reform, as well as leadership qualities. Versatile, you can succeed in such fields as acting, science, brokerage, law, medicine, music, and literature. Cultivate the originality of your Success Number and you will reach the top of your field. You are usually a good moneymaker and are protective and generous toward loved ones. *Birthday of Bobby Darin, singer; George Lucas, film director; and Daniel Gabriel Fahrenheit, scientist.*

May 15   Success Number 20/2 (5 + 15 = 20/2)

You have a good sense of responsibility and strong family values. You work well with groups, and a home of your own is important to you. Often you have innovative ideas and are capable of pioneering work in your field. With 20/2 as your Success Number, you work well in partnership. Your 20/2 may draw you to law, politics, religion, or medicine. Cultivate the idealism of your 20/2 and you could very well become a crusader for a cause. Music may either be a career or a hobby, and you may also have success as a writer of fiction. *Birthday of Jasper Johns, painter; Richard Avedon, photographer; and Florence Nightingale, nurse.*

May 16   Success Number 21/3 (5 + 16 = 21/3)

With 16 as your birthday number and 21/3 as your Success Number, you are a private (16) person with a public persona (21/3). Though seemingly outgoing (21/3), you nevertheless keep a lot to yourself (16). You have natural creative skills and a willingness to work hard to perfect your talents. Your 16/7 may attract you to religious or philosophical subjects, and your 21/3 gives you a talent for getting your ideas across to others. You would make a fine lawyer, teacher, or psychologist. Often you have artistic abilities, an exceptional talent for acting, and a flair for showmanship. *Birthday of Janet Jackson, singer; Henry Fonda, actor; and Pierce Brosnan, actor.*

May 17   Success Number 22/4 (5 + 17 = 22/4)

You have administrative talents and can succeed in such fields as banking and investment counseling. You are a good moneymaker, but must exercise care with spending. With 22/4 as your Success Number, you'll succeed in any field that measures up to your ideals. You have a good intuition, but you are also skeptical. Often you have an exceptional talent for music. Inclined to be nervous and high-strung, you need periods of time by yourself to recharge your energies and soothe your spirit. You are visionary, yet practical. Take care, however, that temperament doesn't get in the way of your overall success. *Birthday of Dennis Hopper, actor; Bill Paxton, actor; and Debra Winger, actress.*

May 18 Success Number 23/5 (5 + 18 = 23/5)

You have administrative talents and may be drawn to a career in politics and public service. You dislike being in subordinate positions and do best as a leader. Usually you have a good head for business and will have success as a head of a corporation or as a financial adviser. With 23/5 as your Success Number, you are innovative and progressive in thought, though at times you can be stubborn. Your 23/5 also gives you a good understanding of human nature and makes you warm and sympathetic. You tend to make the best of any situation and are fond of social contacts. *Birthday of Pope John Paul II, religious leader; Perry Como, singer; and Frank Capra, film director.*

May 19 Success Number 24/6 (5 + 19 = 24/6)

You are independent yet universal in outlook. You have natural leadership abilities and an interest in politics, reform, and public service. Though you can succeed in business, you're usually happier in an artistic or professional career. With 24/6 as your Success Number, you need to keep busy to be happy. Without definite goals, you tend to daydream and drift. Your 24/6 will bring you success in the theater, journalism, music, teaching, and community service. You will learn much from your powers of observation, but you may be inclined to magnify your joys and sorrows. *Birthday of Malcolm X, civil rights leader; Johns Hopkins, philanthropist; and Ho Chi Minh, Vietnamese leader.*

May 20 Success Number 25/7 (5 + 20 = 25/7)

You are sensitive, imaginative, and empathetic. However, with a 25/7 Success Number, you are a private person. You often have intense feelings that you usually keep hidden. Your 25/7 gives you intellectual powers, though, and your 20 birthday number gives you heart. This combination makes you a force to be reckoned with in such fields as writing, acting, music, medicine, religion, and philosophy. In business, you would succeed in publishing and real estate. You may have a passion for collecting things, and you probably have the taste and know-how of a connoisseur. *Birthday of Jimmy Stewart, actor; Honoré de Balzac, writer; and Joe Cocker, rock star.*

May 21 Success Number 26/8 (5 + 21 = 26/8)

You have a flair for communication, which is an asset to you in both business and the arts. You will succeed in such fields as writing, journalism, acting, sales, and teaching. With a 26/8 Success Number, you are ambitious and know how to successfully commercialize your talents. With the organizational skills of your 26/8, you'll overcome a tendency to scatter your energies or waste time in trivial pursuits. You are both intellectual and practical, qualities that will serve you well in such fields as publishing, banking, and promotional work. You are an idealist at heart. *Birthday of Raymond Burr, actor; Harold Robbins, writer; and Henri Rousseau, painter.*

May 22   Success Number 27/9 (5 + 22 = 27/9)

You are inventive and intuitive, but inclined to be nervous and high-strung. You have magnificent potential and need the self-discipline of your birthday number to make the most of your talents. You dislike routine work and need a job that will allow you to use your visionary powers. You can succeed in the arts and sciences, as well as any field that measures up to your ideals. With a 27/9 Success Number, you thrive on challenges and are resilient in crisis situations. Your 27/9 inclines you to literary, philosophical, and humanitarian pursuits. *Birthday of Naomi Campbell, model; Arthur Conan Doyle, writer; and Mary Cassatt, painter.*

May 23   Success Number 28/10/1 (5 + 23 = 28/10/1)

You are versatile and liable to experiment before setting on a career. You're inclined to go from this to that, especially if success is not quickly forthcoming. With 28/10/1 as your Success Number, though, you should avoid having your fingers in too many pies. Your greatest success will come when you find and then do your own thing. You know how to look out for number one, but take care not to make changes without due forethought. Any field involving communications is your natural milieu, and you may have a special talent for either acting or brokerage. *Birthday of Drew Carey, actor; Rosemary Clooney, singer; and Joan Collins, actress.*

May 24   Success Number 29/11/2 (5 + 24 = 29/11/2)

You work well with groups and often become a leader in that capacity. Though you are somewhat restless, you are also capable of being responsible. With a 29/11/2 Success Number, you work best when inspired and are capable of work that is ahead of its time. You can be a trailblazer in the arts, but take care that temperament doesn't sap a good deal of your energies. A home of your own is important to your happiness. You are a dreamer and an idealist, but you need action for success. You have humanitarian interests and are drawn to public life. Dramatic by nature, you can succeed in theatrical pursuits. *Birthday of Queen Victoria, British monarch; Priscilla Presley, actress; and Bob Dylan, singer.*

May 25   Success Number 30/3 (5 + 25 = 30/3)

With 30/3 as your Success Number, you are talkative and self-expressive, but your 25 birthday inclines you to secrecy. Though cheerful in manner (30/3), you often do not reveal your true feelings (25). This characteristic can cause you difficulty in personal relationships. You have the potential to be a deep thinker, but you may be inclined to expediency. If you will develop your talents and resist the temptation to take the easiest way, you can reach great heights, especially in such fields as music, writing, education, psychology, architecture, law, and engineering. *Birthday of Miles Davis, jazz great; Ian McKellen, actor; and Beverly Sills, opera singer.*

May 26   Success Number 31/4 (5 + 26 = 31/4)

You are clever and can get by on your wits. To make the most of your potential, however, you need to cultivate the self-discipline and the willingness to work hard of your 31/4 Success Number. You enjoy travel, have promotional skills, and would make a fine writer, lawyer, teacher, or salesperson. If creatively talented, you seem to have no trouble in successfully commercializing your abilities. You may have a special talent for acting, sculpture, painting, or music. You have a warmth to your nature, which is a great asset to you in business and personal dealings. *Birthday of Peggy Lee, singer; Al Jolson, singer-actor; and James Arness, actor.*

May 27   Success Number 32/5 (5 + 27 = 32/5)

You have fortitude, determination, and an ability to bounce back from adversity. In business, you would have success as a banker, stockbroker, or financier. You often have an interest in politics and public service, but need to cultivate the warmth and the personal touch of your 32/5 Success Number in order not to be too detached and impersonal. You have decided philosophical, intellectual, and literary interests, and your 32/5 Success Number may attract you to theatrical pursuits as well. You have natural leadership abilities and dislike being in a subordinate position. *Birthday of Louis Gossett Jr., actor; John Cheever, writer; and Hubert H. Humphrey, U.S. politician.*

May 28   Success Number 33/6 (5 + 28 = 33/6)

You can succeed in business for yourself, yet you also work well in partnerships. You may have an inclination, though, to scatter your energies and to put things off. Still, with 33/6 as your Success Number you'll come into your own as soon as you develop a sense of responsibility. In fact, you have all the necessary equipment to make a significant contribution to society's betterment. Versatile, you're likely to have success in both the arts and sciences. Your best bet for success, though, is the field of communications—writing, advertising, publishing, and journalism. *Birthday of Ian Fleming, writer; Rudy Giuliani, U.S. politician; and Gladys Knight, singer.*

May 29   Success Number 34/7 (5 + 29 = 34/7)

You are restless, high-strung, and inventive. You are constantly on the go and would not be happy in a routine job. Idealistic, you often gravitate to politics, humanitarian interests, and public service. When interested in a cause, you are truly an inspired leader. With 34/7 as your Success Number, you should obtain a good education and perfect your talents to offset an inclination to get by simply on your wits and charm. In the arts, you're capable of original achievements, and your work is often ahead of its time. Having a home of your own is important for your peace of mind. *Birthday of Rupert Everett, actor; Bob Hope, actor; and Annette Bening, actress.*

May 30   Success Number 35/8 (5 + 30 = 35/8)

You were born with the gift of gab and are a natural for such fields as advertising, public relations, sales, and communication. You have many interests, but need to guard against scattering your energies. With a 35/8 Success Number, you are ambitious and desire a high place in life. However, you will need to cultivate self-discipline in order to reach your goals. Put your 35/8 organizational skills to use; learn how to manage your time wisely. Literature, art, law, painting, and singing are some of the fields that promise you fulfillment. *Birthday of Benny Goodman, bandleader; Keir Dullea, actor; and Barry Bonds, baseball star.*

May 31   Success Number 36/9 (5 + 31 = 36/9)

You like to work with people and enjoy travel in connection with your work. You are quick with repartee and would make a fine news reporter, commentator, or correspondent. It's important that you have a job you like or you won't apply yourself. With 36/9 as your Success Number, you're often drawn to politics, public service, and humanitarian pursuits. You would find much joy in welfare work. Blessed with a keen mind, organizational skills, and a universal outlook, you'll have success in the arts, science, and business. You may have a special talent for music. *Birthday of Brooke Shields, actress; Don Ameche, actor; and Joe Namath, football star.*

JUNE

June 1 Success Number 7 (6 + 1 = 7)

You are independent but sometimes indecisive. You start many things but do not always bring them to completion. With 7 as your Success Number, you need to develop a workable philosophy of life. Cultivate that striving for perfection of 7 and you will overcome a tendency to scatter your energies. You usually put your personal stamp on what you do and you are capable of making original contributions to your field. You have much creative ability and are often drawn to writing and the theater. *Birthday of Morgan Freeman, actor; John Masefield, poet; and Andy Griffith, actor.*

June 2 Success Number 8 (6 + 2 = 8)

You are sensitive, imaginative, and empathetic. You have a strong need for emotional and financial security, and with 8 as your Success Number you are ambitious and willing to work hard to achieve your goals. You usually have a way with words and would make a fine journalist, writer, columnist, or correspondent. Your 8 Success Number will give you the ability to successfully commercialize your artistic talents. Often you have a special talent for acting, dance, photography, poetry, drawing, or music. Sometimes you're drawn to scientific fields. *Birthday of Thomas Hardy, writer; Dana Carvey, actor; and Johnny Weissmuller, actor.*

June 3 Success Number 9 (6 + 3 = 9)

You are witty, verbal, and clever. Versatile, you have an interest in everything in life, but must be careful not to be a dilettante. A born traveler, you're constantly on the go. Often you have an outstanding talent for writing, but need self-discipline to make the most of this potential. Sales, teaching, advertising, law, publishing, travel, and journalism are likely vocations for you. With 9 as your Success Number, you are often drawn to politics and public service. If you'll develop the universal outlook of your 9, those of you who are in creative fields will indeed make your mark on the world. *Birthday of Allen Ginsberg, poet; Tony Curtis, actor; and Alain Resnais, filmmaker.*

June 4 Success Number 10/1 (6 + 4 = 10/1)

You are a realist, and sometimes the opportunist. You know which side your bread is buttered on and are smart enough to get by on your wits. Your 4 birthday number, though, gives you the necessary self-discipline to apply yourself and make the most of your potential. You work well in the corporate structure, but your rise to the top begins when you follow the dictates of your 10/1 Success Number, which are to find and then do your own thing. Strive to be original (1), to be independent (1), to develop your leadership abilities (1), and never allow yourself to get into a rut (negative 4). *Birthday of Rosalind Russell, actress; Angelina Jolie, actress; and Ruth Westheimer, sex therapist.*

June 5   Success Number 11/2 (6 + 5 = 11/2)

You are adventurous and liable to experiment before settling on a career. At times, your emotional life leaves you confused, and you must guard against ill-advised changes. With an 11/2 Success Number, you have a good imagination and can succeed in artistic areas. Hold fast to your ideals (11) and you will make your mark as a visionary thinker, creator, or leader. Your 5 birthday number gives you a way with people and ensures your success in any field where the personal touch is a factor. You love travel, are a bon vivant, and like to be constantly on the go. *Birthday of Bill Moyers, journalist; Ruth Benedict, anthropologist; and Tony Richardson, director.*

June 6   Success Number 12/3 (6 + 6 = 12/3)

Though you crave adventure and are experimental by nature, your birthday number 6 gives you a fine sense of responsibility. You work well with groups, are an asset to the community, and are family-oriented. With 12/3 as your Success Number, personal contacts will be helpful to you in business. If you'll develop the communication skills and sense of humor of your 12/3, you'll go far in such fields as acting, law, journalism, sales, writing, singing, broadcasting, and teaching. Your 12/3 also makes you given to flirtations. A home of your own is important to your happiness. *Birthday of Thomas Mann, writer; Sandra Bernhard, actress; and Harvey Fierstein, actor.*

June 7   Success Number 13/4 (6 + 7 = 13/4)

You are inclined to scatter your energies and need the self-discipline of your 13/4 Success Number to make the most of your capabilities. Your 7 birthday number gives you an analytical mentality, but you still need a good education to fine-tune your talents. You're quite versatile, but your greatest success will come when you become a specialist in your chosen field. With a 13/4 Success Number, you are creative and practical, but sometimes have difficulty reconciling these qualities. It is important that you like your work; otherwise you won't put forth the proper effort. *Birthday of Prince, rock star; Liam Neeson, actor; and Tom Jones, singer.*

June 8   Success Number 14/5 (6 + 8 = 14/5)

You are ambitious, but inclined to expediency. Instead of capitalizing on the opportunity of the moment, you should look to your heart for a vocational direction. You enjoy power and being in a position of authority, and you'll work hard to achieve these ends. Be careful, though, not to take on more than you can handle. With 14/5 as your Success Number, you are innovative and willing to take a chance on the new. Your 14/5 also gives you a good understanding of human nature and often the ability to succeed in such fields as writing, acting, and brokerage. *Birthday of Frank Lloyd Wright, architect; Alexis Smith, actress; and Robert Schumann, composer.*

June 9 Success Number 15/6 (6 + 9 = 15/6)

You are humanitarian in outlook and are often drawn to such fields as law, journalism, and public service. An eye for expediency, though, sometimes sends you barking up the wrong tree. It may take you a while before you find yourself. Cultivate the sense of responsibility that comes with your 15/6 Success Number to offset a tendency to scatter your energies. Your 15/6 draws you to large enterprises and gives you a flair for moneymaking. With 9 as your birthday number, you love travel, work well with groups, and will always shine in creative areas. Theater, especially, is your milieu. *Birthday of Johnny Depp, actor; Natalie Portman, actress; and Michael J. Fox, actor.*

June 10 Success Number 16/7 (6 + 10 = 16/7)

You're independent by nature and are apt to stand out from the crowd as a person who does your own thing. Somewhat restless, you need to check a tendency to become easily bored. You're willing to try anything once, but do best when you develop the mentality and striving for perfection that come with your 16/7 Success Number. Though you enjoy work that brings you before the public, you're a bit of a loner as well. Your 16/7 will draw you to such fields as law, literature, music, religion, and teaching. Your 10 birthday number makes you at home in music and the theater. *Birthday of Judy Garland, singer-actress; F. Lee Bailey, lawyer; and Saul Bellow, novelist.*

June 11   Success Number 17/8 (6 + 11 = 17/8)

You are versatile, clever, inventive, and high-strung. You work best when inspired and can succeed in fields that measure up to your ideals. Often you are the inspired leader of a cause. Your 11 gives imagination, and your 17/8 Success Number offers the practical know-how, ambition, and organizational skills to make your dreams a reality. Though you can succeed in business, you're usually happier in creative fields, most notably music. Take care, though, that temperament doesn't undermine your chances to be successful. Your financial fortunes are likely to fluctuate. *Birthday of Jacques Cousteau, oceanographer; Vince Lombardi, football coach; and William Styron, writer.*

June 12   Success Number 18/9 (6 + 12 = 18/9)

You are socially inclined, are usually popular, and enjoy public life. An ability to get your ideas across to others is an asset to you in both business and creative fields. You have many interests, but must be careful not to scatter your energies. Your 18/9 Success Number will give you administrative talents and may draw you to a career in politics and public service. Your 12/3 makes you a natural for such fields as writing, sales, travel, public relations, banking, teaching, and advertising. Often you are attracted to businesses allied to the arts. *Birthday of; George Herbert Walker Bush, U.S. president; Jim Nabors, actor; and Marv Albert, sportscaster.*

June 13   Success Number 19/10/1 (6 + 13 = 19/10/1)

Mystical and poetic, you can succeed in creative fields. It's important, however, that you like your work, or you won't put in the necessary effort to succeed. Yet sometimes you do find yourself in a rut. That is why it's important that you cultivate the originality and daring of your 19/10/1 Success Number. Reach out to be number one and you will certainly stand out in your field as a person to be reckoned with. You can succeed in business and are often found in the sciences as well. Your 19/10/1 Success Number may draw you to law, politics, medicine, writing, or music. *Birthday of William Butler Yeats, poet; Richard Thomas, actor; and James Clark Maxwell, physicist.*

June 14   Success Number 20/2 (6 + 14 = 20/2)

Your restlessness can cause you to make ill-advised moves, yet you also are sometimes lucky in taking chances. The stage and the stock market are two areas for which you may have a special talent. You have a revolutionary spirit and would make a good spokesperson for a cause. With 20/2 as your Success Number, you're empathetic and may be drawn to such fields as law, medicine, religion, and politics. Your 20/2 Success Number often makes you gifted in music and writing fiction. You like excitement in your work and are capable of original accomplishments in your field. *Birthday of Burl Ives, singer; Steffi Graf, tennis star; and Alois Alzheimer, physician.*

June 15   Success Number 21/3 (6 + 15 = 21/3)

You are an innovator and will inject new life into any business you may be associated with. However, with 21/3 as your Success Number, you are primarily an artist and will enjoy notable achievements in such fields as art, literature, acting, and music. Your 15 birthday number gives you the ability to make things pay, but you are usually happier in a professional career than in business. You also make friends easily, but it may take you a while before you truly warm up to others—you are inclined to be suspicious of their motivations. A home of your own is important to your happiness. *Birthday of Harry Nilsson, singer; Helen Hunt, actress; and Jim Belushi, actor.*

June 16   Success Number 22/4 (6 + 16 = 22/4)

You are a good observer with a natural interest in society and its problems. An original thinker with a philosophical outlook on life, you have high ideals and do best in fields that reflect them. With a 22/4 Success Number, self-discipline will be the key to making the most of your considerable talents. However, you do not fare so well in a routine job and require a vocation that allows you free play of your visionary ideas. You are most at home in such fields as science, law, literature, banking, advertising, architecture, acting, music, painting, and teaching. *Birthday of Joyce Carol Oates, writer; Stan Laurel, actor; and Tupac Shakur, rap star.*

June 17   Success Number 23/5   (6 + 17 = 23/5)

You are naturally curious with an interest in many subjects. Somewhat restless, you may experiment before settling on a career. You have moneymaking skills, though sometimes your own financial fortunes fluctuate. Your 23/5 Success Number makes you adventurous, but take care not to waste your best self in pleasure seeking. Your 23/5 also gives you an understanding of human nature, a gift that will serve you well in both business and the arts. You may have a special talent for music. Other fields that promise you fulfillment are law, science, acting, writing, teaching, and banking. *Birthday of Barry Manilow, singer; Igor Stravinsky, composer; and Venus Williams, tennis star.*

June 18   Success Number 24/6   (6 + 18 = 24/6)

You are clever enough to get by on your wits, but with a 24/6 Success Number you do best in a position of responsibility. You have business acumen, but are happiest in work where you can utilize your fine intellectual gifts. Your 24/6 promises you success in theatrical pursuits, but you can also fare well in such fields as law, journalism, music, politics, real estate, and sculpture. You seem to wilt on the vine unless you have something to keep you busy, so you're never apt to retire. Your 18 birthday makes you universal in outlook, whereas your 24/6 gives you a strong need for family life. *Birthday of Isabella Rossellini, actress; John Hersey, writer; and Roger Ebert, film critic.*

June 19   Success Number 25/7 (6 + 19 = 25/7)

You fare best when given the chance to do your own thing. A natural leader, you may be drawn to politics and public service. With 25/7 as your Success Number, study is the key to perfecting your talents. Your 25/7 gives you an introspective side and inclines you to philosophical and spiritual interests. Though seemingly gregarious, you may have a private side that you keep to yourself. You can succeed in business, but are usually happier in an artistic or professional career. Writing, sales, and acting are fields for which you have a special aptitude. *Birthday of Gena Rowlands, actress; Paula Abdul, singer; and Blaise Pascal, philosopher.*

June 20   Success Number 26/8 (6 + 20 = 26/8)

Your 20 birthday number gives you the ability to work well with others, whereas your 26/8 Success Number makes you ambitious. If you'll cultivate the patience, organizational skills, and broad vision of your Success Number, you'll offset an inclination to throw in the towel if results aren't quickly forthcoming. Imaginative and sensitive, you have the ability to turn these traits into creative accomplishments. Clever and versatile, you like to deal with people and do well before the public. You often are skilled with your hands and have a great love of animals. *Birthday of Nicole Kidman, actress; Errol Flynn, actor; and Lillian Hellman, playwright.*

June 21   Success Number 27/9 (6 + 21 = 27/9)

You are clever, entertaining, and imaginative. You are very much at home in intellectual areas and may also have artistic and literary talents. Your 27/9 Success Number makes you resilient in crisis situations and gives you an interest in the larger issues that affect humankind. Through books, travel, and contacts with others, you will learn much about your fellow man. Though you are a gracious host or hostess, you may be slow to take others into your confidence. At times, you may be given to bouts of depression. Your 27/9 gives you leadership qualities and makes you public-spirited. *Birthday of Mary McCarthy, writer; Jean-Paul Sartre, philosopher; and Prince William, British royalty.*

June 22   Success Number 28/10/1 (6 + 22 = 28/10/1)

You can succeed at practically anything. Blessed with a good intuition, you should learn to trust it. At times, though, you tend to be a skeptic. With 28/10/1 as your Success Number, you're a person meant to do your own thing. Cultivate your originality—dare to be different—and you will be a trailblazer in your field. Sometimes you're nervous and high-strung, but try not to let these traits impede your overall progress. You are capable of work that's ahead of its time, but self-discipline is a requisite for you to make the most of your potential. *Birthday of Kris Kristofferson, singer-actor; Dianne Feinstein, U.S. senator; and Billy Wilder, film director.*

June 23   Success Number 29/11/2 (6 + 23 = 29/11/2)

Your 23 birthday gives you a sense of adventure, whereas your 29/11/2 Success Number makes you idealistic. Often you experiment before settling on a career. Not one to live by the conventions, your Success Number makes you capable of doing highly original work in your field. However, you can be temperamental and must not let your emotions get the best of you. With 29/11/2 as your Success Number, you work well in partnership and have a genuine concern for those less fortunate than you. Affectionate ties are important to you. *Birthday of Bob Fosse, choreographer; Clarence Thomas, U.S. Supreme Court justice; and Wilma Rudolph, track star.*

June 24   Success Number 30/3 (6 + 24 = 30/3)

Sensitive and dramatic, you can succeed in theatrical pursuits. If you will cultivate the optimism, good cheer, and social skills of your 30/3 Success Number, you'll offset an inclination to magnify your joys and sorrows. A person who needs to keep busy to be happy, you'll succeed in such fields as writing, teaching, medicine, music, and finances. Your 30/3 abilities to sell yourself and your ideas are an asset to you in whatever you do. You are good at raising money for a cause and have management skills. You're conscientious by nature, but at times can be fixed in your views. *Birthday of Mick Fleetwood, rock star; Michelle Lee, actress; and Jack Dempsey, boxer.*

June 25 Success Number 31/4 (6 + 25 = 31/4)

You aspire to great things and need a good education to obtain your objectives. Serious-minded and inclined toward introspection, you have an interest in social problems and are drawn to intellectual pursuits. Your 31/4 Success Number gives you the ability to advertise and promote yourself. However, it also inclines you to unrealistic expectations and, sometimes, to trivial interests. Always remember that the 3 + 1 of your 31 adds up to 4, the number of self-discipline and hard work—qualities that you will need to make a success of your life. Though you are a homebody at heart, you also like to travel. *Birthday of Carly Simon, singer; Brad Renfro, actor; and Sidney Lumet, film director.*

June 26 Success Number 32/5 (6 + 26 = 32/5)

You usually are a good moneymaker, but your work must reflect your ideals for you to be truly happy. Your 32/5 Success Number makes you willing to take a chance now and then, but you must guard against expediency in your choice of occupation. You can succeed in business, but are often drawn to show business and creative areas. Rest assured, you won't be a starving artist, for you have the ability to successfully commercialize your creative talents. You may have a special talent for the culinary arts, and you often acquit yourself well in such fields as banking and brokerage. *Birthday of Peter Lorre, actor; Pearl S. Buck, writer; and Babe Didrikson Zaharias, golfer.*

June 27   Success Number 33/6 (6 + 27 = 33/6)

You are resilient in crisis situations and gravitate toward challenges in life. With 33/6 as your Success Number, you're usually a force for betterment in community affairs and are often involved in humanitarian areas. You do best in leadership positions; have great determination; and may resent taking orders. Still, your 33/6 gives you a good sense of responsibility and an ability to work well with groups. You enjoy being before the public and are likely to be drawn to such fields as philosophy, literature, teaching, law, and religion. *Birthday of Erik Ericson, anthropologist; Ross Perot, businessman; and Helen Keller, writer.*

June 28   Success Number 34/7 (6 + 28 = 34/7)

You are independent, yet you work well in partnership. At times, though, you can be a bit of a loner. With 34/7 as your Success Number, you'll need to cultivate a workable philosophy of life to counter a tendency to be moody and fearful. A good education will also help you make the most of your potential. Often you have an outstanding talent for music; you may also be drawn to one of the healing professions. You are practical in outlook and executive by nature—qualities that will enable you to succeed in almost any line you choose. *Birthday of Kathy Bates, actress; Richard Rodgers, composer; and John Elway, football star.*

June 29   Success Number 35/8 (6 + 29 = 35/8)

You are highly sensitive, imaginative, and, at times, high-strung. A dreamer at heart, you often find it hard to keep your feet on the ground. However, if you'll cultivate the organizational skills, ambition, and practical know-how of your 35/8 Success Number, you'll be able to turn your dreams into realities. To reconcile the real with the ideal is your mission in life. You are likely to have an interest in public service and are a willing and ardent worker for causes. In creative areas, you're capable of work that is ahead of its time. *Birthday of Gary Busey, actor; Carlos Santana, musician; and Antoine de Saint-Exupéry, writer.*

June 30   Success Number 36/9 (6 + 30 = 36/9)

You have excellent communication skills, which will serve you well in both business and the arts. You can, however, be a bit self-involved, and you need to cultivate the warmth and genuine concern for others of your 36/9 Success Number. Becoming involved will help you overcome a tendency to be childish and petulant if crossed, or when things don't go your way. When at your best, you're an excellent comrade and an inspiring optimist who will achieve success in such fields as acting, music, teaching, writing, politics, and advertising. You enjoy being before an audience. *Birthday of Martin Landau, actor; Susan Hayward, actress; and Mike Tyson, boxer.*

JULY

July 1 Success Number 8 (7 + 1 = 8)

You are independent and self-reliant. You can succeed in business for yourself and usually are more successful on your own than in partnership. With 8 as your Success Number, you are naturally ambitious. Take care, though, that your 8 Success Number doesn't make you overly materialistic and that your 1 birthday doesn't make you selfish or self-insistent. Somewhat unusual, you often stand out from the crowd as a person who does your own thing. You have a good memory and are a planner and originator. *Birthday of Dan Aykroyd, actor; Charles Laughton, actor; and Twyla Tharp, choreographer.*

July 2 Success Number 9 (7 + 2 = 9)

You are sensitive, with a strong need emotional security. You can succeed in creative areas and may have a special talent for music, poetry, and dance. With 9 as your Success Number, you have an interest in the general welfare and can be an enthusiastic worker for a cause. You can easily become discouraged, however, and then may simply drift with the currents of your imagination rather than making full use of your potential. Empathetic by nature, you would make a fine teacher or physician. *Birthday of Herman Hesse, writer; Dave Thomas, founder of Wendy's; and Jerry Hall, model.*

July 3   Success Number 10/1 (7 + 3 = 10/1)

You are a good talker and a good salesperson. Your ability to communicate your ideas is an asset to you in both business and the arts. Your 3 birthday inclines you to take things easy, but your 10/1 Success Number gives you initiative, originality, and incentive. In other words, you can be a leader in thought and action. You have marked social gifts and are usually popular—that is, if you don't let your 10/1 cause you to become self-centered. Writing, acting, sales, and teaching are some of the fields that promise you success and fulfillment. *Birthday of Tom Stoppard, playwright; Dorothy Kilgallen, journalist; and Tom Cruise, actor.*

July 4   Success Number 11/2 (7 + 4 = 11/2)

Your 4 birthday number makes you practical, whereas your 11/2 Success Number makes you an idealist at heart. This combination indicates that you're a person who will work (4) hard to make your dreams (11) come true. You work (4) best when inspired (11) and may have a special talent for acting, music, writing, or painting. Real estate, teaching, and banking are other fields that promise you fulfillment. However, you are more likely to be found in an artistic career than in business. You have a strong code of ethics, but take care not to be dictatorial. *Birthday of Neil Simon, playwright; Ann Landers, advice columnist; and Eva Marie Saint, actress.*

July 5 Success Number 12/3 (7 + 5 = 12/3)

Your 5 birthday makes you adventurous, and your 12/3 Success Number gives you a way with words. You can buy, sell, and promote and usually do well in fields that involve an element of risk taking. You have a fine sense of what the public wants and are a people person. You often are public-spirited and interested in philanthropy. You enjoy travel, but at times you can be self-indulgent. Cultivate the charm and friendliness of your 12/3 Success Number and you will go far. Put your communication skills to good use, and avoid any inclination to be lazy. *Birthday of John Cecil Rhodes, South African financier-statesman; Georges Pompidou, French statesman; and Shirley Knight, actress.*

July 6 Success Number 13/4 (7 + 6 = 13/4)

You work well with groups and have strong family ties. With 13/4 as your Success Number, you are both practical and creative, but sometimes you have difficulty reconciling these qualities. It is important that you like your work, or you won't put forth the proper effort to succeed. Community-minded, with a strong set of principles, you are conscientious and often quite patriotic. Businesses allied to the arts sometimes appeal to you, though you may be creatively talented yourself. You have an interest in causes and may be drawn to government service. *Birthday of Janet Leigh, actress; Frida Kahlo, painter; and Nancy Reagan, U.S. first lady.*

July 7 Success Number 14/5 (7 + 7 = 14/5)

Your 7 birthday inclines you to introspection, but your 14/5 Success Number makes you adventurous. If you will cultivate your 14/5 desire to experience life to the fullest, you will offset your 7 tendency to withdraw into yourself. Your 14/5 gives you the ability to get along with others, yet your 7 birthday indicates there are times when you need to be alone. Behind your 14/5 need for travel and to experience a variety of life experiences lies your 7 birthday, which gives you a sincere desire to find the meaning of life. You're not apt to wear your heart on your sleeve. *Birthday of Ringo Starr, rock star; Satchel Paige, baseball star; and Gustav Mahler, composer.*

July 8 Success Number 15/6 (7 + 8 = 15/6)

Your 8 birthday number gives you a good head for business, and your 15/6 Success Number attracts you to large enterprises. You can be a good moneymaker, but you should refrain from being too acquisitive or overly materialistic. You also like to put on a good front, but you may need to watch your spending. Your 15/6 attracts you to the arts and makes you community-minded. Often you succeed in businesses allied to the arts. Doing for others seems to bring out the best in you and keeps you from being too self-involved. Sometimes you are drawn to a political career. *Birthday of Kevin Bacon, actor; Anjelica Huston, actress; and Nelson Rockefeller, U.S. vice president.*

July 9   Success Number 16/7 (7 + 9 = 16/7)

You have an interest in public service and do not belong in a subordinate position. Questions concerning social conditions, politics, and the world in general are of natural interest to you. With 16/7 as your Success Number, you could be drawn to an academic career; you'd make a fine psychologist or political analyst. Take care, though, not to let your 16/7 Success Number make you too critical of others. You have many interests, but should learn to specialize for your greatest success. You can succeed in both the arts and sciences. *Birthday of David Hockney, painter; Barbara Cartland, writer; and O. J. Simpson, football star.*

July 10   Success Number 17/8 (7 + 10 = 17/8)

Though fearful at times, you can become known as a person who does your own thing. You are capable of striking originality, especially in the arts and sciences. Your 10 birthday number makes you independent, and your 17/8 Success Number makes you ambitious and capable of succeeding in business for yourself. You have a talent for management, but may be inconsistent in the handling of your own funds. You can be set in your ideas and must be careful not to insist that others live up to your high standards. Practice a *live-and-let-live* philosophy in your dealings with others. *Birthday of Marcel Proust, writer; David Brinkley, TV news analyst; and James Whistler, painter.*

July 11   Success Number 18/9   (7 + 11 = 18/9)

You are sensitive, emotional, and high-strung. You need to be careful that temperament doesn't get in the way of your overall success. You work best when inspired and are blessed with fine imaginative powers. With 18/7 as your Success Number, you have administrative talents and are humanitarianly inclined. Though you can succeed in business, you're better suited for public service, politics, and the arts. Financial and emotional security are highly important to you. You are an idealist at heart, however, and you enjoy being in the limelight. *Birthday of John Quincy Adams, U.S. president; Yul Brynner, actor; and Giorgio Armani, designer.*

July 12   Success Number 19/10/1   (7 + 12 = 19/10/1)

Your ability to express yourself is an asset to you in both business and the arts. Often you have a great sense of humor. You can succeed in the entertainment world, though your 19/10/1 Success Number may incline you to politics and reform as well. You are smart enough to get by on your wits, but you still should get a good education in order to make the greatest use of your potential. Cultivate the originality of your 19/10/1 Success Number and you'll become known as a person who does your own thing. Refrain, though, from being selfish, and take care not to scatter your energies. *Birthday of Milton Berle, comedian; Van Cliburn, pianist; and Bill Cosby, comedian.*

July 13   Success Number 20/2 (7 + 13 = 20/2)

You are creative and practical, but sometimes have difficulty reconciling these qualities. It is important that you like your work or you won't put the forth the proper effort to succeed. Whether or not you choose a career in the arts, you should have some artistic outlet for your emotions. You can succeed in acting, writing, music, painting, and sculpture. With a 20/2 Success Number, you work well in partnership and may be drawn to such fields as law, religion, publishing, and politics. Businesses allied to the arts are also likely to appeal to you. *Birthday of Patrick Stewart, actor; Harrison Ford, actor; and Cameron Crowe, film director-writer.*

July 14   Success Number 21/3 (7 + 14 = 21/3)

You like excitement in your work and may be drawn to such fields as travel, brokerage, theater, and sales. Though ambitious, at times you can be expedient and may not always be willing to put in the hard work that's necessary to succeed. Too many interests can cause you to scatter your energies. Your 21/3 Success Number ensures you success in such fields as writing, education, and publishing. Cultivate the friendliness and charm of your 21/3 and you'll cultivate important contacts that will help you get ahead. Accent positive thinking to quell a tendency to be too sensitive. *Birthday of Ingmar Bergman, filmmaker; Woody Guthrie, folksinger; and Gerald Ford, U.S. president.*

July 15   Success Number 22/4   (7 + 15 = 22/4)

You work well with groups and often serve the community in some advisory capacity. You'd make a fine teacher, psychologist, or counselor. Often you have musical ability or a talent for writing or painting. With 22/4 as your Success Number, you can succeed in any line that measures up to your ideals. Somewhat nervous and high-strung, you need a job that allows you freedom of self-expression. You have advanced ideas, and your work is often ahead of its time. Hard work and self-discipline will be the keys to making the most of your considerable talents. *Birthday of Rembrandt, painter; Linda Ronstadt, singer; and Iris Murdoch, writer.*

July 16   Success Number 23/5   (7 + 16 = 23/5)

You have an interest in helping others and have a strong religious or philosophical streak. Though you are something of a loner, your 23/5 Success Number lends you warmth and gives you a good understanding of human nature. Your 23/5 ensures that you will do well in public life, especially in such fields as acting or writing on subjects that concern public interests and welfare. Some other fields that promise you fulfillment are law, politics, education, and literature. In love, though, you often feel misunderstood and need to open up more with others. *Birthday of Ginger Rogers, actress; Barbara Stanwyck, actress; and Mary Baker Eddy, religious leader.*

July 17   Success Number 24/6 (7 + 17 = 24/6)

You are something of the artist—but more of a businessperson and always a potential moneymaker. However, you're not always consistent in the way you handle your finances, and are prone to experience financial ups and downs. With 24/6 as your Success Number, you're likely to have a considerable talent for acting, music, writing, art, or sculpture. You also have a strong need for a home of your own and enjoy being involved in community affairs. Remember to always keep yourself busy, for you're inclined to become listless if you have nothing constructive to do. *Birthday of Diahann Carroll, actress; James Cagney, actor; and Phyllis Diller, actress.*

July 18   Success Number 25/7 (7 + 18 = 25/7)

You have administrative talents and may be drawn to public service. Usually diplomatic, you can succeed in politics as well. With 25/7 as your Success Number, you have a decided metaphysical streak and gravitate to fields where your fine intellect can be put to good use. You tend to perfectionism and need to be careful not to be too hard on yourself. Your critical talents are marked, and you often have writing ability. You will also have success in such fields as science, law, religion, and acting. You may need, though, to curb a tendency to be faultfinding. *Birthday of Richard Branson, businessman; Red Skelton, comedian; and Joe Torre, baseball player-manager.*

July 19   Success Number 26/8 (7 + 19 = 26/8)

You are a person meant to do your own thing and are usually successful in marketing yourself and your ideas. You can succeed in the business world, but are at your best when your work measures up to your ideals. With 26/8 as your Success Number, you are a good money-maker and know how to commercialize your creative gifts. You enjoy being before the public and will succeed in acting, law, medicine, politics, and public service. You often have decided leadership qualities and are ambitious to do good for others and make a name for yourself. *Birthday of Edgar Degas, painter; George McGovern, U.S. politician; and Kathleen Turner, actress.*

July 20   Success Number 27/9 (7 + 20 = 27/9)

You work well in partnership and often are drawn to politics and religion. Naturally empathetic, you'd make a fine teacher, counselor, or social worker. With 27/9 as your Success Number, you gravitate toward challenges and have the ability to bounce back from setbacks readily. Your 20 birthday number inclines you to be laid-back and retiring, but your 27/9 Success Number invites you think big, to see the larger picture, and to get involved with the larger issues that affect humankind. Your 27/9 will help you offset a tendency to get into a rut or to suffer from bouts of laziness. *Birthday of Edmund Percival Hillary, mountaineer; Natalie Wood, actress; and Petrarch, poet.*

July 21 Success Number 28/10/1 (7 + 21 = 28/10/1)

You are versatile, but inclined to scatter your energies. Often you're blessed with outstanding creative talents and will succeed as an actor, playwright, painter, musician, or writer. Cultivate the originality of your 28/10/1 Success Number and you will create work that is unique and ahead of its time. Your gift for self-expression will also serve you well in such fields as advertising, publishing, banking, sales, and businesses allied to the arts. You enjoy being in the limelight and are inclined to do your own thing. Though independent, you are also cooperative. *Birthday of Isaac Stern, violinist; Cat Stevens, rock star; and Hart Crane, poet.*

July 22 Success Number 29/11/2 (7 + 22 = 29/11/2)

You are creative, inventive, and often high-strung. You require periods by yourself to avert and alleviate tension. With 29/11/2 as your Success Number, you do well in partnership and are at your best when your work reflects your ideals. Both the arts and sciences are likely to appeal to you. Sensitive by nature, you need to be careful not to let temperament and hurt feelings interfere with your efforts to get ahead. A true visionary, you would not be happy in a routine job. Often, you stand out from the crowd as a person who is unique—an original! *Birthday of Bob Dole, U.S. politician; Alexander Calder, sculptor; and Jason Robards Jr., actor.*

July 23   Success Number 30/3 (7 + 23 = 30/3)

You have an adventurous approach to life and dislike routine. Somewhat restless, you need to cultivate more patience to make a success of things. With 30/3 as your Success Number, you're usually skilled at getting your ideas across to others, though you tend to be outspoken and fixed in your viewpoints. If you'll cultivate the charm and friendliness of your 30/3 Success Number, you will excel in such fields as public relations, acting, writing, law, brokerage, medicine, and businesses allied to the arts. Learn to persist, though, when you feel like throwing in the towel. *Birthday of Michael Wilding, actor; Woody Harrelson, actor; and Harry Connick Jr., singer-actor.*

July 24   Success Number 31/4 (7 + 24 = 31/4)

You work well with groups and often achieve a position of leadership in that capacity. You're smart enough to get by on your wits, but do best when you apply yourself. You need the self-discipline of your 31/4 Success Number to keep you from scattering your energies. Dramatic by nature, you can succeed in creative areas and may also be drawn to such fields as banking, real estate, and promotional work. You seem happiest, though, when you become involved in humanitarian endeavors. You enjoy public life, prominence, and being in a leadership position. *Birthday of Amelia Earhart, aviatrix; Gus Van Sant, film director; and Jennifer Lopez, singer-actress.*

July 25   Success Number 32/5 (7 + 25 = 32/5)

Your 25 birthday number inclines you to introspection, whereas your 32/5 Success Number makes you a seeker of adventure. Obtaining a good education is mandatory for those born on the 25th, yet with a 32/5 Success Number your greatest teacher will be experience. Through your Success Number you will be strongly attracted to business, but you'll also shine in such fields as acting, music, painting, antiques, writing, and architecture. Often you prefer to work from behind the scenes—to be the power behind the throne. You're not always understood, for you sometimes keep your feelings to yourself. *Birthday of Walter Brennan, actor; Estelle Getty, actress; and Eric Hoffer, writer.*

July 26   Success Number 33/6 (7 + 26 = 33/6)

You have a terrific drive for success, power, and recognition. You thrive on large enterprises and have the know-how to successfully commercialize your creative talents. You're at your best, though, when your work reflects your ideals. Often you have a talent for writing, music, or art, and usually you gravitate to the top of your field. With 33/6 as your Success Number, you can make a strong impact on the social consciousness and cultural values of humanity. Your 33/6 gives you a sense of responsibility, and your 26 birthday gives you abilities for organization and management. *Birthday of Stanley Kubrick, film director; Carl Jung, psychiatrist; and Aldous Huxley, writer.*

July 27 Success Number 34/7 (7 + 27 = 34/7)

You sometimes have a feisty nature and thrive on challenges. Something of a law unto yourself, you dislike taking orders and are at your best in a leadership position. With a 34/7 Success Number, obtaining a workable philosophy of life will be the key to making a success of your life. Your 34/7 promises you fulfillment in such fields as writing, law, art, theater, teaching, philosophy, and merchandising. You are ambitious and will work hard to get ahead in life. Though generous with others, you must guard against a tendency to be dictatorial. *Birthday of Peggy Fleming, skater; Leo Durocher, baseball manager; and Elizabeth Hardwick, writer.*

July 28 Success Number 35/8 (7 + 28 = 35/8)

You are sympathetic, warm, and appreciative. However, you are also quite independent and will not be coerced or cajoled into doing anything that goes against your better judgment or your need to be your own person. With 35/8 as your Success Number, you are a good organizer and are endowed with a sense of practicality. Your 28 birthday gives you the desire to do your own thing; your 35/8 Success Number, the ambition to make the most of your capabilities. You're apt to be drawn to law, acting, publishing, writing, teaching, politics, and social service. *Birthday of Gerard Manley Hopkins, poet; Bill Bradley, basketball star–politician; and Beatrix Potter, writer.*

July 29   Success Number 36/9 (7 + 29 = 36/9)

You are inventive, intuitive, and possibly high-strung. You are drawn to both business and the arts, but sometimes have difficulty in deciding which route to take. With 36/9 as your Success Number, you have strong humanitarian leanings and enjoy being in the public eye. If you'll let your 36/9 infuse you with universal principles and a desire to work for the common good, you'll offset a wish to always have your own way. In creative areas, your work is usually ahead of its time. Versatile, you can succeed in any line that matches your ideals. *Birthday of Henry Moore, sculptor; Melvin Belli, lawyer; and Alexis de Tocqueville, historian.*

July 30   Success Number 37/10/1 (7 + 30 = 37/10/1)

Your communication skills will serve you well in both business and the arts, but at times you can be stubborn and fixed in your viewpoints. Friends will be helpful to you once you overcome a tendency to be suspicious of their motivations. Your 37/10/1 Success Number is a mandate to you to do your own thing. Strive to develop your originality and you can become a leader in thought and action. You can succeed in business for yourself and are likely to be drawn to such fields as law, acting, journalism, writing, promotional work, and merchandising. *Birthday of Arnold Schwarzenegger, actor-politician; Emily Brontë, writer; and Henry Ford, industrialist.*

July 31   Success Number 38/11/2 (7 + 31 = 38/11/2)

Your 31 birthday makes you practical, and your 38/11/2 Success Number makes you idealistic. In combination, these two numbers make you the practical idealist—a person whose eyes are glued to heaven but whose feet are on the ground. With a 38/11/2 Success Number, you are capable of unique accomplishments in creative areas. Other fields that will provide you with fulfillment are law, medicine, politics, music, science, writing, and promotional work. If you're in business, you should still cultivate music, painting, or writing as a sideline and emotional outlet. *Birthday of Wesley Snipes, actor; J. K. Rowling, writer: and Jean Dubuffet, painter.*

AUGUST

August 1   Success Number 9 (8 + 1 = 9)

You thrive on being in the limelight, but you can be too egotistical. By following the lead of your 9 Success Number, you will come into your own. Your 9 invites you to devote your considerable talents to the larger concerns that affect humankind. When you lose yourself in service to others, you find yourself—and your true calling, which is to be a leader of the people. Politics, the arts, sales, writing, law, and science are some of the fields that promise you fulfillment and success. *Birthday of Jerry Garcia, rock star; Herman Melville, writer; and Claudius, Roman emperor.*

August 2   Success Number 10/1 (8 + 2 = 10/1)

Your 2 birthday number inclines you to lean on others, but your 10/1 Success Number will give you the push that you need to be independent. Your 2 needs for security can be limiting if they keep you from taking a chance on your originality (10/1). Dare to follow the lead of your 10/1 Success Number to do your own thing, and then you will come into your own. You may have a talent for teaching, and you can succeed in business for yourself. Take care, though, to avoid dead-end careers. Your creativity will serve you well in artistic fields. *Birthday of Peter O'Toole, actor; James Baldwin, writer; and Edward Furlong, actor.*

August 3   Success Number 11/2 (8 + 3 = 11/2)

You get along well with others and will find social contacts helpful in business. You're a real charmer with the gift of gab, but take care that you don't use people for your ends. With 11/2 as your Success Number, you work best when inspired and when you let your ideals dictate your choices in life. Your fine communication skills will serve you well in both business and the arts. You have selling ability and would be a successful stockbroker or advertising executive—and you will also make money in creative fields. Ambitious and warmhearted, you are often loved by many, and you're capable of unique accomplishments. *Birthday of Leon Uris, writer; Martha Stewart, entrepreneur; and Martin Sheen, actor.*

August 4   Success Number 12/3 (8 + 4 = 12/3)

You are practical, serious, and a hard worker. At times, you may have to guard against a tendency to be dictatorial. Your 12/3 Success Number, though, gives you a wonderful sense of humor and a zest for living life to the fullest. Cultivate the communication skills of your 12/3 and you will succeed in such fields as show business, writing, music, and design. You can also succeed in the corporate world, as head of your own business, and as a teacher or physician. Whether you choose art, science, or business, you always seem to have a knack for making money. *Birthday of Louis Armstrong, jazz great; Helen Thomas, journalist; and Maurice Richard, hockey star.*

August 5   Success Number 13/4 (8 + 5 = 13/4)

You are versatile and gifted, but may be inclined to be restless and overly intent on pleasure seeking. To make the most of your considerable talents, cultivate the self-discipline and application to duty of your 13/4 Success Number. You thrive on change, are enterprising, and like to keep things moving. You have a good understanding of human nature and know how to promote yourself and your ideas. You can succeed in both business and creative fields and sometimes are attracted to law, medicine, writing, politics, and science. *Birthday of Guy de Maupassant, writer; Neil Armstrong, astronaut; and Patrick Ewing, basketball star.*

August 6 Success Number 14/5 (8 + 6 = 14/5)

You have a keen sense of social values and are a fine organizer of groups, clubs, and gatherings. Your 6 birthday number gives you a love and need for home and family life, but your 14/5 Success Number invests you with a spirit of adventure and a love for travel. To reconcile these contradictory needs is a lifelong task for you. You must neither stay in a rut (6) nor make needless changes (14/5). Dramatic by nature, you often have an outstanding talent for acting and are usually skilled in sales and brokerage as well. You have a good head for business and are a born moneymaker. *Birthday of Lucille Ball, actress; Robert Mitchum, actor; and Alfred, Lord Tennyson, poet.*

August 7 Success Number 15/6 (8 + 7 = 15/6)

You strive to bring perfection to your work. Mental and analytical, you can succeed in research and you are introspective. You would be tempted to dwell in your ivory tower, except for the fact that with 15/6 as your Success Number you're dynamic, progressive, and enjoy being in the limelight. You have a flair for business and usually are a good moneymaker. You think big and are most at home in large enterprises. If you'll cultivate the warmth of your 15/6, you'll overcome your 7 tendencies to be too critical of others. You'll also have success in professional and creative fields. *Birthday of Louis B. Leakey, archaeologist; Taylor Caldwell, novelist; and Ralph Bunche, diplomat.*

August 8   Success Number 16/7 (8 + 8 = 16/7)

You have a good head for business, yet with a 16/7 Success Number you would also make a good critic of society and its values. You are a curious mixture of the philosopher and the materialist. You are a perfectionist in what you do, and will drop a project or a career if you think your chances of making it are slim. You have a talent for show business and can make a name for yourself in such fields as art, film, literature, education, law, politics, investing, and science. Your 8 birthday number may incline you to bluff or show off, but your 16/7 Success Number will make you more circumspect. *Birthday of Dustin Hoffman, actor; Esther Williams, actress; and Connie Stevens, singer.*

August 9   Success Number 17/8 (8 + 9 = 17/8)

You are first and foremost an artist. If you do not choose some kind of creative work as your career, you should still have some form of art as a hobby. With 17/8 as your Success Number, you are ambitious and have good organizing skills. You can succeed in business for yourself and are good at managing the affairs of others. However, you may be erratic in handling your own funds. At times, you're generous, but you may also be extravagant in spending. You have strong humanitarian leanings and may be drawn to politics and public service. *Birthday of Melanie Griffith, actress; Whitney Houston, singer; and Gillian Anderson, actress.*

August 10 Success Number 18/9 (8 + 10 = 18/9)

Independent and self-sufficient, you can succeed in business for yourself. With 18/9 as your Success Number, you're often drawn to politics, public service, and humanitarian concerns. You are a born leader, and your 18/9 promises you success in large endeavors that require efficient administration. You're equally at home in the arts. Most often, though, you're found in such fields as law, merchandising, banking, teaching, and medicine. At times, you may need to guard against a tendency to be aloof or withdrawn. *Birthday of Antonio Banderas, actor; Herbert Hoover, U.S. president; and Eddie Fisher, singer.*

August 11 Success Number 19/10/1 (8 + 11 = 19/10/1)

You are sensitive and imaginative and work best when you are inspired. Somewhat high-strung and nervous, but always dynamic, you need to keep a check on your temperament at times. With 19/10/1 as your Success Number, you can succeed in business, but you are usually happier in a professional or artistic career. Your 19/10/1 gives you leadership abilities and inclines you to politics and public service. If you'll listen to your intuition and hold fast to your ideals, you can be a trail-blazer in your field, especially if it involves the arts. You'll also do well as head of your own business. *Birthday of Mike Douglas, TV personality; Louise Bogan, sculptor; and Lloyd Nolan, actor.*

August 12   Success Number 20/2 (8 + 12 = 20/2)

You find joy in living and have a good sense of humor. Though you'll have your ups and downs emotionally, basically you're a cheerful and optimistic person. You are a natural showman, but take care not to be carried away by the sound of your own voice. With 20/2 as your Success Number, doors will open for you, if you're diplomatic and cooperative in your dealings with others. Your 20/2 gives you marked creative talents and inclines you to politics, religion, and social service. A person who thinks big, you have the ability to promote what you believe in. *Birthday of Pete Sampras, tennis star; Cantinflas, actor; and Buck Owens, country singer.*

August 13   Success Number 21/3 (8 + 13 = 21/3)

Your 21/3 Success Number endows you with much creativity, while your 13 birthday number inclines you to practicality and conservatism. Sometimes, though, you have difficulty reconciling these qualities. It is important that you like your work or you won't put forth the proper effort. If you'll cultivate the good humor and optimism of your Success Number, you'll offset an inclination to let life's difficulties get you down. You have an intuitive side that is an asset to you in whatever you do. Thoroughly dramatic, you're at home in the world of show business. Often you have writing ability. *Birthday of Annie Oakley, sharpshooter; Bert Lahr, actor; and Fidel Castro, Cuban dictator.*

August 14   Success Number 22/4   (8 + 14 = 22/4)

You would be dissatisfied in a routine job. You have an adventurous attitude toward life and are likely to experiment before settling on a career. You must guard against a tendency to be expedient and learn to take a chance on your creative gifts, which are many. With 22/4 as your Success Number, you work best when inspired and can succeed in any line that measures up to your ideals. You'll need the self-discipline of your Success Number to overcome an inclination to burn the candle at both ends. You often achieve outstanding success in business. *Birthday of Danielle Steele, writer; Steve Martin, actor; and Halle Berry, actress.*

August 15   Success Number 23/5   (8 + 15 = 23/5)

You have a flair for large enterprises, are a good moneymaker, and are thoroughly dramatic. A natural for show business, you know how to sell yourself and your product. Your 15 birthday gives you a need for roots and family ties, but your 23/5 Success Number invests you with the spirit of adventure. You can successfully commercialize your creative gifts and can be both generous and extravagant. Your 23/5 gives you push and daring, qualities that will offset any tendency of your 15 birthday to become complacent and self-satisfied. You do well in positions of authority and have leadership skills. *Birthday of Napoleon Bonaparte, French emperor; Ben Affleck, actor; and Ethel Barrymore, actress.*

August 16   Success Number 24/6   (8 + 16 = 24/6)

Your 16 birthday inclines you to solitude, but your 24/6 Success Number is a mandate to be less faultfinding and to cultivate warmth, tolerance, and understanding. If you follow 24/6 by taking an active role in community affairs and the problems of others, you'll overcome your 16 inclinations to magnify your own joys and sorrows. You are strongly allied to both the arts and sciences, but will also enjoy financial success in the business world. You have an interest in helping others and may be drawn to philanthropy. Though practical, you are also a dreamer. *Birthday of James Cameron, film director; Angela Bassett, actress; and Madonna, singer.*

August 17   Success Number 25/7   (8 + 17 = 25/7)

You are a master of organization and efficiency. Well suited to being a leader, you will succeed as the head of your own business. Though progressive in outlook, you still have a fondness for old and choice things and could be an art or antiques dealer. With 25/7 as your Success Number, a good education in your field is a must. Your 25/7 will teach you the true value of things and will offset your occasional tendency to show off your position and possessions. Dramatic and dynamic, you can succeed in creative areas. Public-spirited, you often have humanitarian interests. *Birthday of Maureen O'Hara, actress; Sean Penn, actor; and Robert De Niro, actor.*

August 18   Success Number 26/8 (8 + 18 = 26/8)

Your birthday number of 18 indicates that you have administrative skills and would succeed as head of a large organization that requires efficient management. With 26/8 as your Success Number, you are ambitious and want to be at the forefront of your field. Though you're a good moneymaker, you are happiest when your work reflects your ideals. You have strong theatrical leanings, and your 26/8 Success Number ensures that you will be successful in commercializing your creative talents. Though you like the limelight, you have an introspective side as well. *Birthday of Robert Redford, actor; Shelley Winters, actress; and Christian Slater, actor.*

August 19   Success Number 27/9 (8 + 19 = 27/9)

You are ambitious with leadership qualities. With 27/9 as your Success Number, an interest in reform often attracts you to a political career. Though you can succeed in business, you're usually happier in an artistic or professional career. You do not like to be dictated to, and you often have philosophical and literary interests. Your 27/9 gives you the ability to readily bounce back from adversity. Both clever and original, you're apt to stand out from the crowd as a person who does your own thing. It's when you identify with a cause bigger than self-interest that you come into your own. *Birthday of Bill Clinton, U.S. president; Orville Wright, inventor; and James Gould Cozzens, writer.*

August 20   Success Number 28/10/1   (8 + 20 = 28/10/1)

You are both independent and cooperative. Your 20 birthday number gives you the ability to work well in partnership, yet with 28/10/1 as your Success Number, you're also a person meant to do your own thing. You have a genuine concern for others and may be drawn to a medical or humanitarian career. Naturally diplomatic, you would do well in politics and government service. Financial security is important to you, but it should not be attained by the sacrifice of your individuality. Strive to develop the leadership skills of your Success Number. *Birthday of Connie Chung, TV journalist; Robert Plant, rock star; and Edgar A. Guest, poet.*

August 21   Success Number 29/11/2   (8 + 21 = 29/11/2)

You certainly have the genius and temperament of the creative artist, but you'll need to take care not to let temperament get the upper hand. Your creativity is marked, and with a 29/11/2 Success Number you work best when inspired. With 29/11/2 as your guide, either you'll heed your intuition, hold fast to your ideals, and create work that is ahead of its time—or you can be erratic with a need to cultivate stability. Friends help you out, once you overcome a tendency to be suspicious of them. To reconcile the ideal with the practical may be a lifetime job for you—but you can do it if you try. *Birthday of Kenny Rogers, singer; Peter Weir, film director; and Aubrey Beardsley, illustrator.*

August 22   Success Number 30/3 (8 + 22 = 30/3)

With 30/3 as your Success Number, you often choose a creative medium through which to express your individuality. You should accent 3 rather than 30, however, if you want others to respond to you and your ideas. 30 inclines to be stubborn, fixed in ideas, and outspoken, whereas 3 has a sense of humor and a lighter touch. You often have an outstanding talent for acting, writing, or music—and you may be inclined toward humanitarianism . Both practical and idealistic, your eyes may be on the heavens, but your feet are on the ground. You'll succeed in any field that matches your ideals. *Birthday of Carl Yastrzemski, baseball star; Ray Bradbury, writer; and Dorothy Parker, writer.*

August 23   Success Number 31/4 (8 + 23 = 31/4)

You are adventurous and naturally drawn to show business and creative pursuits. Mentally curious, you have an interest in many things, but are inclined to wanderlust. You are progressive in outlook, but need the self-discipline of your 31/4 Success Number to make the most of your talents. It is important that you like your work; otherwise you may have a tendency to drift. You can succeed in both the arts and sciences and may have special talents for writing and teaching. You have a fine intuition, but ultimately it will be through diligence and practicality that you make your mark on the world. *Birthday of Gene Kelly, dancer; River Phoenix, actor; and Shelley Long, actress.*

August 24   Success Number 32/5 (8 + 24 = 32/5)

You have a keen sense of responsibility and a strong sense of duty. You take pride in your accomplishments, but must resist any inclination to become listless or to fall into a rut. Your 32/5 Success Number, though, will prompt you to vary your routine and explore new horizons, through either books, travel, or personal adventures. In business, you can succeed in real estate and banking. Often you are exceptionally talented at writing, music, teaching, and sculpture. Never give a thought to retiring, for you are happiest when you are engaged in meaningful work. *Birthday of Jorge Luis Borges, writer; Cal Ripken Jr., baseball star; and Jean Rhys, writer.*

August 25   Success Number 33/6 (8 + 25 = 33/6)

You have a good critical sense and are also highly intuitive—a combination that will bring you success in such fields as writing, research, science, medicine, counseling, and teaching. If you'll embrace the potential of your 33/6 Success Number, you can make an original contribution to the cultural betterment of humankind. Your 33/6 will prompt you to become interested in the greater problems that affect humanity and will help offset your occasional 25 tendencies to be narrow-minded. You can succeed in theatrical pursuits and are often blessed with exceptional musical abilities. *Birthday of Elvis Costello, singer; Leonard Bernstein, composer; and Sean Connery, actor.*

August 26 Success Number 34/7 (8 + 26 = 34/7)

You're usually blessed with financial acumen. With 34/7 as your Success Number, you have an interest in society and its problems and would make a good teacher, writer, or counselor. Your 26 birthday number indicates the ability to succeed in the arts in a big way, whereas your 34/7 inclines you to science and research. You are happiest, though, when your work reflects your ideals. With a 34/7 Success Number, obtaining a workable philosophy of life will be the key to making the most of your talents. *Birthday of Antoine-Laurent Lavoisier, chemist; Branford Marsalis, jazz great; and Christopher Isherwood, playwright.*

August 27 Success Number 35/8 (8 + 27 = 35/8)

Your 27 birthday number gives you philosophical and literary talents, and your 35/8 Success Number gives you the ability to successfully commercialize these gifts. Because your 27 is a humanitarian number and your 35/8 indicates the ability to make money, you would be a fine fund-raiser for a worthy cause. *Think big* should be your motto with a 35/8 Success Number; try not to get bogged down by minutiae and worrying about small concerns. You're good at managing the affairs of others, for you are both efficient and well organized. You have leadership skills and can succeed in politics. *Birthday of Lyndon Baines Johnson, U.S. president; Theodore Dreiser, writer; and Joan Kroc, philanthropist.*

August 28   Success Number 36/9 (8 + 28 = 36/9)

Your 28 birthday number will bring you success in intellectual fields. However, you will achieve your greatest fulfillment when you develop the warmth, love of humanity, and global consciousness of your 36/9 Success Number. Your 28 gives you originality and inclines you to do your own thing, but your 36/9 indicates that you'll also make a contribution to the betterment of humankind. Your talents for literature, music, and the arts are likely to be outstanding, and you'll also enjoy success in such fields as law, teaching, lecturing, engineering, architecture, and show business. *Birthday of Shania Twain, singer; Johann von Goethe, writer: and Donald O'Connor, actor.*

August 29   Success Number 37/10/1 (8 + 29 = 37/10/1)

You are idealistic, yet you also have a strong need to make money. Financial security is important to you, and you often achieve your monetary goals through an artistic profession. You have a genuine interest in helping others and will be found on the side of the underdog. You're a sound craftsman and know how to put technique in the service of inspiration. To truly make something of your life, though, you'll need the initiative, fire, and fearless individualism of your 37/10/1 Success Number. Dare to be original and have the courage to go after what you want from life. *Birthday of Michael Jackson, rock star; Ingrid Bergman, actress; and Dinah Washington, blues singer.*

August 30   Success Number 38/11/2 (8 + 30 = 38/11/2)

You are creatively talented and idealistic. Your 30 birthday number gives you the gift of self-expression, which is an asset to you in both business and the arts. With 38/11/2 as your Success Number, you work best when inspired, and you are charismatic. You'd do well as a spokesperson for a cause; you may find yourself drawn to politics and humanitarian pursuits. At times, you can be set in your ideas and need to cultivate a tolerance for those whose opinions differ from your own. Your Success Number is a mandate for you to listen to your intuition and hold fast to your ideals. *Birthday of Cameron Diaz, actress; Mary Shelley, writer; and Warren Buffet, financier.*

August 31   Success Number 39/12/3 (8 + 31 = 39/12/3)

You are a perfectionist and a hard worker, but you may fail to see opportunities outside of what you have set up for yourself as your main interest. Take care not to become narrow-minded. With 39/12/3 as your Success Number, you are quite adept at selling your ideas to others. Cultivate the optimism and good cheer of your Success Number, and you'll offset a tendency to take yourself too seriously. You can write, teach, and act. Often you are greatly talented in music. *Birthday of Richard Gere, actor; Itzhak Perlman, violinist; and Frank Robinson, baseball star.*

SEPTEMBER

September 1   Success Number 10/1   (9 + 1 = 10/1)

With 1 as a birthday number and 10/1 as your Success Number, there is a double accent on the qualities of 1—originality and independence. You are a real go-getter, a person who is every inch the individual and destined to do your own thing. 1 at its worst can be egotistical, self-important, and selfish, so it would be best if you reached out for the higher vibration of 10, that of the leader whose progress benefits others. Though you can succeed in business for yourself, you're usually happiest in an artistic or professional career. *Birthday of Rocky Marciano, boxer; Gloria Estefan, singer; and Ann Richards, politician.*

September 2   Success Number 11/3   (9 + 2 = 11/2)

You are sensitive and cooperative, but inclined to let the little things of life upset you. With an 11/2 Success Number, you often are visionary, but you are also inclined to be fearful (2). A need for financial security (2) can keep you from taking a chance on your dreams (11). You work best with encouragement and are easily upset by criticism. When you learn not to take things so personally, you can rise to the top of your field. You are a natural for such fields as acting, writing, art, and music. You also would make a fine diplomat, teacher, or member of the clergy. *Birthday of Keanu Reeves, actor; Salma Hayek, actress; and Jimmy Connors, tennis star.*

September 3   Success Number 12/3 (9 + 3 = 12/3)

You have an interest and knowledge of many things, but are at times prone to scatter your energies. With 12/3 as your Success Number, you can organize, promote, and sell. Let your 12/3 help you develop a sense of humor to offset an inclination to be overly critical. Your 3 birthday gives you a talent for self-expression, and your 12/3 Success Number gives you showmanship. You can succeed in any field where personal contacts and a facility with words are assets. Your flair for design would make you a fine architect, and you'll also succeed in such fields as show business, advertising, and publishing. *Birthday of Sarah Orne Jewett, writer; Louis Sullivan, architect; and Alan Ladd, actor.*

September 4   Success Number 13/4 (9 + 4 = 13/4)

You are serious-minded—and no wonder, your birthday number is 4, the number of hard work, practicality, and self-discipline. Your Success Number of 13/4 only further emphasizes the necessity for you to work hard to achieve your goals. You're apt to experiment with pleasure seeking during your youth, but with maturity you'll enjoy work for its own sake and will take great pride in your achievements. You'll succeed in business, science, writing, medicine, real estate, and teaching. You often achieve a distinguished position in the arts. *Birthday of Anton Bruckner, composer; Henry Ford II, manufacturer; and Mitzi Gaynor, actress.*

September 5 Success Number 14/5 (9 + 5 = 14/5)

You are blessed with intellectual curiosity, and your thirst for knowledge is likely never to be satiated. You're also adventurous. You thrive on excitement in your work and excitement in your life. Take care, though, that pleasure seeking doesn't get out of hand. With 14/5 as your Success Number, you're a bit of a rebel, or in some cases an innovator who creates work that's ahead of its time. Your 14/5 promises you success in show business and as a stockbroker. You can also succeed in science, medicine, writing, teaching, music, criticism, and real estate. *Birthday of Bob Newhart, actor; Rose McGowan, actress; and Jesse James, outlaw.*

September 6 Success Number 15/6 (9 + 6 = 15/6)

You work well with groups and are often involved in community projects. A home is important to your happiness, and your sense of duty gives you a good sense of responsibility. If you'll cultivate the inventive genius and progressive outlook of your 15/6 Success Number, you'll avoid your 6 birthday number's tendency to be provincial and complacently comfortable in a familiar rut. Your 15/6 urges you to continually explore new horizons and better yourself. Your 15/6 also makes you good at earning money. You'll have success in law, medicine, music, literature, science, and theater. *Birthday of Jane Curtin, actress; Marquis de Lafayette, French statesman; and Rosie Perez, actress.*

September 7 Success Number 16/7 (9 + 7 = 16/7)

You have an analytical mentality but at times can be too harsh in judging others. Put to constructive use, however, your critical tendencies make you a good researcher and—with 16/7 as your Success Number—an insightful critic of society and its values. Your 16 will draw you to such fields as education, law, literature, and science. Usually you work better on your own than in partnership. Try not to make too much of little things, though, especially in your personal relationships. Music, painting, and acting are other fields that promise you success and fulfillment. *Birthday of Elizabeth I, British monarch; Devon Sawa, actor; and Buddy Holly, rock star.*

September 8 Success Number 17/8 (9 + 8 = 17/8)

You have a strong drive and are anxious to make the most of your potential. You have a talent for handling details, but with 17/8 as your Success Number, you must think big to achieve your greatest success. Your 17/8 gives you a philosophical bent and an ability to manage the affairs of others. You function well in the corporate structure and can succeed in such fields as finance, real estate, businesses allied to the arts, antiques, and promotional work. You also may be drawn to the arts, especially theater, music, sculpture, and writing. *Birthday of Peter Sellers, actor; Patsy Cline, country singer; and Jonathan Taylor Thomas, actor.*

September 9   Success Number 18/9 (9 + 9 = 18/9)

You have leadership qualities. Outer-directed, you find your greatest fulfillment when you become involved in causes larger than self-interest. Your 18/9 Success Number gives you administrative talents and will enable you to succeed in large fields that require efficient management. Something of a perfectionist, you must learn to make allowances for others' shortcomings. Both your 9 birthday number and your 18/9 Success Number give you a sense of drama and the ability to succeed in such fields as acting, art, writing, and music. However, try not to be too fussy. *Birthday of Hugh Grant, actor; Leo Tolstoy, writer; and Otis Redding, singer.*

September 10   Success Number 19/10/1
(9 + 10 = 19/10/1)

You are independent with leadership abilities. With 19/10/1 as your Success Number, you have a natural interest in politics, reform, and public service. Your 19 gives you the ability to make things pay, so you shouldn't have trouble commercializing your creative talents, which usually are considerable. Though you have a flair for business, you're generally happier in an artistic or professional career. You will come into your own when you find and then do your own thing. Never let financial considerations keep you from taking a chance on cultivating your individuality. *Birthday of Ryan Phillippe, actor; Arnold Palmer, golfer; and Fay Wray, actress.*

September 11   Success Number 20/2 (9 + 11 = 20/2)

You usually are blessed with some outstanding talent. Intuitive and imaginative, you often find your niche in the arts. You have highly original ideas, but are nervous and high-strung. Cultivate the tact, warmth, and cooperative spirit of your 20/2 Success Number to get your ideas across to others and to offset a tendency to let temperament undermine your accomplishments. Though you'll succeed in business, you'll achieve greater distinction as a playwright, architect, actor, musician, lawyer, or leader of some movement for civic improvement or public welfare. *Birthday of Brian De Palma, film director; Hedy Lamarr, actress; and D. H. Lawrence, writer.*

September 12   Success Number 21/3 (9 + 12 = 21/3)

You are both artistic and literary. You have a way with words and can succeed in such fields as writing, teaching, acting, advertising, and publishing. You have many interests, but must be careful not to scatter your energies. With 21/3 as your Success Number, friends will be helpful to you, though it may take you a while before you warm up to them. Inclined to be suspicious, you'd do well to cultivate the sense of humor that is associated with both the numbers 12 and 21. Music, painting, law, architecture, and journalism are other fields that will bring you a sense of fulfillment. *Birthday of Jesse Owens, Olympic athlete; Maurice Chevalier, entertainer; and Barry White, singer.*

September 13 Success Number 22/4 (9 + 13 = 22/4)

You have a good intuition, a sense of inner values, and a fine critical sense. Though idealistic, you are also practical, but at times may be skeptical. You are easily bored, so it is important that you find work that you indeed enjoy. With 22/4 as your Success Number, you will succeed in any line that measures up to your ideals. You are mental and analytical, and often have a love and talent for music. Somewhat nervous and high-strung, you often need time by yourself to recharge your energies. Other promising fields for you are writing, acting, education, publishing, and engineering. *Birthday of Fiona Apple, singer; Jacqueline Bisset, actress; and Claudette Colbert, actress.*

September 14 Success Number 23/5 (9 + 14 = 23/5)

With a 23/5 Success Number and a 14/5 birth date, it may be hard for you to sit still. This double accent on the qualities of 5 makes you extremely restless and adventurous. You like to go places and do things; you have an investigative and inventive mind. Because you are always willing to explore new horizons, you are often an innovator in your field. You must, though, quell a tendency to be expedient in the choice of a job. Dare to take a chance on your potential. Your 14 gives you a talent for acting and investment, whereas your 23/5 will bring you success in science, teaching, publishing, law, and the arts. *Birthday of Zoe Caldwell, actress; Ivan Pavlov, scientist; and Cherubini, composer.*

September 15   Success Number 24/6   (9 + 15 = 24/6)

You work well with groups and are a good money-maker. Often you're drawn to businesses allied to the arts, though you yourself are creative and talented as well. With a 24/6 Success Number, you're a person who needs to keep busy to be happy. Without something constructive to do, you tend to wilt. Your 24/6 gives you a dramatic flair and promises you success in such fields as acting, journalism, creative writing, music, and art. Law, medicine, and diplomacy would also suit you. A home of your own is important to your happiness. *Birthday of Tommy Lee Jones, actor; Prince Harry, British royalty; and James Fenimore Cooper, writer.*

September 16   Success Number 25/7   (9 + 16 = 25/7)

You are a natural critic of society and its values. You have an interest in the human psyche and may be drawn to psychology, counseling, and social work. You would make an excellent teacher. With 25/7 as your Success Number, you have a philosophical bent and may be drawn to both science and religion. Some other fields that promise you fulfillment are music, painting, writing, acting, law, and architecture. You're usually more drawn to the professions than business. Sometimes, though, you're not always understood, as you have a tendency to conceal your real feelings and emotions. *Birthday of Lauren Bacall, actress; B. B. King, musician; and J. C. Penney, department store owner.*

September 17   Success Number 26/8 (9 + 17 = 26/8)

You are shrewd in business and can succeed in such fields as law, banking, and accounting. You can be generous at times, but sometimes are tight-fisted. With 26/8 as your Success Number, you are happiest in work that reflects your ideals. Your 26/8 also gives you the ability to successfully commercialize your artistic talents and draws you to such fields as writing, acting, music, and painting. You are intellectual and practical, but are also a bit of a dreamer, inclined to introspection, soul searching, and reminiscence. You must learn to finish what you start. *Birthday of Anne Bancroft, actress; William Carlos Williams, poet; and Roddy McDowell, actor.*

September 18   Success Number 27/9 (9 + 18 = 27/9)

You have executive talents and leadership abilities and would make a fine administrator. With 27/9 as your Success Number, you have a strong will and gravitate toward challenges. You are resilient in crisis situations and can achieve success and distinction in the theater and as a writer, lawyer, or public servant. A perfectionist, you can be overly concerned about details and may be exacting with others. If you'll develop your Success Number's genuine concern for the welfare of others, you'll overcome a tendency to live within yourself. Otherwise you may feel alone and unfulfilled. *Birthday of Greta Garbo, actress; James Gandolfino, actor; and Lance Armstrong, cyclist.*

September 19   Success Number 28/10/1
(9 + 19 = 28/10/1)

You are a true individualist, yet you're also reform-minded with a desire to help other people. Though you have a good head for business, you are more inclined to the arts. With a 28/10/1 Success Number, you should strive to do your own thing. Your 28/10/1 invites you to dare to be original. Develop confidence in your abilities; heed your intuition; and give vent to your creative urges, and you will become a trailblazer in your field. You often have a talent for acting, law, and science. *Birthday of Joe Morgan, baseball star-announcer; Cass Elliot, singer; and Jeremy Irons, actor.*

September 20   Success Number 29/11/2
(9 + 20 = 29/11/2)

You have a good intuition that you should learn to trust. With 29/11/2 as your Success Number, you work best when inspired and are often drawn to an artistic career. Your 2 birthday gives you a strong need for financial and emotional security, but you should not sell out your dreams in order to attain them. You wouldn't be happy in a rutlike job; you need a career that allows your ideas to soar. Subject to mood swings, you need a creative outlet for your feelings. Empathetic by nature, you would make a good counselor, actor, writer, lawyer, or teacher. *Birthday of Sophia Loren, actress; Red Auerbach, basketball coach; and Maxwell Perkins, editor.*

September 21   Success Number 30/3 (9 + 21 = 30/3)

You are clever and truly artistic, but don't let a tendency to perfectionism cause you to undervalue your abilities. You're somewhat nervous and given to depression, but usually have a good sense of humor. With 30/3 as your Success Number, you can succeed in any line involving books and communication skills, especially writing. You are conscientious, but your 30/3 Success Number inclines you to be stubborn. Banking, acting, music, publishing, and real estate also promise you success. Try not, though, to be overly suspicious of others. Cultivate trust and faith. *Birthday of Leonard Cohen, singer; H. G. Wells, writer; and Faith Hill, singer.*

September 22   Success Number 31/4 (9 + 22 = 31/4)

You have progressive ideas and high ideals, and these will be the cornerstone of your success. With 31/4 as your Success Number, you have the ability to promote yourself and your ideas, a quality that will serve you well in both business and the arts. You can succeed in any line that interests you, but you may be especially gifted as an actor, musician, scientist, educator, writer, painter, sculptor, architect, lawyer, or physician. You do best in a job that allows freedom of expression. Usually you have strong humanitarian leanings and will do your part to make the world a better place to live. *Birthday of John Houseman, actor; Paul Muni, actor; and Scott Baio, actor.*

September 23   Success Number 32/5 (9 + 23 = 32/5)

Both your 23 birthday number and your 32 Success Number add up to 5, the number of sex, travel, and adventure, so you will have an exciting life! With a double accent on 5, your mission in life is to achieve an understanding of your fellow man. Try not, though, to let 5 cause you to be self-indulgent and let your emotions get out of hand. However, you have a knack for throwing off worry and making the best of things. You are a progressive thinker with original ideas and will enjoy success in acting, investment, sales, literature, sports, and music. *Birthday of Jason Alexander, actor; Julio Iglesias, singer; and Ray Charles, singer.*

September 24   Success Number 33/6 (9 + 24 = 33/6)

You are inclined to an artistic or professional career. Dramatic by nature, you can succeed in such fields as acting, music, and literature. With 33/6 as your Success Number, you should choose work that takes you into public life, for you are an ideal public servant. At your best, you will make original contributions to the social progress and cultural betterment of humankind. Law, science, and statesmanship are also fields in which you'll excel. Always keep yourself busy, for you tend to wilt without meaningful work to keep yourself occupied. *Birthday of John Marshall, U.S. Supreme Court justice; Anthony Newley, actor; and Phil Hartman, actor.*

September 25   Success Number 34/7 (9 + 25 = 34/7)

You are practical and productive, visionary, and at times eccentric. Though you'll have success in business, your flair is mental and you would be happier in a writing, teaching, or professional career. Your 34/7 Success Number adds to your tendencies to be philosophical, introspective, intuitive, and perhaps to live too much within yourself. Open up more with others, and you'll do better in personal relationships. You usually are blessed with artistic talents and will succeed as an actor, painter, musician, sculptor, dancer, poet, or architect. *Birthday of Catherine Zeta-Jones, actress; Michael Douglas, actor; and Christopher Reeve, actor.*

September 26   Success Number 35/8 (9 + 26 = 35/8)

You are practical and an idealist. Your tendency to dream may interfere with your productivity, yet often the products of your imagination have great merit and practical value. For your best success, you need to cultivate the organizational skills and ambition of your 35/8 Success Number. You are inventive and creative, with the ability to commercialize your artistic talents successfully. Sculpture, design, music, writing, singing, acting, and painting are some of the fields that promise you recognition, success, and fulfillment. Having a home of your own is important to you. *Birthday of Serena Williams, tennis star; George Gershwin, composer; and Linda Hamilton, actress.*

September 27   Success Number 36/9 (9 + 27 = 36/9)

Both your 36 Success Number and your 27 birthday number add up to 9, the number of universal love and service to others. You are a humanitarian and always ready to give others the benefit of the doubt. Though you are a law unto yourself, you are charitable and have a spirit of goodwill to all. An interest in law could easily lead to a political career, and you often have an outstanding talent for writing. You are a creator and an idealist with leadership skills, artistic talents, and an appreciation for beauty—qualities that will serve you well in whatever vocation you may choose. *Birthday of Wilford Brimley, actor; Jayne Meadows, actress; and Peter Sellers, actor.*

September 28   Success Number 37/10/1
(9 + 28 = 37/10/1)

You are sweet and affable, but you also know how to look after number one. Because both your 37/10 Success Number and your 28/10 birthday number add up to 1, the number of individuality, your mission in life is to find and then do your own thing. You can succeed in business for yourself and often are found in an artistic career. Very effective at communicating your ideas, you would make a fine orator, writer, teacher, salesperson, lawyer, or diplomat. Your birthday also has an affinity with the study of birds, flowers, and nature. *Birthday of Gwyneth Paltrow, actress; Marcello Mastroianni, actor; and Brigitte Bardot, actress.*

September 29   Success Number 38/11/2
(9 + 29 = 38/11/2)

You are inventive, nervous, and high-strung. With a 38/11/2 Success Number, you work best when inspired and have the potential to be a pioneer in the arts and sciences. Financial and emotional security are important to you, but you should never sell out on your dreams. Work hard to achieve your ideals and you will achieve your greatest success. Once you overcome an inclination to be temperamental, you'll get along better with partners. Often you have strong humanitarian leanings; you would be outstanding as a leader of a cause. *Birthday of Gene Autry, actor; Stanley Kramer, film director; and Michelangelo Antonioni, film director.*

September 30   Success Number 39/12/3
(9 + 30 = 39/12/3)

You are gifted with the written and spoken word. With 39/12/3 as your Success Number, you can succeed in such fields as advertising, law, public relations, banking, and publishing. Though you do not warm up to people readily, you'll still find social contacts an asset to you in getting ahead in life. The arts are where you usually shine. At times, you will need to guard against laziness and self-indulgence. Usually you're tactful and diplomatic, but on occasion you can be too outspoken and fixed in your viewpoints. *Birthday of Deborah Kerr, actress; Truman Capote, writer; and Angie Dickinson, actress.*

362

OCTOBER

October 1   Success Number 11/2 (10 + 1 = 11/2)

You'll always stand out from the crowd as someone unique. With 11/2 as your Success Number, you have a strong intuition. Your Success Number makes you an idealistic and inspired leader. You're at home in the political arena and will also enjoy success as an actor, writer, or musician. Though independent (1), you work best with cooperation (11/2). In business, you can sell and promote. A love of nature may attract you to planting and agriculture. *Birthday of Jimmy Carter, U.S. president; Walter Matthau, actor; and Richard Harris, actor.*

October 2   Success Number 12/3 (10 + 2 = 12/3)

You are the epitome of cooperation, gentleness, patience, and diplomacy. Inclined, though, to be overly sensitive, you need to cultivate the good humor of your 12/3 Success Number to offset a tendency to take things too personally. You can achieve notable success in life as a great painter, writer, musician, poet, designer, actor, or singer. Your statesmanship qualities are also marked; you would make a skilled politician or government leader. A healer by nature, you would make a fine physician. Always heed your intuition. *Birthday of Graham Greene, writer; Groucho Marx, actor; and Don McLean, singer.*

October 3　Success Number 13/4　(10 + 3 = 13/4)

You are quite expressive, with a natural facility and ease in getting your ideas across to others. If you cultivate the self-discipline of your 13/4 Success Number, you'll overcome a tendency to be overly carefree and easygoing. Your 13/4 gives you creativity and practicality, but at times you may have difficulty in reconciling these talents. You have natural writing ability, and your sense of drama will attract you to theatrical pursuits. Your charm will win you many friends, but try not to let the pleasures of the primrose path deter you from achieving your goals. *Birthday of Pierre Bonnard, painter; Thomas Wolfe, writer; and Stevie Ray Vaughan, singer.*

October 4　Success Number 14/5　(10 + 4 = 14/5)

Your 4 birthday makes your practical, whereas your 14/5 Success Number gives you a taste for adventure. The good life has a strong attraction for you, and you must guard against self-indulgence. Though you're conservative, you are not averse to taking a risk now and then. You must be careful, however, not to be expedient in making life's choices. Be sure to follow a path in line with your true desires. By tapping the originality of your Success Number, you can rise to a position of accomplishment. You can succeed in real estate and teaching and are also likely to have strong artistic leanings. *Birthday of Anne Rice, writer; Susan Sarandon, actress; and Frederic Remington, painter.*

October 5   Success Number 15/6 (10 + 5 = 15/6)

You are adaptable, agreeable, and popular. You like freedom in your personal life, though your 15/6 Success Number will give you a desire for home and family. Your 15/6 also gives you the ability to be responsible and will help you overcome a tendency to flit from one thing to another. You would thrive in the entertainment world, especially acting. Your 15/6 makes you a good money-maker and inclines you to large enterprises in business. You can also succeed in science, engineering, law, politics, sales, medicine, and any field where the personal touch is a factor. *Birthday of Kate Winslet, actress; Josuha Logan, director; and Ray Kroc, entrepreneur.*

October 6   Success Number 16/7 (10 + 6 = 16/7)

You are family-oriented, but you also need periods of time by yourself. Your 6 birthday will attract you to the stage, whereas your 16/7 Success Number will bring you success with mental interests and will incline you to a professional career. You need a good education and a workable philosophy of life to help offset your tendencies to be vacillating and to put things off. In youth, you're likely to experiment and make frequent changes, but as you mature you'll be inclined to settle down. Though you have a strong need for love and affection, you do not always show your feelings. *Birthday of Janet Gaynor, actress; Carole Lombard, actress; and Elizabeth Shue, actress.*

October 7 Success Number 17/8 (10 + 7 = 17/8)

You are refined and often have a love of and affinity for nature. Naturally reflective and philosophical, you have an analytical mentality and require a good education to make the most of your fine academic potential. With 17/8 as your Success Number, you have a good head for management and business, though your financial fortunes are liable to fluctuate. Usually, though, you are happier in artistic and contemplative fields than you would be in business and industry. Often you have a great spiritual awareness, and you may be blessed with psychic gifts as well. *Birthday of R. D. Laing, psychiatrist; Vladimir Putin, Russian president; and John Cougar Mellencamp, rock star.*

October 8 Success Number 18/9 (10 + 8 = 18/9)

You have executive talents and a good business sense. With 18/9 as your Success Number, you may be drawn to politics and public service. You would make an excellent fund-raiser (8) for a cause (18/9). You're naturally drawn to large enterprises and sometimes have humanitarian interests. You are strongly attracted to acting. Writing, intellectual pursuits, and law are also likely to appeal to you. Your 8 gives you strength, determination, and courage. Magnetic, charming, and personable, you will do well in fields where personality counts. *Birthday of Matt Damon, actor; Sigourney Weaver, actress; and Chevy Chase, actor.*

October 9   Success Number 19/10/1 (10 + 9 = 19/10/1)

Though you are diplomatic, you are also a law unto yourself. You have leadership qualities and dislike being in a subordinate position. With a 19/10/1 Success Number, you are often interested in reform and may be drawn to social work and politics. On the negative side, your 19/10/1 increases your 9 tendencies to take things too personally. When you are thwarted, you can become brusque and stormy. You belong in the realm of creation. You are often outstandingly talented in the arts, especially music, and enjoy success in a professional career. You know how to make things pay. *Birthday of John Lennon, rock star; Camille Saint-Saëns, composer; and Scott Bakula, actor.*

October 10   Success Number 20/2 (10 + 10 = 20/2)

You often stand out from the crowd as a person who does your own thing. You have leadership qualities and can succeed in business for yourself. With 20/2 as your Success Number, however, you'll find that cooperation and diplomacy will be the keys to attaining your objectives. Your 20/2 promises you success in the fields of law, diplomacy, religion, and philosophy. You're not likely to be a domestic type, but you have a love for the arts—an area in which you usually shine. Music, acting, painting, poetry, drama, and fiction are especially favored as vocations or hobbies. *Birthday of Thelonious Monk, jazz great; Ben Vereen, actor; and Harold Pinter, writer.*

October 11   Success Number 21/3   (10 + 11 = 21/3)

You are idealistic and work best when inspired. With 21/3 as your Success Number, you're usually adept at getting your ideas across to others and will succeed in any field involving communications, especially public speaking and writing. You enjoy being before the public and place a high premium on financial and emotional security. You may be, however, too impractical and temperamental to make a success of anything that requires adherence to routine. You belong in a profession—as an architect, painter, poet, musician, lawyer, or leader of a spiritually uplifting movement. You have much magnetism. *Birthday of Jerome Robbins, director; François Mauriac, writer; and Luke Perry, actor.*

October 12   Success Number 22/4   (10 + 12 = 22/4)

You are versatile, imaginative, and creative. You have a natural gift for self-expression, but may be inclined to scatter your energies. With 22/4 as your Success Number, you need to cultivate stability (4) and discipline (4), as well as the urge to put your ideals into practical workable form (22). You have an engaging personality and work well with others. Totally at home in creative areas, you may have an outstanding gift for music, writing, acting, law, or architecture. You would not be happy in a routine job and need a career where you can feel free to be innovative. *Birthday of Luciano Pavarotti, opera star; Ralph Vaughan Williams, composer; and Kirk Cameron, actor.*

October 13   Success Number 23/5 (10 + 13 = 23/5)

Yours is not always an easy birthday. If you place too much emphasis on the 1 and 3 of your 13, you could become selfish (1) and self-concerned (3). It is through work (4) that you will find your fulfillment. Your 23/5 Success Number, though, will cause you to experiment before settling on a career. Through your 23/5, you will gain an understanding of people; this will offset an inclination to be critical, nagging, or bossy with others. You can succeed in business and often have a talent for writing, design, music, acting, and real estate. *Birthday of Ian Thorpe, Olympic athlete; Margaret Thatcher, British political leader; and Yves Montand, actor.*

October 14   Success Number 24/6 (10 + 14 = 24/6)

You are adventurous, versatile, and progressive in outlook. Your 24/6 Success Number, though, is a stabilizing influence and will teach you the value of being responsible. Without its influence, you could easily waste time and energy in pleasure seeking. Still, you are good at taking chances and extricating yourself from difficult situations. Like all people born on the 14th, you have a talent for acting and making money through the stock market and real estate. Writing, teaching, and music will also bring you fulfillment. You are a person who must always stay busy to be happy. *Birthday of Dwight Eisenhower, U.S. president; Lillian Gish, actress; and Roger Moore, actor.*

October 15 Success Number 25/7 (10 + 15 = 25/7)

If attracted to business, you gravitate toward large enterprises and have the ability to put new life into old ventures. Usually, though, you're found in an artistic or professional career. You have a love of and talent for art, music, poetry, writing, and acting, as well as the ability to successfully commercialize these gifts. With 25/7 as your Success Number, you'll be inclined to be a perfectionist in whatever you undertake. Your 25/7 gives you intuition and discrimination, qualities that will further abet your career strivings. *Birthday of Friedrich Nietzsche, philosopher; Mario Puzo, writer; and Lee Iacocca, business executive.*

October 16 Success Number 26/8 (10 + 16 = 26/8)

You have good insights into society and its problems. You often serve the group in some advisory capacity and may be religiously and humanitarianly inclined. You are at home in intellectual fields and would make a fine teacher, lawyer, psychologist, or writer. Your 26/8 Success number gives you ambition and the ability to commercialize your artistic talents successfully. Not usually drawn to the business world, you are happiest in work that reflects your ideals. You are both intellectual and practical and you are inclined to reminisce. *Birthday of Tim Robbins, actor; Angela Lansbury, actress; and Eugene O'Neill, playwright.*

October 17   Success Number 27/9 (10 + 17 = 27/9)

You usually have personal magnetism and are a lover of art and beauty. You will do well in theatrical areas, but you also have a flair for business. Often you are found in businesses allied to the arts. Though cooperative by nature, you dislike taking orders and are not one to be told what to do. With 27/9 as your Success Number, you thrive on challenges and are resilient in crisis situations. Your 27/9 gives you strong philosophical, artistic, and literary leanings and also draws you to humanitarian pursuits. Still, a part of you is inclined to be aloof. *Birthday of Montgomery Clift, actor; Rita Hayworth, actress; and Eminem (Marshall Bruce Mathers), rap star.*

October 18   Success Number 28/10/1
(10 + 18 = 28/10/1)

You have a strong desire for material success, but shouldn't let the need to get ahead keep you from taking a chance on your own individuality. Your 28/10/1 Success Number gives you leadership abilities, whereas your 18 inclines you to public service. The combined influence of these numbers gives you the ability to be a leader for a worthy cause. Your 28 makes you independent and cooperative, with a pleasing personality that will serve you well in all your activities. Law, politics, acting, music, and administration are apt to appeal to you. *Birthday of Jean Claude van Damme, actor; Martina Navratilova, tennis star; and George C. Scott, actor.*

October 19   Success Number 29/11/2
(10 + 19 = 29/11/2)

You can succeed in business for yourself and are inclined to do your own thing. You have a flair for making things pay, though you also have a natural interest in reform and society's betterment. Your 29/11/2 Success Number gives you much originality and the ability to create work that's ahead of its time. You'll need to cultivate the cooperative spirit of 2 to ensure your success, however, because at times you can let temperament get the best of you. Writing, music, acting, politics, law, and public service are likely to appeal to you. *Birthday of John le Carré, novelist; Lewis Mumford, historian—urban planner; and Evander Holyfield, boxer.*

October 20   Success Number 30/3   (10 + 20 = 30/3)

You are sensitive and imaginative. You work well in partnership and have a strong need for financial security. A diplomat by nature, you can succeed in politics, though at times you can be vacillating. With 30/3 as your Success Number, you have a gift for self-expression, but may be inclined to be fixed in your views. Though you are conscientious, you may lack trust in others and can be suspicious of their motivations. Writing may be a special talent. You are also drawn to teaching, acting, law, religion, counseling, music, and businesses allied to the arts. *Birthday of Snoop Dogg (Calvin Broadus), rap star; Mickey Mantle, baseball star; and Tom Petty, rock star.*

October 21   Success Number 31/4 (10 + 21 = 31/4)

You are versatile, but must guard against a tendency to scatter your energies. If you'll cultivate the self-discipline of your 31/4 Success Number, you'll be able to successfully commercialize your considerable artistic talents. You're gifted at getting your ideas across to others and will enjoy success as a writer, teacher, or publicist. Other fields that may interest you are music, publishing, banking, advertising, travel, and sales. You have a good sense of humor and a great personality, qualities that will serve you well in all your activities. *Birthday of Dizzie Gillespie, jazz great; Whitey Ford, baseball star; and Samuel Taylor Coleridge, poet.*

October 22   Success Number 32/5 (10 + 22 = 32/5)

You are independent, inventive, visionary, and a bit high-strung. Though you are people-oriented, you still need periods by yourself to recharge your energies. If you'll cultivate the adventurous spirit of your 32/5 Success Number, you'll ward off a tendency to get yourself in a rut. More than most people, you need a job that gives you plenty of freedom to express your ideas. Versatile, you can succeed in many areas, but usually you're happiest in work that reflects your ideals. Quite often, you have a great talent for acting, art, or music. You also may be humanitarianly inclined. *Birthday of Christopher Lloyd, actor; Joan Fontaine, actress; and Timothy Leary, teacher.*

October 23   Success Number 33/6 (10 + 23 = 33/6)

You have a love of freedom, are adventurous, and are inclined to be impulsive. However, if you'll cultivate the social responsibility of your 33/6 Success Number, you'll offset a tendency to scatter your energies. With 33 as your guide, you can make a strong impact on the social consciousness and cultural values of humanity. Your engaging personality is usually a factor in your success, though you're liable to experiment before settling on a career. You have a fine intuition that you should learn to trust. Sometimes you have a talent for music. *Birthday of Dwight Yoakam, singer; Michael Crichton, writer; and Johnny Carson, talk show host.*

October 24   Success Number 34/7 (10 + 24 = 34/7)

You're capable of great enthusiasms and are inclined to give your all to whatever you have your heart set on. You're clever enough to get by on your wits, but with a 34/7 Success Number, you need a good education to make the most of your abilities. Your 34/7 gives you a reflective side and inclines you to science, religion, law, and writing. A born humanitarian and responsible by nature, you would make a fine physician, teacher, or counselor. The arts, though, are your best milieu, especially acting, music, sculpture, and literature. You're happiest when busy and are not likely to retire. *Birthday of Kevin Kline, actor; Bill Wyman, rock star; and Sybil Thorndike, actress.*

October 25   Success Number 35/8 (10 + 25 = 35/8)

You are intellectual, practical, and intuitive. You're likely to have academic interests, and you have a talent for painting, music, writing, and sculpture. If you'll cultivate the ambition of your 35/8 Success Number, you can rise to the top of your chosen field. You have leadership qualities, though you do not like being to be told what to do. You also have a strong need for affection, but are not inclined to wear your heart on your sleeve. Still, it's important not to let your feelings get bottled up. You're likely to demand perfection from yourself and others. *Birthday of Helen Reddy, singer; Georges Bizet, composer; and Henry Steele Commager, historian.*

October 26   Success Number 36/9 (10 + 26 = 36/9)

You place a great importance on getting ahead in life and are at home in the business world. You're drawn to large enterprises and can become quite the wheeler-dealer. Your 26 birthday gives you executive strengths, whereas your 36/9 Success Number will incline you to the arts, politics, and humanitarian endeavors. You would make an excellent fund-raiser for a cause and will also excel as a government leader. You would also enjoy a profitable career as a creative artist, physician, or financier. You are intuitive, intellectual, idealistic, and practical. *Birthday of Mahalia Jackson, singer; François Mitterand, French statesman; and Hillary Rodham Clinton, U.S. senator.*

October 27 Success Number 37/10/1 (10 + 27 = 37/10/1)

You are independent and do not like to be in a subordinate position. You're always ready for a challenge and pride yourself on your ability to overcome adversity. Your 37/10/1 Success Number only increases these qualities, making you a person who is fearless and perhaps intimidating. Yet you are sympathetic by nature and have a natural concern for the general welfare. Cultivate the leadership abilities and the individuality of your Success Number and you'll rise to the top of your field. Do not let materialistic considerations deter you from doing your own thing. *Birthday of Sylvia Plath, poet; Roy Lichtenstein, painter; and Theodore Roosevelt, U.S. president.*

October 28 Success Number 38/11/2 (10 + 28 = 38/11/2)

You are at home in both the arts and sciences. There are many things in life that you feel strongly about, but you must guard against being fixed in your opinions. With 38/11/2 as your Success Number, you are an inspirational thinker and are often at the forefront of your field. Writing, medicine, acting, law, engineering, and research are some of the fields that promise you happiness. You have an investigative mind and won't rest until you have achieved your goals. You can be stubborn, but with diplomacy and cooperation you will succeed in getting your message across to others. *Birthday of Bill Gates, Microsoft founder; Dennis Franz, actor; and Jonas Salk, physician.*

October 29   Success Number 39/12/3 (10 + 29 = 39/12/3)

You are idealistic and practical, but at times have difficulty reconciling these qualities. Often nervous, inventive, and high-strung, you need to have periods by yourself to overcome an inclination to be temperamental. Your feelings are intense, but you are a magnetic individual, capable of inspired leadership. If you'll cultivate the charm and sense of humor of your 39/12/3 Success Number, others will be more receptive to your highly original ideas. Your Success Number promises you success in communications and creative fields. Your work is likely to be ahead of its time. *Birthday of Winona Ryder, actress; Richard Dreyfuss, actor; and Jean Giraudoux, playwright.*

October 30   Success Number 40/4 (10 + 30 = 40/4)

You are a gifted communicator, but are inclined to be fixed in your viewpoints. Friends will be helpful to you once you overcome a tendency to be suspicious of their motivations. To make the most of your extraordinary creative potential, you'll need to cultivate the self-discipline, organization, and applied direction of your 40/4 Success Number. Highly dramatic, you're capable of notable accomplishments in literature and the theater. You will also enjoy success in medicine, politics, banking, teaching, law, music, and sculpture. You enjoy being in public life. *Birthday of Ruth Gordon, actress; Ezra Pound, poet; and Louis Malle, film director.*

October 31   Success Number 41/5 (10 + 31 = 41/5)

You are creative and practical but sometimes have difficulty reconciling these qualities. You enjoy travel, are highly intuitive, and are sincerely interested in the welfare of others. If you'll cultivate the spirit of adventure of your 41/5 Success Number, you'll offset a tendency to get into a rut. Self-discipline and a willingness to work hard are the keys for making the most of your capabilities. You'll enjoy success as a reformer, leader, writer, architect, sculptor, physician, or actor. Take care, though, not to place a premium on obtaining the luxuries of life. *Birthday of Barbara Bel Geddes, actress; Jan Vermeer, painter; and Peter Jackson, film director.*

NOVEMBER

November 1   Success Number 12/3 (11 + 1 = 12/3)

You are self-reliant, creative, intense, and dynamic. With 12/3 as your Success Number, you often choose a creative medium through which to express your individuality. Your 12 gives you the ability to organize, sell, promote, and publish. If you'll cultivate the sense of humor of your Success Number, you'll offset a tendency to take yourself too seriously. Whether you choose politics, science, law, medicine, literature, or acting for a career, you will always be a leader—and perhaps a pioneer as well. *Birthday of Lyle Lovett, singer; Larry Flynt, publisher; and Gary Player, golfer.*

November 2 Success Number 13/4 (11 + 2 = 13/4)

You are sensitive, intuitive, and imaginative. You work well in partnership and have a genuine concern for the welfare of those you care for. Both financial and emotional security are extremely important to you, and you will work hard to achieve these ends. You can succeed in business, medicine, and politics, and you'll also enjoy success in creative fields. With 13/4 as your Success Number, self-discipline and strict application will be the key to making the most of your abilities. It is important, though, that you like your work or you won't put in the necessary effort to succeed. *Birthday of K. D. Lang, singer; Burt Lancaster, actor; and Daniel Boone, frontiersman.*

November 3 Success Number 14/5 (11 + 3 = 14/5)

Your ability to get along with others is an asset in whatever you do. Naturally skilled with words, you can succeed in writing, poetry, and sales. With 14/5 as your Success Number, you are adventurous and an opportunist. Often you have a special talent for acting and investing, but must avoid taking the easiest way. You're clever enough to get by on your wits and good at extricating yourself from emergency situations. Your best field is science or literature—but you also have a good business head and a great appreciation (and talent) for the arts. Engineering, architecture, and medicine may also appeal to you. *Birthday of Charles Bronson, actor; Monica Vitti, actress; and Roseanne Barr, actress.*

November 4   Success Number 15/6 (11 + 4 = 15/6)

Your 4 birthday number gives you the ability to work hard; your 15/6 Success Number, a sense of responsibility. Your 15 also gives you the ability to make a good income, and it draws you to large enterprises. If you'll cultivate the ingenuity and inventiveness of your 15, you'll ward off your 4 tendency to get into a rut. Medicine, law, acting, sculpture, writing, journalism, and music are other promising fields for you. Usually you have a good understanding of human nature, and may be inclined to keep your woes to yourself. *Birthday of Matthew McConaughey, actor; Laura Bush, U.S. first lady; and Robert Mapplethorpe, photographer.*

November 5   Success Number 16/7 (11 + 5 = 16/7)

Your 5 birthday number gives you a flair for adventure and the theater, but your 16/7 Success Number gives you a philosophical bent and promises you success in such fields as teaching, research, law, medicine, music, religion, and writing. A good education (16/7) coupled with what you learn from experience (5) will give you a sound, workable code to live by. You get along well with others, but you're something of a loner, too. You are well suited for public life, though, and can succeed in business on a large scale. You are a person who's inclined to practice what you preach. *Birthday of Roy Rogers, singer-actor; Vivien Leigh, actress; and Bryan Adams, singer.*

November 6   Success Number 17/8 (11 + 6 = 17/8)

You work well with groups and often achieve a leadership position in that capacity. With 17/8 as your Success Number, you have a strong drive for success and financial well-being. Sometimes, though, you're inconsistent in the way you handle money and may veer from overgenerosity to penuriousness. Fields that promise you success are music, acting, literature, law, and medicine. You will also fare well in business allied to the arts. Emotional, sensitive, and psychic, you treasure your freedom, yet have a keen sense of responsibility. *Birthday of John Philip Sousa, bandleader; Sally Field, actress; and James Jones, writer.*

November 7   Success Number 18/9 (11 + 7 = 18/9)

You are a deep thinker with an interest in the mysteries of life and are equally drawn to science and religion. With 18/9 as your Success Number, you have an interest in broad social issues and want to help humanity. Your 18 gives you administrative talents and an ability to reach out and touch the masses with your message. At the same time, though, a part of you remains aloof. Your best fields are scientific research and literature. You would also have success as a business adviser, though you're more at home in intellectual spheres. You have keen insights about others, but be careful not to be too critical. *Birthday of Marie Curie, physicist: Al Hirt, jazz great; and Albert Camus, writer.*

November 8   Success Number 19/10/1 (11 + 8 = 19/10/1)

You are executive by nature. Intense and dynamic, you won't let anything stand in your way in your reach for the top. With 19/10/1 as your Success Number, you have leadership skills and may be politically inclined. Sympathetic to the plight of the underdog, you may be reform-minded. A born moneymaker, you would be a good fund-raiser for a cause. Cultivate the individuality of your 19/10/1 Success Number and you'll stand out from the crowd as someone who is unique. Material success means much to you, but don't sacrifice your individuality in the pursuit of it. The arts and the professions often appeal to you. *Birthday of Bonnie Raitt, singer; Margaret Mitchell, writer; and Christiaan Barnard, surgeon.*

November 9   Success Number 20/2 (11 + 9 = 20/2)

You have a natural interest in public affairs and may be drawn to a political career. You dislike playing second fiddle and are happiest in a position of leadership. If you'll cultivate the diplomacy and tact of your 20/2 Success Number, you'll offset tendencies to be temperamental, too intense, or argumentative. You have strong feelings and often seek an emotional outlet for them in creative work. You would make an excellent actor, though you'll also enjoy success as an author, poet, painter, physician, psychologist, scientist, public servant, or businessperson. *Birthday of Carl Sagan, astronomer; Dorothy Dandridge, actress; and Ivan Turgenev, novelist.*

November 10   Success Number 21/3 (11 + 10 = 21/3)

You are independent and creative. You're usually found in a professional career, though you can also succeed in business. You have natural leadership abilities and are a true individual. Take care to avoid the negative traits of egotism, pride, and jealousy. With 21/3 as your Success Number, you have a flair for self-expression, which is an asset to you in both business and the arts. If you'll develop the charm, flexibility, and good humor of your Success Number, you'll overcome a tendency to be insistent or to take yourself too seriously. *Birthday of Richard Burton, actor; Martin Luther, religious leader; and Roy Scheider, actor.*

November 11   Success Number 22/4 (11 + 11 = 22/4)

You are intense, dramatic, and charismatic. You are also high-strung and emotional and need a creative outlet for your strong, feeling nature. You are inclined to march to the beat of your own drummer. Your 22/4 Success Number will give you the ability to make your dreams and inspirations practical. A routine job is not for you, however, because you have a visionary nature and require the freedom to be an independent thinker. You'll have success in both the arts and sciences, and you are often found in such fields as writing, acting, metaphysics, public service, medicine, and engineering. *Birthday of Demi Moore, actress; Fyodor Dostoyevsky, writer; and Kurt Vonnegut, writer.*

November 12   Success Number 23/5 (11 + 12 = 23/5)

You have a friendly manner and a magnetic personality. Gifted in the area of communications, you'll have success in a writing or speaking occupation. You also have strong artistic leanings and may be drawn to such fields as acting and painting. With 23/5 as your Success Number, you are adventurous and are likely to experiment before settling on a career. Your 23 gives you a special talent for science, medicine, and work with the public. You are popular and fond of social contacts. You also have a good intuition, are a progressive thinker, and are a loyal friend. *Birthday of Neil Young, singer; Grace Kelly, actress; and Sammy Sosa, baseball star.*

November 13   Success Number 24/6 (11 + 13 = 24/6)

You are both creative and practical, but may have difficulty reconciling these qualities. It is essential that you like your work or you're apt to feel unappreciated, underpaid, and resentful. With 24/6 as your Success Number, you are happiest when busiest and capable of assuming great responsibilities. Your 24/6 promises you success in such fields as journalism, acting, art, and music. You have great inner resources and should choose a job where they will be allowed to evidence themselves. A home of your own is important for your happiness. *Birthday of Robert Louis Stevenson, writer; Whoopi Goldberg, actress; and Joe Mantegna, actor.*

November 14 Success Number 25/7 (11 + 14 = 25/7)

Your 14 birthday number promises you an adventurous life, whereas your 25/7 Success Number inclines you to reflection and introspection. This is a powerful combination that gives you the ability to learn (25/7) and profit from your experiences (14/5). You have strong emotions that you often conceal. As a result, you are not always understood. Pleasure seeking and sex can be your downfall if you allow them to usurp control of your life. If you do not—then you will enjoy success in such fields as acting, investing, painting, engineering, science, law, business, and politics. *Birthday of Prince Charles, British royalty; Claude Monet, painter; and Veronica Lake, actress.*

November 15 Success Number 26/8 (11 + 15 = 26/8)

You work well with groups and are an innovator. A born moneymaker, you can succeed in business and are drawn to large enterprises. With 26/8 as your Success Number, you are happiest in work that reflects your ideals. Your 26/8 gives you ambition and the ability to successfully commercialize your creative talents. At times, though, you can be stubborn and fixed in your opinions. Remember that it makes good sense to give in once in a while. You can succeed in medicine and would make a fine lawyer, actor, artist, musician, statesman, diplomat, or scientist. *Birthday of Georgia O'Keeffe, painter; Sam Waterston, actor; and Petula Clark, singer.*

November 16   Success Number 27/9 (11 + 16 = 27/9)

You are a good promoter of the causes you espouse, but are inclined to be set in your views. Your 16 gives you philosophical and literary tendencies and makes you a natural critic of society and its values. With 27/9 as your Success Number, you are public-spirited, but you dislike taking orders. You thrive on challenges and are resilient in crisis situations. Often you have an outstanding talent for music. You are good with details and can also see the big picture. Writing, teaching, law, politics, and public service are likely to appeal to you. *Birthday of Burgess Meredith, actor; W. C. Handy, composer; and George S. Kaufman, playwright.*

November 17   Success Number 28/10/1
(11 + 17 = 28/10/1)

With a 28/10/1 Success Number and a 17 birthday, you will rise to success (17/8) when you learn to do your own thing (28/10/1). Executive by nature, you will have success as an architect, engineer, teacher, lawyer, or writer. You do well in public life and may have an exceptional talent for acting. A deep thinker, you like to dig deep and get to the root of things. You may not always handle your money wisely. At times, you can be extravagant; at other times, penurious. You are dramatic, affectionate, and intense. *Birthday of Rock Hudson; actor; Martin Scorsese, film director; and Lauren Hutton, model-actress.*

November 18   Success Number 29/11/2
(11 + 18 = 29/11/2)

You have determination and are anxious to get ahead in life. You usually have a fine intuition and good administrative qualities as well. You can succeed in such fields as law, politics, and teaching. With 29/11/2 as your Success Number, you do best when inspired and are capable of original work in the arts. You're also capable of going to emotional extremes and must be wary that temperament doesn't undermine your prospects for success. You can, however, succeed in anything that you undertake. *Birthday of Linda Evans, actress; Johnny Mercer, songwriter; and Susan Sullivan, actress.*

November 19   Success Number 30/3 (11 + 19 = 30/3)

You are versatile and can succeed in a wide variety of occupations. However, you must guard against a tendency to be inflexible and stubborn. With 30/3 as your Success Number, you are highly magnetic and have great powers of persuasion, qualities that will serve you well in such fields as sales, diplomacy, writing, acting, and law. You are a good moneymaker, but are more likely to be found in an artistic or professional career than in business. Your natural leadership skills can take you to the heights in a political career. You can always be counted on to do more than your share in getting things accomplished. *Birthday of Calvin Klein, designer; Meg Ryan, actress; and Indira Gandhi, Indian political leader.*

November 20   Success Number 31/4 (11 + 20 = 31/4)

You're likely to have more than one interest at the same time. You work well in partnership and are good at bringing out the best in others. You can succeed in such fields as teaching, writing, law, medicine, science, and real estate. You have a fine intuition, which you should learn to trust. You also have strong feelings and are capable of going to extremes. To make a success of your life, you need to cultivate the self-discipline of your 31/4 Success Number. Once you do, you can achieve grand results, for you are capable of big deeds. Of the arts, you may be most drawn to music. *Birthday of Robert F. Kennedy, U.S. senator; Edwin Hubble, astronomer; and Bo Derek, actress.*

November 21   Success Number 32/5 (11 + 21 = 32/5)

Your 21 birthday number gives you a love of pleasure, money, display, and excitement, and these qualities are further emphasized by your adventurous 32/5 Success Number. Take care that the allure of the primrose path doesn't interfere with your overall progress. However, your 32/5 gives you a talent for acting and promises you success in fields where the personal touch and risk taking are factors. Your 21 gives you a gift for self-expression, which will be an asset to you in such fields as writing, sales, and promotional work. *Birthday of Troy Aikman, football star; Stan Musial, baseball star; and Voltaire, philosopher.*

November 22   Success Number 33/6 (11 + 22 = 33/6)

You have an iron will and great determination. You have strong humanitarian leanings, but can be fanatical in your beliefs. Intense, inventive, and high-strung, you are capable of accomplishments that are ahead of their time. With 33/6 as your Success Number, you often make a notable contribution to cultural values and society's betterment. Both the arts (especially music, acting, and literature) and the sciences are likely to appeal to you. You're happiest in work that reflects your ideals. Responsibility seems to bring out the best in you, and you often have outstanding skills as a leader. *Birthday of André Gide, writer; Charles de Gaulle, French statesman; and Geraldine Page, actress.*

November 23   Success Number 34/7 (11 + 23 = 34/7)

Your 23 birthday number makes you people-oriented, whereas your 34/7 Success Number makes you a bit of a loner and inclined to introspection. You have progressive new ideas, yet are also practical. You have strong humanitarian leanings and are likely to succeed in such fields as teaching, medicine, law, science, and government service. Often you have an outstanding talent for acting or music. With a 34/7 Success Number, you should obtain as good an education as possible and learn to specialize; this will help you overcome an inclination to scatter your energies and talents. *Birthday of Maxwell Caulfield, actor; Boris Karloff, actor; and Billy the Kid, outlaw.*

November 24   Success Number 35/8 (11 + 24 = 35/8)

You are smart enough to get by on your wits, and usually you're a good student of human nature. You work well with groups and can achieve a position of leadership in that capacity. Your 24 birthday number gives you an excellent sense of responsibility, whereas your 35/8 Success Number gives you ambition and a willingness to work hard to make something of yourself. With this combination of numbers, you will achieve success as a writer, lawyer, painter, musician, sculptor, statesman, teacher, or actor. Never think of retiring—you are happiest when working. *Birthday of Scott Joplin, ragtime great; Henri de Toulouse-Lautrec, painter; and Zachary Taylor, U.S. president.*

November 25   Success Number 36/9 (11 + 25 = 36/9)

You are introspective and concerned about the meaning of life. Teaching, religion, writing, law, psychology, and counseling are some the fields that will bring you fulfillment. With a 36/9 Success Number, you are genuinely concerned about the welfare of others and would enjoy a career in politics, reform, public service, and work of a humanitarian nature. Your 36/9 also gives you creative talents, and you'll achieve success in any line of the arts. You are a private (25/7) person with a universal (36/9) outlook. Take care, though, not to procrastinate. *Birthday of John F. Kennedy Jr., publisher; Pope John XXIII, religious leader; and Amy Grant, singer.*

November 26   Success Number 37/10/1
(11 + 26 = 37/10/1)

You are intellectual and practical, with strong imaginative powers. You are at your best in mental spheres and will have success in such fields as writing and teaching. You are also highly artistic and have the capability to commercialize your creative gifts successfully. With 37/10/1 as your Success Number, it is important to find and then do your own thing. Your 37/10/1 gives you the ability to be the head of your own business or to attain a position of leadership in the corporate world. For you to be truly happy, though, you must find work that reflects your ideals. *Birthday of Rich Little, comedian; Eugene Ionesco, playwright; and Robert Goulet, singer-actor.*

November 27   Success Number 38/11/2
(11 + 27 = 38/11/2)

You would enjoy a job that allows you to travel. Independent, you do not fare well in a subordinate position. You belong on top—and since you have a genuine desire to help others, you would make a fine leader of a cause. With 38/11/2 as your Success Number, you work best when inspired. Idealistic and inventive, you are capable of creating work that's ahead of its time, especially in artistic fields. Though you are resilient in crisis situations, you still may need to check a tendency to be temperamental and high-strung. *Birthday of Bruce Lee, actor; Robin Givens, actress; and Jimi Hendrix, rock star.*

November 28   Success Number 39/12/3
(11 + 28 = 39/12/3)

You can succeed in any line you choose and may be especially talented in music. With 39/12/3 as your Success Number, you often choose a creative medium through which to express your individuality. Naturally ambitious, you will make sacrifices to get ahead, but periodically you might have to fight off an inclination to be lazy or too easygoing. Some of the fields that promise you success are acting, writing, sales, electrical engineering, law, science, teaching, and architecture. Some 28s are mechanical geniuses. *Birthday of Agnieszka Holland, film director; Gloria Grahame, actress; and Jon Stewart, comic.*

November 29   Success Number 40/4 (11 + 29 = 40/4)

You are inclined to be nervous, restless, and high-strung, but you have a sincere desire to make the world a better place to live. You are an idealist and a dreamer who must cultivate the self-discipline and practicality of your 40/4 Success Number to make the most of your capabilities. Imaginative and inventive, you have the potential to spin magic and create work that's ahead of its time, especially in artistic fields. You'll also have success as a writer, teacher, lawyer, publisher, actor, public servant, or political leader. *Birthday of Jacques Chirac, French president; Louisa May Alcott, writer; and Kim Delaney, actress.*

November 30 Success Number 41/5 (11 + 30 = 41/5)

Your 30 birthday gives you a way with words, whereas your 41/5 Success Number gives you a way with people. The combination makes you an ideal salesperson, a gifted writer, a skilled politician, or an entertainment personality with showmanship. The 4 in your 41/5 Success Number will help offset the inclination of 30 to drift or to be careless and indolent. However, you will still need to develop tact and diplomacy, for you can be too outspoken and fixed in your opinions. You are conscientious and caring, but can be too exacting with others. *Birthday of David Mamet, playwright; Dick Clark, TV personality; and Billy Idol, rock star.*

DECEMBER

December 1 Success Number 13/4 (12 + 1 = 13/4)

You have much creative talent and are inclined to do your own thing. However, you need the self-discipline of your 13/4 Success Number to make a success of your life. With a willingness to work hard, you can rise to the top in your field. You are creative and practical, but sometimes have trouble reconciling these qualities. It is essential that you find work that you like to do or you won't put forth the necessary effort to get ahead. You are an explorer, a trailblazer, a creator, and a leader. *Birthday of Richard Pryor, comic; Lou Rawls, musician; and Lee Trevino, golfer.*

December 2   Success Number 14/5 (12 + 2 = 14/5)

You work best in an atmosphere of friendliness and hate disharmony. Magnetic and warmhearted, you have a good sense of what the public wants and will have success in fields where the personal touch is a factor. With 14/5 as your Success Number, you are adventurous and may have a special talent for acting or investing. You work best in partnership, but are apt to experiment before settling down. You may also have a talent for writing poetry or fiction. Interior design, music, dancing, medicine, and teaching may appeal to you as well. *Birthday of Britney Spears, singer; Lucy Liu, actress; and Monica Seles, tennis star.*

December 3   Success Number 15/6 (12 + 3 = 15/6)

You are naturally gifted with the written and spoken word. Your gift for self-expression is an asset to you in both business and the arts. You'll find that social contacts will be helpful to you in business, for you're friendly and personable. If you'll cultivate the sense of responsibility of your 15/6 Success Number, you'll offset a tendency to scatter your energies. Your 15/6 also gives you a talent for making a good income. Writing, sales, acting, editing, painting, music, publishing, advertising, and banking are some of the fields that are apt to appeal to you. *Birthday of Daryl Hannah, actress; Brendan Fraser, actor; and Jean-Luc Goddard, film director.*

December 4   Success Number 16/7 (12 + 4 = 16/7)

You'll work hard to achieve your goals, but at times you can be too hard on yourself. You can succeed in business and work well in the corporate structure. With a 16/7 Success Number, you need to develop a workable philosophy of life to offset a tendency to get down in the dumps. Your 16/7 inclines you to introspection and makes you a good critic of society and its values. You'll have success with mental interests and would make a fine writer, teacher, psychologist, lawyer, or banker. Music, sculpture, acting, and interior design are your best avenues in the arts. *Birthday of Jeff Bridges, actor; Marisa Tomei, actress; and Rainer Maria Rilke, poet.*

December 5   Success Number 17/8 (12 + 5 = 17/8)

You are restless, progressive, and thrive on change, travel, excitement, and adventure. You love variety and would feel confined by a routine job. Business, though, is your natural milieu, but you will also enjoy success as an engineer, lawyer, physician, politician, salesperson, or writer. You are a good talker and can sell both yourself and your ideas. With 17/8 as your Success Number, you are ambitious and have the know-how to successfully commercialize your creative talents. You enjoy public life and are often an innovator in your field. You may also have dramatic gifts or musical talent. *Birthday of Strom Thurmond, U.S. senator; Little Richard, rock star; and Walt Disney, filmmaker.*

December 6   Success Number 18/9 (12 + 6 = 18/9)

You have a keen sense of responsibility and work well with groups. You are at home in the arts and may have a special talent for acting, literature, design, and music. Businesses allied to the arts will also appeal to you. With 18/9 as your Success Number, you have an interest in the world around you and may be drawn to politics and public service. You will do well in any field that requires efficient administration. You will also succeed as a lawyer, business adviser, or teacher. Though emotional, you are also intellectual. You handle money well, but may dislike taking orders and advice. *Birthday of Dave Brubeck, jazz great; Joyce Kilmer, poet; and Wally Cox, actor.*

December 7   Success Number 19/10/1 (12 + 7 = 19/10/1)

You are an analyst, a searcher after hidden truths, and a critic with a passion for perfection. However, you must learn to come out of your shell and be more expressive. To ensure your success, cultivate the drive, courage, and initiative of your 19/10/1 Success Number. Otherwise you can be a person who is all thought and no action. Still, your 19 will give you the ability to lead and direct. Though you are a good moneymaker, you're usually happier in an artistic or professional career than in business. Law, acting, writing, and teaching are fields where you'll shine. *Birthday of Ellen Burstyn, actress; Tom Waits, singer; and Willa Cather, writer.*

December 8   Success Number 20/2 (12 + 8 = 20/2)

You are practical and productive. Your 8 birthday number gives you a good head for business, whereas your 20/2 Success Number gives you magnetism and a flair for the dramatic and poetic. If you'll cultivate the tact and diplomacy of your Success Number, you'll have success in such fields as law, politics, business, banking, publishing, and religion. You work well in partnership, and being successful financially is very important to you. Your 8 gives you executive talents, and your 20 makes you community-minded. Acting, music, writing, and education are other areas that promise you fulfillment. *Birthday of Sammy Davis Jr., actor; Kim Basinger, actress; and Jim Morrison, rock star.*

December 9   Success Number 21/3 (12 + 9 = 21/3)

You are universal in outlook and naturally drawn to public service and politics. You dislike taking orders and you have a strong need for personal freedom. With 21/3 as your Success Number, you're good at getting your ideas across to others and will have success in such fields as public relations, sales, law, writing, acting, publishing, science, painting, and education. Take care, though, to avoid the negative sides of your Success Number, which are inclinations toward escapism, procrastination, and the scattering of energies. Take care also not to be self-righteous. *Birthday of Kirk Douglas, actor; Douglas Fairbanks Jr., actor; and Judi Dench, actress.*

December 10 Success Number 22/4 (12 + 10 = 22/4)

You are independent and do well in business for yourself and in positions of authority. Intuitive and practical, you can commercialize any talent. With 22/4 as your Success Number, you are visionary in outlook and can succeed in both the arts and sciences. You are at your best, however, when your occupation measures up to your ideals. You would feel confined in a routine job—you need the freedom to be innovative. Some of the fields that promise you fulfillment are law, acting, painting, music, writing, medicine, psychology, banking, and real estate. Often you're drawn to philosophy and religion. *Birthday of Kenneth Branagh, actor; Dorothy Lamour, actress; and Emily Dickinson, poet.*

December 11 Success Number 23/5 (12 + 11 = 23/5)

You are imaginative, nervous, and sometimes high-strung. Take care that temperament doesn't get in the way of your overall progress. You are an innovator who often works best when inspired. You have definite humanitarian leanings and would make a fine government official. You're usually happier in an artistic career than business. Your 23/5 Success Number will help you to develop warmth and human understanding, qualities that will offset the tendency of your 11 birthday number to be detached and impersonal. *Birthday of Aleksandr Solzhenitsyn, writer; Rita Moreno, actress; and Hector Berlioz, composer.*

December 12   Success Number 24/6 (12 + 12 = 24/6)

You have promotional skills and are good at selling yourself and your ideas. Sales, teaching, banking, and advertising are some of the fields that promise you fulfillment. If you'll cultivate the sense of responsibility of your 24/6 Success Number, you'll offset an inclination to scatter your energies. Your 24 makes you dramatic by nature and gives you the ability to succeed in show business. You would be a great asset in public affairs and would make a fine journalist or creative writer. You're happiest when busy, so don't count on an early retirement. A home of your own is important to your happiness. *Birthday of Edward G. Robinson, actor; Dionne Warwick, singer; and Gustave Flaubert, writer.*

December 13   Success Number 25/7 (12 + 13 = 25/7)

You have a love of freedom, but are often burdened with responsibility. Both creative and practical, you sometimes have difficulty reconciling these qualities. Your 25/7 Success Number gives you an introspective side and may incline you to religion and philosophy. Your 25 makes you a perfectionist, but you may also be given to procrastination. To be inwardly content, it is essential that you develop a workable philosophy of life. Some of the fields that promise you fulfillment are writing, acting, painting, music, teaching, law, real estate, engineering, and businesses allied to the arts. *Birthday of Christopher Plummer, actor; Dick Van Dyke, actor; and Archie Moore, boxer.*

December 14   Success Number 26/8 (12 + 14 = 26/8)

You have an adventurous approach toward life and are inclined to take risks. A born speculator, you like things to move quickly and must be careful not to be expedient in your choice of occupation. You have your eye out, though, for the main chance and know which side the bread is buttered on. With 26/8 as your Success Number, you have the ability to make money through your creative talents. Your 26/8 gives you ambition, and the 14 birthday gives you originality—a combination that will ensure your success in such fields as law, science, writing, acting, and sales. Take care, though, not to be reckless. *Birthday of Nostradamus, seer; Lee Remick, actress; and Tycho Brahe, astronomer.*

December 15   Success Number 27/9 (12 + 15 = 27/9)

You have a need for a home of your own to be happy. You work well for a cause and are blessed with a sense of responsibility. Imaginative and intuitive, you can succeed in creative areas. In business, you have a talent for making money and are at home in large enterprises. With 27/9 as your Success Number, you gravitate toward challenges and are resilient in crisis situations. Cultivate the universal outlook of your Success Number to offset a tendency to be too bound to home and hearth. Your 27/9 gives you an interest in literature and philosophy. *Birthday of Tim Conway, actor; Don Johnson, actor; and Alexandre Eiffel, engineer.*

December 16 Success Number 28/10/1
(12 + 16 = 28/10/1)

You need a good education for your best success. Intuitive and perceptive, you will learn much from your powers of observation and will have success as a critic or an adviser to the community. With 28/10/1 as your Success Number, you'll learn to be a doer (1) as well as a thinker (16/7). With the courage and initiative of 1, you'll act upon your ideas. Teaching, law, music, art, writing, architecture, and science are likely to appeal to you more than a business career. If you will be open with others, your love life will be a lot less complicated. *Birthday of Liv Ullman, actress; Arthur C. Clarke, science-fiction writer; and Ludwig van Beethoven, composer.*

December 17 Success Number 29/11/2
(12 + 17 = 29/11/2)

You are idealistic and practical. With 29/11/2 as your Success Number, you work best when inspired, but often you can let temperament get in the way of success. You are original in thought, and your work is often ahead of its time. Though you're restless by nature, you need to find an anchor in your home to be happy. Money is important to you, but you should avoid long-shot gambles. You would, however, be successful as a fundraiser for a cause. You can succeed in creative areas and business. *Birthday of John Greenleaf Whittier, poet; Erskine Caldwell, writer; and Arthur Fiedler, conductor.*

December 18 Success Number 30/3 (12 + 18 = 30/3)

You have administrative talents and may be drawn to politics and public service. Somewhat restless, you need to be careful not to scatter your energies. With 30/3 as your Success Number, you're good at getting your ideas across to others, but must guard against being dictatorial or fixed in your ideas. Your 30/3 promises you success in such fields as sales, art, writing, publishing, music, acting, law, medicine, and teaching. Though sociable, you may be slow to take others into your confidence. You also have a philanthropic side and a genuine interest in helping people. *Birthday of Keith Richards, rock star; Christina Aguilera, singer; and Brad Pitt, actor.*

December 19 Success Number 31/4 (12 + 19 = 31/4)

You have an excellent head for business and have the ability for making everything pay for itself. Good at promoting yourself and your ideas, you can succeed in sales and real estate. You shine best, though, in an artistic or professional career, most notably music, law, science, medicine, writing, aviation, and publishing. If you are to succeed, it is essential that you develop self-discipline and persistence, qualities associated with your 31/4 Success Number. Despite your love of people, you are sometimes the loner. You have leadership skills, but may be overly emotional. *Birthday of Edith Piaf, singer; Leonid Brezhnev, Soviet leader; and Cicely Tyson, actress.*

December 20   Success Number 32/5 (12 + 20 = 32/5)

Your 32/5 Success Number gives you magnetism, and your 20 birthday number makes you a good mixer or diplomat. This combination promises you success in such fields as law, politics, medicine, psychology, and acting. You would be at home in government service and you are humanitarian in outlook. You also have a religious or philosophical side and would make a fine teacher, counselor, or writer. You work well in partnership and are empathetic. Financial security is important to you, but with 32/5 as your Success Number you're willing to take a chance now and then. You are adventurous (32/5) and sensitive (20/2). *Birthday of Anita Baker, singer; Irene Dunne, actress; and Susanne Langer, philosopher.*

December 21   Success Number 33/6 (12 + 21 = 33/6)

You are versatile and creative. You work well with others, but may be slow to take people into your confidence. With 33/6 as your Success Number, you're an idealist who has a sincere desire to contribute to the general welfare. If you'll cultivate the sense of responsibility of your 33/6, you'll overcome an inclination to scatter your energies. Often you're drawn to politics as well as creative pursuits. Though your eyes may be on the stars, your feet are usually on the ground. You're good at promoting yourself and your ideas and would excel as a teacher, writer, actor, or publicist. *Birthday of Kiefer Sutherland, actor; Jane Fonda, actress; and Benjamin Disraeli, statesman.*

December 22   Success Number 34/7 (12 + 22 = 34/7)

You are both idealistic and practical and usually have no trouble in reconciling these qualities. Though visionary, you also have your feet on the ground. If you'll cultivate the philosophical outlook of your 34/7 Success Number, you'll offset a tendency to be high-strung. Periodically, you need time by yourself to replenish your energies. In business, you're capable of handling big projects, though you will fare best in work that reflects your ideals. You can succeed in both the arts and sciences. Rise above skepticism and heed your inner voice (34/7), then you'll find your mission in life (22). *Birthday of Lady Bird Johnson, U.S. first lady; Ralph Fiennes, actor; and Diane Sawyer, TV journalist.*

December 23   Success Number 35/8 (12 + 23 = 35/8)

You like excitement in your work and are likely to experiment before settling on a career. Somewhat opportunistic, you have your eye out for the main chance and you know which side your bread is buttered on. Your 35/8 Success Number gives you extraordinary ambition, and your 23 birthday number gives you the ingenuity to be an innovator in your field. You have a way with people, and your pleasing personality contributes to your success in life. Often you're drawn to a financial career or the business side of the arts, though you may be creatively talented as well. *Birthday of Corey Haim, actor; Susan Lucci, actress; and Robert Bly, poet.*

December 24   Success Number 36/9 (12 + 24 = 36/9)

You are ambitious, serious-minded, and responsible. Though artistically talented, you're more often found in business. You work well with groups, are self-reliant, and have good organizational skills. With 36/9 as your Success Number, you should cultivate a universal outlook to achieve your greatest success. Your 36/9 may attract you to administration, politics, and public service, for you are at your best when your energies are directed to a cause larger than self-interest. Other promising fields for you are banking, real estate, manufacturing, and acting. *Birthday of Ricky Martin, singer; Ava Gardner, actress; and Howard Hughes, industrialist.*

December 25   Success Number 37/10/1
(12 + 25 = 37/10/1)

You are intuitive yet practical. With 37/10/1 as your Success Number, you can stand out in your field as an innovator. If you'll develop the positive outlook and initiative of your Success Number, you'll overcome a tendency to be vacillating. Cultivate the courage of 1 to do your own thing; at the same time, however, do not become too self-absorbed (also 1). You can succeed in the academic world and usually have no trouble commercializing your artistic or scientific gifts. Basically altruistic, you may be drawn to politics and public service. *Birthday of Humphrey Bogart, actor; Clara Barton, nurse; and Rickey Henderson, baseball star.*

December 26   Success Number 38/11/2
(12 + 26 = 38/11/2)

You are both intellectual and practical. Though your eyes may be fixed on the heavens, your feet are always on the ground. You are happiest in work that reflects your ideals. With 38/11/2 as your Success Number, you are often charismatic. Your tendency is to think big, and you feel right at home in large enterprises. You have the practical know-how (26/8) to make your dreams (38/11/2) come true. Often you achieve outstanding success in creative areas. You enjoy being in a position of authority. *Birthday of Mao Tse-tung, Chinese leader; Henry Miller, writer; and Richard Widmark, actor.*

December 27   Success Number 39/12/3
(12 + 27 = 39/12/3)

You thrive on challenges and do well in crisis situations. Highly ambitious, you enjoy life before the public. You also have a highly developed philosophical or literary side and can succeed in both the arts and sciences. Not one to be contented in a subordinate position for long, you will make you way to the top in your own way. With 39/12/3 as your Success Number, you have communication skills and a good sense of humor. These qualities will help offset your tendency to dwell on worries too much. You would make a fine executive and are also humanitarianly inclined. *Birthday of Gerard Depardieu, actor; Louis Pasteur, scientist; and Johannes Kepler, astronomer.*

406

December 28   Success Number 40/4 (12 + 28 = 40/4)

Your 40/4 Success Number indicates that you're willing to work hard to achieve the high place you desire in life, whereas your 28 birthday inclines you to do your own thing. More likely to be drawn to a professional career than business, you'll have success as a teacher, lawyer, writer, architect, engineer, or scientist. Music, acting, and government service are also likely to appeal to you. At times, you can be stubborn, and you may suffer from periodic bouts with laziness, but in the long run you will succeed with patience, perseverance, and persistence. *Birthday of Denzel Washington, actor; Maggie Smith, actress; and Woodrow Wilson, U.S. president.*

December 29   Success Number 41/5 (12 + 29 = 41/5)

You have a good intuition, but may be overly concerned about financial security. You are both practical and idealistic, but sometimes have difficulty reconciling these qualities. You work best when inspired and are capable of original achievements in the arts and sciences. You have strong humanitarian inclinations, but may want to keep a distance between yourself and the masses. That is why you must cultivate the warmth and understanding of your 41/5 Success Number. Your 41/5 will teach you to be expressive and outgoing and will keep you from being detached and aloof. *Birthday of Ted Danson, actor; Mary Tyler Moore, actress; and Pablo Casals, cellist.*

December 30 Success Number 42/6 (12 + 30 = 42/6)

At times you can be fixed in your views, but you still are convincing in arguments and can excel in such fields as writing, teaching, advertising, and sales. Cultivate the willingness to accept responsibility that comes with your 42/6 Success Number and you will offset a tendency to scatter your energies or to be lazy. The 4 in your 42 gives you the capacity to work hard, and its 2 will make you sensitive to others' feelings. These qualities combined will ensure your success in life. However, don't expect everyone to live up to your own high standards—in other words, don't nag. *Birthday of Tracey Ullman, actress; Sandy Koufax, baseball star; and Tiger Woods, golfer.*

December 31 Success Number 43/7 (12 + 31 = 43/7)

You are a combination of the introvert and the extrovert. Your 31 birthday makes you cheerful and sociable, but your 43/7 Success Number inclines you to introspection and aloofness. Used positively, your 43/7 gives you the ability to think deeply, and your 31 birthday gives you communication skills. With this combination, you are a person who has something meaningful to say. It's not surprising that you would excel as a teacher, counselor, lawyer, writer, or researcher. You also love travel and will work hard when interested. Take care, though, not to spend unwisely. Also, learn to forgive and forget. *Birthday of Anthony Hopkins, actor; Henri Matisse, painter; and Val Kilmer, actor.*

CHAPTER 10

WHAT NUMBERS ARE IMPORTANT TO YOU RIGHT NOW?

What happens if you don't like the number of your first pinnacle? Does this mean you'll just have to wait until the pinnacle number changes? Or let's say your life path number differs from the number of your ruling passion. Does this mean you'll never get the chance to enjoy yourself fully?

The answer to all these questions is no! Each of us gets our chance to experience all nine numbers, plus the Master Numbers of 11 and 22. And to do so, we don't have to wait for the pinnacle and cycle numbers to change.

Every day, every month, and every year the calendar date changes. Remember how you found your life path number? Well, take today's date and add up the day, the month, and the year—just as you did for your life path number—and you'll find what kind of day it is for the human race. To find the kind of month it is for the world, add the number of the calendar month to that of the year. February 1977 was an 8 month. If you want to know what kind of a year 1977 was, reduce it to a single digit: $1 + 9 + 7 + 7 = 24 = 6$.

As a Universal Vibration, 6 meant the public was susceptible in 1977 to stories about families. No wonder the TV production *Roots,* based on the family tree of author **Alex Haley**—a descendant of Kunta Kinte, a West African youth enslaved in America before the Civil War—stirred the consciousness of its viewers. The ABC miniseries reached a record 80 million viewers and was shown eight nights in a row, an unprecedented scheduling feat.

On any particular day, humanity is subject to these three important vibrations: the *Universal Year*, the *Universal Month*, and the *Universal Day*. If you are dealing with the world at large, it is helpful to be familiar with them.

Take the case of the famous composer **Achille Claude Debussy**, born on August 22, 1862, with a birth name that adds up to the Master Number of 11. The first performance of his *Prelude à l'Après-midi d'une Faune* (prelude to Afternoon of the Faun) was on December 22, 1894. For the world, it was a 22 year, a 7 month, and an 11 day; for Debussy it was a day that matched his 11 expression, and a year that matched the 22 of the day he was born. Certainly it was a perfect day for 11 and 22 abilities to be well received by the world.

410

The Calendar Day

Often major events and turning points in your life will occur on a day that has the same number as the day you were born. For example, actor **George Burns** was born on January 20, a number that relates to partnerships. Since the birthday number relates to vocation, we can expect some major events relating to career and partnerships to have occurred for George Burns on the 20th. And indeed, he got married on September 20, 1936. On that same day it was announced that he and Gracie had signed a major contract. Note also that *The George Burns and Gracie Allen Show* ran for almost 20 years on TV.

If the number of the calendar day matches your soul urge, it is a good time to go after what you want from life. You'll often get a chance to showcase your talents on a calendar day that matches your expression. Pivotal turns in your destiny that will give you insights into the meaning of your life may occur on a calendar day that matches your life path number.

Other Key Factors

Often the key numbers in your name or birth date will show up in your life in other significant ways. **Henry Ford** was born with a 19 life path, and his Model T Ford was manufactured for a period of 19 years. **Nelson Mandela** was born on the 18th and spent 18 years in prison. **Mother Seton** (Elizabeth Ann

Bayley), with a 16 expression, spent 16 years of her life as a nun. **Richard Buckminister Fuller** was born with 25 letters in his name and published 25 books during his lifetime. Actor **Gerard Depardieu** was born with a 16 life path and began acting at age 16. Actress **Demi Moore** was born on the 11th, and her marriage to Bruce Willis lasted 11 years. Playwright **Tennessee Williams** (Thomas Lanier Williams) was born with a 14 expression, and his relationship with his lover Frank Merlo lasted 14 years, until Frank's death of cancer.

Baseball star **Peter Edward Rose** was born with a 14/5 quiet self on April 14, 1941, and he wore the number 14 on his uniform. On August 23, 1989, he was banned from baseball for allegedly gambling on baseball games, a charge Rose vehemently denied. However, 14 years later, in his book *My Prison Without Walls* (published January 8, 2004, a day that adds up to 14), Rose finally admitted that he had in fact bet on baseball games.

The Personal Year, Month, and Day

How to Find Your Personal Year

In addition to these Universal Vibrations, each person has his or her own Personal Year, Personal Month, and Personal Day numerical vibrations. Let's say you were born on February 5, 1963, and you want to know the number of your Personal Year in 1971. To find out, add the day and the month of your birth to the number of the Universal Year. 1971 was a 9 Universal Year, so you add 9 + 2 + 5 to find your Personal Year, which would be 16, or 7.

Every January, the number of your Personal Year changes. If the number of the new year matches your expression, you'll get the opportunity to show your natural abilities. If it matches your soul urge, then opportunities will come your way in accordance with your heart's desire. If it is the same as your ruling passion, then you'll get the chance to do something you really enjoy. Go over all the important numbers you've learned in this book and compare them with the opportunities provided by the current year.

If the number of the Personal Year does not match any of your major numbers, it is still a significant year for you. Because the numbers of the Personal Years have their own sequence from 1 through 9, it is important for you to tune in to their rhythms.

A *1 Year* is a time to go after what you want, to keep moving, and to exercise initiative. 1 Years always signify new starts. In chapter 7, you learned that the cycle numbers change at around ages 28 and 56. To find the exact year of change, find the 1 Year nearest your 28th and 56th birthdays.

A *2 Year* is a time to be cooperative, to follow rather than to lead. Things begun in a 1 Year grow slowly during a 2 Year. Don't expect immediate results. Do small things that will make last year's new start work. This is a time to be receptive. The accent is on partnerships and on give-and-take in close relationships.

A *3 Year* means social activity with both old and new friends. You may scatter your energies and undertake too many things at once. It is a time to be happy but not frivolous. The accent is on charm and creativity. Buy some new clothes and express the joy of life.

A *4 Year* means facing reality. Sometimes it means digging in and doing the hard work. Not a time for 3 loafing or 5 restlessness, this is a time to be practical, to take care of health, and to be patient. Increased responsibilities require attention to duty.

A *5 Year* means investigating the new. Expand your horizons. It is a time for travel, excitement, and adventure. Some of you will do a lot of dating. Be ready for surprises, and be open to change and to opportunity outside the usual routine.

A *6 Year* is a stabilizing influence. Some will find a steady girl- or boyfriend; others will spend more time with their families. You may be asked to help around the house or to pitch in on some group project. Those without a steady friend will find themselves going along with the crowd. Be ready to assume responsibility with or for others.

A *7 Year* is a time to get it together and to spend some time by yourself. The accent is on self-examination, study, and meditation. If you find yourself dwelling on the past, know that tomorrow is going to be a brighter day. Keep the faith; investigate the unknown. Get in touch with inner strengths, with soul power.

An *8 Year* means recognition for those who have earned it. After last year's sabbatical, it's time to face the world again and assume your rightful place in it. Think big and aim for the top. Deal with important people. It is a time for power in the material world and for attending to financial affairs.

A *9 Year* is a time to finish old projects and to get ready for next year's new start. Tune in to current events; realize the common humanity you share with others. You can afford to give now, for next year you are starting something new. It is a period of endings.

An *11 Year* accents ideals, dreams, and inspirations. It is not a time for practical affairs. Always read the fine print on contracts. Some will be sensitive to music, poetry, and art, while others will express their sensitivity as a 2, which means consideration for others. Avoid escapism, fast cars, and drugs.

A *22 Year* favors success for the artist, the musician, and the sculptor. You can succeed at any work that matches your ideals. Think big and don't be skeptical about what comes to you via intuition. Most people will respond to this vibration as a 4, unless they are in the position to do something for the progress of humanity. Though you are inclined to be nervous during this period, try to remain calm and be careful not to break the law.

How to Find Your Personal Month

Once you have found your Personal Year, it is easy to find the Personal Month and Day. Let's say your Personal Year was 9 in 1971 and you want to know what kind of a month July was then. Since July is the 7th month of the year, you would add 7 to 9 to get the number of the Personal Month. The number 16, reduced to 7, would be the number of your Personal Month.

How to Find Your Personal Day

Add the number of the Personal Month to that of the calendar day to find your Personal Day. July 5 would be a 3 Personal Day, as 7 + 5 = 12/3. For the influences of the Personal Month and Day, read the descriptions given for the Personal Years, but apply them to these shorter periods of time.

Example

On July 5, 1971, a fictitious person was under the numerical influences of a 3 Personal Day, a 7 Personal Month, and a 9 Personal Year. For him, it was a day to talk with others (3) about some insights gained (7) regarding the common humanity we all share (9).

Times That May Be Difficult

Times that may be difficult are indicated when the number of the Personal Year, Month, or Day is the *same number* as one of the *missing* numbers in your birth name.

Example: Richard Nixon and Watergate

On June 17, 1972, the day of the Watergate break-in, Richard Milhous Nixon was under the numerical influences of an 11/2 Personal Year, an 8 Personal Month, and a 7 Personal Day. The number 7 always has a secretive quality. As the number of a Personal Day in an 8 month, the secrecy would be related to matters of power (8). 11 as a Personal Year always carries with it the danger of thinking yourself above the law because of your special mission in life.

If we think of the 11 as also bearing the quality of 2, it becomes especially revealing. Richard Nixon is missing 2 in his birth name. People missing 2 in their names tend to gloss over small things and are invariably tripped up by them. They are also sometimes extremely hypersensitive and have delusions of persecution. The former president was under the 11/2 vibration for a full year. What made this 7 day doubly critical for him was the factt that he was also missing 7 in his birth name. Because of this, June 17, 1972, was a day when his philososophy of life would be tested.

CHAPTER 11

THE NUMBERS OF KARMA—
13, 14, 16, 19

✡ ✡
✡

In chapter 5, you learned that the missing numbers in your name are called *karmic lacks;* the absence of these numbers represents principles or experiences that you have avoided in former lives. These missing numbers represent your *personal karma.* In this chapter, we will look at the numbers of *universal karma*—13, 14, 16, and 19. These numbers deal with *universal* principles and the misuse of those principles; they also relate to myths, to archetypes from the collective unconscious, to race memories and experiences shared by all of us. Their origins date back to the dawn of civilization, mythology, and the Bible.

Historically 13 also relates to the Middle Ages; 14 to the Age of Discovery and the Renaissance; 16 to the Age of Reason and Enlightenment; and 19 to the 19th and 20th centuries. Perhaps some of us with a karmic number in our names or birth dates have had past lifetimes related to these periods of time.

Whether or not we have these karmic numbers in our names or birth dates, all of us get to experience these numbers at ages 13, 14, 16, and 19. If you've ever wondered why adolescence is universally considered to be a painful period, it's because during that time we all have to deal with these four karmic numbers. People with 13 in their names or birth dates are apt to have difficulty expressing their feelings, often keeping them deeply hidden—and this is true of most 13-year-olds. Sexuality and freedom are concerns of the 14-year-old and for those with 14 in their numberscopes; many people with 16 in their birth names or birth dates experience difficulties with love—and that is also true for many adolescents who at age 16 experience their first romantic crushes and their first broken hearts; and coming to terms with individuality, power, and one's upcoming place in the world are often the concern of the 19-year-old—and for people with 19 prominent in their names or birth dates.

It was **Saint Augustine** (born November 13, A.D. 354) who said that Time (or karma) as we know it began with the original sin and subsequent fall of Adam and Eve from the Garden of Eden into the cycle of death and rebirth—in other words, the cycle of the four seasons, winter, spring, summer, and fall. The reason why there are four karmic numbers is that there are four seasons, and the four seasons can be correlated with the numbers 13, 14, 16, and 19. In the words of the poet **John Keats** (13/4 expression), "There are four seasons in the mind of man" who has "his winter too of pale misfortune / Or else he would forego his mortal nature."

13 is associated with the Death Card in the Tarot deck and wasting time when we should be working; 14 means misuse of freedom and sex in a former lifetime, with a likelihood of accidents and/or sexual indiscretions; 16 means crucifixion of the self on the cross of love due to a past lifetime of illicit love; and 19, a misuse of power in a former lifetime. If you have one of these numbers in your name or birth date, you'll be put into similar situations that you experienced in former lifetimes, with the chance to do it right this time around.

Karma, though, deals with principles and not events. If something bad happens to you, it's not because of your karma; rather, it's because you misused the principle(s) associated with that karmic number. Karma is not Mosaic Law; it is not tit for tat, or "an eye for an eye, a tooth for a tooth"; it is not cosmic revenge. People with karmic numbers have the karma of doing something with their lives to correct the misuse of the principles associated with that number.

Here's an example of a person who turned a negative (karma) into a positive. **Abraham Lincoln** was born with a 14 life path and the karma of misuse of freedom in a former lifetime. In his lifetime, though, he freed the slaves. In other words, karma for him became a mandate to correct a misuse of freedom. The writer **Erich Segal** was born on June 16, a day associated with misuse of the universal principle of love. He wrote the best seller *Love Story.* **Karen Silkwood,** who was born on February 19, the number of misuse of power in a former lifetime, was the whistleblower who exposed her company's dangerous misuse of plutonium.

Though we do not have full access to the origins of numerology, and its karmic side for the most part remains occulted, in the examples of contemporary writers, poets, statesman, and so on, who have dealt with these numbers, we have the legacy of how modern people in a modern civilization have dealt with the ancient truth of karma.

It may be hard for us, divorced as we are from the spirit that informed many of our traditions with the truth of their meanings, to understand such concepts as death, birth, karma, and reincarnation. However, in their lives and works our Lincolns, our Freuds, and our Hemingways have updated, so to speak, karma, and have not only shown us how they personally have dealt with karma, but also have given us insights into the universal meanings of 13, 14, 16, and 19.

For those of you who don't believe in karma, suffice it to say that these four numbers are difficult, and we can learn how best to handle them from those who have already done so.

The Number 13

13 has traditionally been thought of as an unlucky number, so it shouldn't surprise us to see it listed as one of the karmic numbers. Though some people with 13 prominent in their name or birth date are inclined to be mystical (think of poets **W. B. Yeats** born on June 13 and **William Blake**, with a 13 quiet self), the number itself has an unfortunate heritage because there were 13 at the Last Supper (Jesus and the 12 apostles), and one died. As a side note, **Leonardo da Vinci** (4/15/1452), whose *Last Supper* is one of the most widely appreciated master-pieces in the world, was born with a 13 life path.

Supposedly, it is unlucky for 13 people to be seated at a table together, and whoever is the first to leave will die within a year. (This is partly based on the fact that **Judas Iscariot**, with 13 letters in his name, was the first to leave the Last Supper.)

The poet **Matthew Arnold** (with 13 letters in his name), upon hearing of this superstition while attending a dinner for 13, decided to test fate and purposefully was the first to leave the party. With typical Victorian faith in rationality, he left with two companions, believing that Death would note the fact that there were three of them instead of one, and the Grim Reaper would be proven the fool.

Apparently, however, Fate doesn't add the same way we do, and since three people were the first to leave, Matthew Arnold died of heart failure six months later;

one of the companions who left with him was found dead shortly thereafter with a revolver at his side; and the third that same year went off to sea and drowned.

I doubt the number 13 killed Matthew Arnold, but this anecdote reveals an important aspect of the number 13 as it shows itself in human behavior: an overreliance on the logic of 4 (which is 13 reduced to a single digit) and a subconscious fear of the irrational as symbolized by the hidden 2 in 13 (found by subtracting the 1 from the 3).

13 relates to Death, the 13th Tarot card, but the Death Card shouldn't be interpreted literally. Death in the case of the number 13 is itself a symbol of the unknown and has two significant meanings as symbol for those with this karmic number: First, what happens to us after death remains a mystery; and second, the fact of *death brings to us a consciousness of time—a consciousness that we must work and accomplish something meaningful on the physical plane before we die.*

Many 13s have a fear of the unknown, of what the subconscious (the hidden 2) might reveal, and of work (4), which is a reminder of time, mortality, and how long we have to live. Often they scatter (3) their energies (1) because of subconscious emotional problems, as represented by the hidden 2. At times, they live the philosophy of *Let's eat, drink, and be merry, for tomorrow we die,* and neglect to do the work that will bring meaning and purpose to their lives.

Many 13s have a tendency to waste (3) time (4), to act

(1) childishly (3), and to procrastinate—if not in this incarnation, then perhaps in some former lifetime. A disdain or dislike of work can make them shy away from long-term projects, and they are often contented to occupy the self (1) with trivial (3) pursuits (4). Other 13s, in their efforts to make up for the karma that numerologist Florence Campbell associates with this number—tests and trials in proficiency due to an "insistence (1) on the path of Dalliance (3) when the goal is work and construction" (4)—overcompensate by becoming workaholics.

13s must learn to retain a balance between the logic of 4 and the feelings of 2, the "real" and the "unreal." Too often, 4 logic represses the intuitional power of the hidden 2. Many 13s have a horror of showing their feelings because of the underlying sensitivity of the hidden 2, yet often these repressed feelings erupt explosively, causing hurt to those around them. Some 13s are especially hard to live with; others are male (1) chauvinists (3); and a few are known as domestic tyrants, yet home is vital to their happiness.

Some 13s never get married. The nearest composer **Johannes Brahms** (13 soul urge) ever came to marriage was in his affair with Agathe von Siebold in 1858; from this he recoiled suddenly, and he never thereafter seriously entertained the prospect. No doubt his immense reserve and his inability to express emotions in any other way but musically were responsible. According to the *Encyclopaedia Britannica,* music critics have noted the concentrated inner reserve of his music that hides and sometimes dams powerful currents of feeling.

Some 13s feel that partnerships, with their emotional demands, interfere with their work; still others sublimate their emotions into work and then are plagued with feelings of boredom or emptiness. Often work is a way out from coming to terms with feelings. Such a 13 can become hard, repressed, unfeeling, negative, cold, and materialistic.

Freudian Psychology and the Number 13

If the above sounds like a classic problem from a psychology textbook, it should, for **Sigmund Freud** (5/6/1856) spent a great deal of his life dealing with these problems, and his life path was 13. Freud's celebrated work on the subconscious and the revelation of hidden instincts at work suggests the hidden 2 of the number 13. The child's secret longing for the mother (2) and the need to accept the reality principle (4)—as symbolized by the father (4) and popularized as the Oedipus complex—is another instance of the hidden 2 in confrontation with the dominant reality principle of 4.

Some other Freudian concepts that have their basis in 13 and its root digit of 4 are:

• The importance of childhood (3) interaction with the early environment (4) as the source of later problems (4) for the individual (1).

- Freud's formulation of both the reality (4) and pleasure (3) principles.
- His work on hysteria (the word is taken from the Greek for "womb" and refers to the hidden 2, the mother).
- His interpretation of dreams as the expression of the unconscious, the hidden 2.
- The need to sublimate instincts (2) into work (4).
- Finally, his postulation of the death instinct (13) as the goal of all life.

In Freudian theory and 13, the individual (1) insists on the path of the pleasure principle (3) in order to avoid both the potential pain coming from the inner needs of 2 and the environmental pressures of 4.

13: Work on the Physical Plane

"Of man's first disobedience, and the fruit
Of that forbidden tree whose mortal taste
Brought death into the world, and all our Woe
With loss of Eden."
—*Paradise Lost* I, 1.1, **John Milton,** 13 expression

Like 14, 16, and 19, the other numbers of karma, 13 relates to original sin and the fall of man. All 13s have a subconscious memory of Eden and feel the separation from God most keenly. 13's job in life is to give us insights into the human condition. With the fall of

Adam, the cycle of death and rebirth began. Cold winters and the need to work for a living; to obtain food and shelter; to cope with disease and hardship; to face sorrow, suffering, and death; to survive in body, yet triumph in spirit—all these matters come under the province of 13.

However, it's hard for many 13s to accept the fact that pain and sorrow are part of the human condition. Some 13s succumb to either negativity or escapism, while others do their part to alleviate pain and suffering and to provide us with insights about how the principles of 13 operate in this world.

All 13s have karma in connection with work and a preoccupation with death and the meaning of life. 13s must forgo fantasy and deal with the real world, the only possible world for human beings to achieve the ideal by confronting the real. In the mystery of 13, we have the mystery of incarnation, why humans in fact must undergo the cycle of death and rebirth.

13: Trials and Tests of Proficiency

Ulysses Grant and Edgar Rice Burroughs

U.S. president and general **(Hiram) Ulysses Grant** (13 expression) had a history of business failures during the early part of his life. Later, when he was first appointed a general, his father said, "Be careful, Ulysses, you are a general now—it's a good job, don't lose it!"

Grant not only kept this job, however, but also went on to become one of history's most celebrated U.S. Army leaders, perhaps partly because the number 13 has an affinity with the military.

Edgar Rice Burroughs (9/1/1875), with a 13 life path, spent 13 years (1897 to 1911) in numerous unsuccessful jobs and business ventures in Chicago and Idaho before beginning his career as a writer. Though he is celebrated for his Tarzan stories, he also wrote a novel called *The Efficiency Expert* (1919), which is, in many respects, a slightly embellished autobiography of his own difficulties in keeping a job during his youth. Both Grant and Burroughs did not come into their own until they found work that they truly enjoyed.

H. G. Wells

Many 13s look back on their early job histories with disdain and even hatred. **Herbert George Wells** (13 soul urge), who is best known for his science fiction *(The Time Machine, The War of the Worlds, The Island of Dr. Moreau)*, also wrote two novels—*Kips* and *The History of Mr. Polly*—that were based on his childhood experiences as a draper's apprentice. Though these novels are comic, the experiences upon which they were based were not.

Wells wrote in his memoirs, *Exasperations*, "The hours I unpacked my bag in the 'prentices' dormitory was the most frightful in my life. I thought I was caught and damned to a life of suffocating servitude beyond any hope of escape. I could see no way out." As biographer Brian Murray notes (*H. G. Wells*, 1990), "The frustration and rage that Wells now experienced stayed with him for the rest of his life. As a novelist, he repeatedly portrays characters who find themselves stuck in circumstances that fail to match their talents and expectations; whose sense of suffocation is matched by an equally intense yearning for flight."

Scott Adams and Dilbert

Scott (Raymond) Adams (13 soul urge) held a variety of—in his words—"humiliating and low paying jobs" after graduating from college. These jobs included bank teller, computer programmer, financial analyst, product manager, loan officer, corporate strategist, and pseudo-engineer. Says Adams, "I was incompetent in each of those fields, but for some reason no one ever noticed." However, Scott would try to stave off some of the mind-numbing boredom he faced each day by doodling a little comic strip about a hapless office drone he called Dilbert. Today *Dilbert* is the fastest-growing cartoon of all time, and is enjoyed daily by 150 million people in 1,900 newspapers and 56 countries.

Adams's first attempt writing an actual book was 1996's *The Dilbert Principle*, which became a number one *New York Times* best seller and one of the top-selling business books of all time. Since then, there have been more than 20 other *Dilbert* books on the best-seller lists. More than just a compilation of Adams's cartoons, the books include essays on the trials and tribulations of corporate culture.

13 is said to bring tests and trials in proficiency for those with this number, and this is the subject matter of Scott Adams's *Dilbert* books, in which the author satirically attacks management fads, large organizations, pointless bureaucracy, corporate inefficiency, and sadistic rule makers who glory in control of office supplies, to name just a few of his pet targets. In the potato-shaped, abuse-absorbing Dilbert, he has given voice to the millions of Americans buffeted by the many adversities of the workplace. In his books and comic strip, he smartly points the way to a saner and a more productive work environment for employees and managers alike—and in doing so has done his part to offer a better understanding of the principles of 13 as they pertain to the workplace in today's world.

What Should I Do with My Life? by Po Bronson

Po Bronson (13 Key) worked as an aerobics instructor, litigation consultant, greeting-card designer, bond salesman, political-newsletter editor, high school teacher, book publisher, and other various occupations before finding his true calling as a successful writer. What may prove surprising to some readers is that Po was offered a job as a bond salesman that would have brought him $300,000 annually—and he turned it down in order to pursue his childhood dream to become a writer.

Since then, he has written several books, including *Bombardiers, The First $20 Million Is Always the Hardest,* and *The Nudist on the Late Shift*. Although all three of these books have been critically acclaimed best sellers, author Po Bronson began work on his fourth book, *What Should I Do with My Life?* (2003) because he was asking himself that very question.

For answers, Bronson traveled the country in search of individuals who have struggled to find their calling, their true nature—people who made mistakes before getting it right. Drawn from interviews and personal observations, the book skillfully crafts 55 fascinating profiles of individuals searching for meaning in what they do for a living. They are the stories of people who had the courage to overcome fear and confusion to find a larger truth about their lives by changing their careers.

As said earlier in this book, the birthday number is the chief vocational indicator in numerology, and the first name is the Key that unlocks that door. Po Bronson, with his 13 Key, has in *What Should I Do with My Life?* helped many individuals unlock the door to finding their true callings. His true-life stories shed light on the human psyche and how people go through the some-times painful but liberating process of finding their true destinies.

Death and God

> *"...a physical world creates a spiritual haze."*
> —from "Day by Day," *on the DC Talk album*
> *"Jesus Freak,"* **Stephen Schwartz,** March 6,
> 1948, 13 life path

The Graveyard Poets

Today's fascination with horror films and gothic novels dates back to the mid-18th century and the Graveyard Poets, so called because of the presence of graves, darkness, night, and the supernatural in their poetry. Graveyard Poetry was an exploration into man's fascination with the origins of death. It was the intent of these poets to introduce the end of life as a beginning to a *spiritual* existence that was both welcomed and feared.

> *"Death's but a path that must be trod
> If man would ever pass to God."*

These lines are from "A Night Piece on Death," which is often regarded as the last work of the Graveyard School of poetry.

The Irish poet **Thomas Parnell,** who was born with a 13 soul urge and 13 letters in his name, wrote this in 1714. The most celebrated of the Graveyard Poets was **Thomas Gray** (13 quiet self), whose "Elegy Written in a Country Churchyard" is one of the best-known poems in the English language.

Ingmar Bergman and The Seventh Seal

Not all 13s see death as a welcome beginning to a spiritual existence. Take, for example, **Antonious Block** (13 letters in his name)—the knight who returns from the Crusades to a 14th-century Sweden that has been visited by the black plague in filmmaker **Ingmar Bergman**'s *The Seventh Seal*. As Block approaches home, Death, appropriately dressed in a hooded black cape, appears to the knight and tells him it is his time. The knight is not afraid of dying, but is afraid of what comes after. He offers Death a bargain: They will play chess for the knight's soul. The game continues during the entire film.

In one of the best scenes in *The Seventh Seal,* the knight and his squire visit a church. The knight decides to make his confession to what he thinks is a priest behind the bars. We learn that he seeks answers about life, death, and the existence of God. He pours his heart out, only to find that the priest was actually Death disguised as a monk. Death has ruthlessly tricked him.

There is an especially moving exchange during the confession scene between Death and the knight:

> *Death: "What are you waiting for?"*
> *Knight: "Knowledge."*
> *Death: "You want a guarantee."*
> *Knight: "Call it what you will. . . . What will become of us, who want to believe but cannot?*

*And what of those who neither will nor can
believe? I want knowledge. Not belief. Not
surmise. But knowledge. I want God to put out His
hand, show His face, speak to me."*

As reviewer Andrew Chan notes in *1999–2001 Film
Written Magazine*, "*The Seventh Seal* doesn't dictate to
us that God does not exist. It never discusses that. It is
about our weariness of God's distance, not about God's
existence." It is about our separation from God.

Throughout this film, God remains silent. Ingmar
Bergman, too, remains silent: He does not provide us
with answers, only questions. Yet these are the questions
that define the human condition.

With 13 as his life path number, Ingmar Bergman in
this film and others has asked the right questions, even if
that means that each and every one of us in our own way
must find in God's absence a sign of his presence. The
knight in this film could not apprehend God through the
use of his intellect. Perhaps there is another way.

Woody Allen

The celebrated filmmaker **Woody Allen** (12/1/1935)
was born with a 13 life path and a 13 Success Number.
In his films, he touches on a variety of topics, but, as
critics have noted, three subjects continually reappear:
the existence of God, the fear of death, and the nature of
morality. Woody Allen is a seeker who wants answers to

the Ultimate Questions. His movie characters differ, yet they are all, in some way, asking these questions. They are all surrogate "Woody Allens" wrestling with the same issues. He explains:

> *"Maybe it's because I'm depressed so often that I'm drawn to writers like Kafka, Dostoevski and to a filmmaker like Bergman. I think I have all the symptoms and problems that their characters are occupied with: an obsession with death, an obsession with God or the lack of God, the question of why we are here. Almost all of my work is autobiographical—exaggerated but true."*
> —*Woody Allen* (from Annie Hall)

In his early writings, fear of death provided Woody Allen with some great one-liners.

> *"I don't want to achieve immortality through my work. I want to achieve it through not dying."*

> *"It's not that I'm afraid to die, I just don't want to be there when it happens."*

> *"It is impossible to experience one's own death objectively and still carry a tune."*

Allen's fear of death is inextricably linked to his uncertainty about the existence of God:

> *"To you I'm an atheist, to God I'm the loyal opposition."*

> *"Not only is there no God, but try getting a plumber on weekends."*

> *"If it turns out that there is a God, I don't think that he's evil. But the worst that you can say about him is that basically he's an underachiever."*

It may seem that Woody utilizes humor to escape, and even mock, the deeper implications of death, dying, and lack of religious certitude, but that is far from the case. Though he is not an adherent of any organized religion, he once said in an interview, "I have full appreciation for the search for genuine religious faith that people go through." Woody's collected work, some 41-plus films and various writings (including a one-act play called *Death,* and another one called *God*), are a testament to his never-ending search to find meaning in life and make sense of the human condition, but—like Ingmar Bergman—he provides us only with questions, not answers. Woody Allen is a work in progress. Perhaps it is the job or karma of 13s to ask the questions so the rest of us can find the answers for ourselves.

Milton and Richard Eberhart

Despite **John Milton**'s (13 expression) noble effort "to explain the ways of God to Man" in his magnificent epic poem *Paradise Lost,* the questions of what happens to us after death and if there is a God remain with us. As Woody Allen said, "If only God would cough" or do something else to show that he is around, but as the American poet **Richard (Ghormley) Eberhart** (13 quiet self) says in his poem "The Fury of Ariel Bombardment": "the infinite spaces are still silent."

Eberhart believes there are no answers to the questions that death raises. Still, of this Eberhart is sure: Death is not extinction, and God is present in the natural world—in "Rainscapes, Hydrangeas, Roses, and Singing Birds."

He also sees death in nature. He muses about a dead "Groundhog" in his celebrated poem by the same name; he just misses running over "A Squirrel Crossing the Road in Autumn, in New England." Eberhart's God is capricious and hard to know, but as he says in the just-cited poem, "It is what man does not know of God / Composes the visible poem of the world."

Man (1) must have a set of values and ideas (3) that he can live by (4). Eberhart finds inspiration in the hidden 2 of his 13 (3 - 1 = 2) and his values in the 3 of his 13—that is, in poetry. As he says in the foreword to his *Selected Poems 1930–1965,* published by New Directions (1965):

> *"Poetry is like the mystery of the world. It comes from secret wells; it is a fresh draft from heaven, warmed in earth. . . . Every time a man dies we*

realize that it means more than it did before. . . .
Poetry . . . states the case for mankind. Without it
we lack something central; with it we are rich. We
understand what it is to live, to suffer, to hope."

Anne Sexton and Stephen Schwartz

Another 13 who looked to poetry for meaning in life was **Anne Sexton** (11/9/1928), who was born with a 13 life path. Her last two books of poetry were titled *The Death Notebooks* and *The Awful Rowing Toward God*, anthologies that contain powerful poems about life, death, despair, suicidal thoughts, love, and God.

Composer **Stephen Schwartz** (*Godspell*), who was born on March 6, 1948, with a 13 life path, is also concerned about the mystery and distance of God:

"Oh dear Lord, three things I pray
To see thee more clearly
To love thee more dearly
To follow thee more nearly."

These words from the 1971 song "Day by Day" from *Godspell* are from an Episcopal hymn first written in the 13th century as a prayer by **Richard Backedine** (13 quiet self), who was the bishop of Chichester (England) from 1244 until his death in 1253. A holy man who was known for his laughter, self-discipline, and kindness to the poor and homeless, he was canonized as a saint in 1262.

Many miracles of healing were attributed to St. Richard both during his lifetime and afterward. For example, a student at Oxford owned a bird with a lovely singing voice. The student refused to give his pet to a friend who coveted it. In rage, his friend cut out the bird's tongue when the student was absent. When the owner found his pet bird drooping and songless, he said a prayer to St. Richard of Chichester, who had a love of birds. Immediately, the bird perked up and began to sing. As Stephen Schwartz says in the song "When you Believe," from the 1998 film *The Prince of Egypt,* "there can be miracles when you believe."

The Number 14

14 and Freedom

"We hold these truths to be self-evident: that all men are created equal."
—**Thomas Jefferson,** 14 soul urge

The above lines from the Declaration of Independence, written by **Thomas Jefferson**, capture the heart, soul, and spirit of the United States, a nation that was born on July 4, 1776, with a life path of 14—a destiny to correct misuses of freedom.

How fitting that this nation with a 14 destiny would elect as its first president **George Washington**, a man with a 14 soul urge, to lead and guide it through its first years. That this American experiment in democracy would succeed was partly due to the fact that many of our other founding fathers also had the number 14 prominent in their numbers.

John Jay (12/12/1745) was appointed the first chief justice of the Supreme Court. He was born with a 14 soul urge and a 14 life path. **Alexander Hamilton**, the first secretary of the Treasury, had a 14 expression; **Edmund Randolph**, the first attorney general, was born with 14 letters in his name; **John Adams**, the first vice president, was born with a 14 quiet self; and the first secretary of state, **Thomas Jefferson** (4/13/1743), was born with a 14 soul urge as well as a 14 life path.

Other American patriots with 14 prominent in their names or birth dates include **Benjamin Franklin** (1/17/1706 = 14 life path); **Francis Marion**, "the Swamp Fox," 14 expression; **Paul Revere**, 14 Key; and naval hero **John Paul Jones** (7/6/1747 = 14 life path).

Emma Lazarus and the Statue of Liberty

"I saw the angel in the marble and carved until I set her free."

—**Michelangelo,** 14 expression

The United States began as the sole democracy in a world of monarchies. It was not until after the Civil War that democratic government spread throughout Europe and the rest of the world. The American example, in the words of **Abraham Lincoln** (14 soul urge), of a "government of the people, by the people, and for the people" became a role model for other nations to emulate. In the post–World War II years, the American Revolution became more relevant than ever, as countries throughout the Third World sought independence from European colonial powers. With the collapse of communism in Europe during the late 1980s and 1990s, the American Revolution once more served as a source of inspiration for the peoples of Eastern Europe and the former Soviet Union who were aspiring to achieve a democratic way of life.

As Abraham Lincoln, with simple eloquence, put it in his Gettysburg Address, "our forefathers founded a new nation conceived in liberty and dedicated to the proposition that all men are created equal." The United States as a beacon of light for other nations to follow is best symbolized by the Statue of Liberty. The poem written on the base of the statue by **Emma Lazarus**, whose first name adds up to 14, concludes with the lines:

"Give me your tired, your poor,
Your huddled masses yearning to breathe free,
The wretched refuse of your teeming shore.
Send these, the homeless, tempest-tossed, to me:
I lift my lamp beside the golden door."

These haunting words remind us that the United States is a nation that was founded and built by immigrants. From Plymouth Rock in the 17th century to refugees from Indochina in the 20th century, people born elsewhere came to America. Many immigrants experienced poverty, religious persecution, political turmoil, imprisonment, a lack of freedom and civil rights, or other hardships in their native lands.

The 4 in the number 14 is the number of hardships. America's life path or destiny (14/5) has always been, and will always be, to provide freedom (5) to individuals (1) who have suffered oppression and hard times (4).

Slavery and Civil Rights

"An' we gazed upon the chimes of freedom flashing."

—from "Chimes of Freedom," **Bob Dylan** (Robert Allen Zimmerman), 14 soul urge

Harriet Beecher Stowe

The ideals of liberty, equality, and democracy that America has always stood for, stood in marked contrast to the institution of African slavery, certainly an example of the misuse of the principle of freedom that the dark side of 14 represents. Clearly, slavery violated the most sacred rights of life and liberty, a point that was skillfully and poignantly brought home in **Harriet Beecher Stowe**'s

Uncle Tom's Cabin, the novel that Abraham Lincoln said helped cause the Civil War. It's no doubt a cosmic coincidence, but the name of the cruel slave trader in the book, **Simon Legree**, adds up to the number 14.

Harriet Beecher Stowe was born on June 14, 1811. The soul urge of her birth name, Harriet Elizabeth Beecher, is 14.

Abraham Lincoln

One of the greatest of American presidents, **Abraham Lincoln** was born on February 12, 1809, with a 14 life path. His achievements, though, are well known and won't be reiterated in these pages. Suffice it to say that his Emancipation Proclamation, which abolished slavery, was a good start toward creating equality among the races. It was left to others, though, to continue his work, for Lincoln was assassinated on April 14, 1865, by **John Wilkes Booth**, a man with a 14 soul urge.

Martin Luther King Jr.

Martin Luther King was the guiding light of the civil rights movement from the mid-1950s until his death in 1968. His leadership was the catalyst to that movement's success ending the legal segregation of African Americans in the South and other parts of the U. S.

He had "a dream that one day this nation will rise up and live out the true meaning of its creed: We hold these truths to be self-evident that all men are created equal." He believed with his heart and soul that "when we allow freedom to ring, when we let it ring from every village and every hamlet, from every state and every city, we will be able to speed up that day when all of God's children, black men and white men, Jews and Gentiles, Protestants and Catholics, will be able to join hands and sing in the words of the old Negro spiritual, 'Free at last, free at last—Thank God Almighty, we are free at last.'"

Martin Luther King's original name was Michael Luther King, a name that adds up to 14. Martin Luther King was assassinated on April 4, 1968, a day that adds up to the number 14.

Other Voices of Freedom

Freedom is not only an American phenomenon.

In Ireland, **Eamon de Valera** (10/14/1882), Irish patriot and revolutionary, in 1937 took the Irish Free State out of the British Commonwealth and made his country a "sovereign" state, renamed Ireland or Eire. **T(homas) E(dward) Lawrence**, better known as Lawrence of Arabia, with his 14 expression, fought as a soldier and diplomat for Arab independence.

South American soldier and statesman **Simón Bolívar**, born July 24, 1783, with a 14 life path, was known as The Liberator. He led the revolutions against Spanish rule in what is now Colombia, Venezuela, Ecuador, Peru, and Bolivia.

Eva Perón, second wife of Argentine president Juan Perón, was a political leader in her own right. She was born on May 7, 1919, with a 14 life path. She was largely responsible for the passage of the woman suffrage law and helped institute reforms in education, health care, and labor.

Oscar Schindler

Think of all the atrocities **Adolf Hitler** (4/20/1889) committed with his 14 life path and you'll have some understanding of 14 at its very worst. Not all the evil of Hitler's actions, though, can be attributed to 14, because Hitler manifested the dark side of his 11 expression as well.

But this is not Hitler's story—it is that of **Oscar Schindler**, the German industrialist and war profiteer who, confronted with the horror of the extermination camps, gambled his life and fortune to rescue over 1,100 Jews from the gas chambers.

Oscar Schindler was born with 14 letters in his birth name on April 28, 1908, with a 14 life path. In his lifetime, he manifested both the positive and negative aspects of the number 14. Many 14s are *love 'em and leave 'em* types, and that was true of Schindler—an alcoholic playboy and shameless womanizer. Many 14s thrive in work that involves taking a chance, and that, too, was true of Schindler, who was a black marketeer. Some 14s love gambling and are good at it—again, Schindler qualifies.

However, 14s' legendary ability to extricate themselves from emergency situations proved an invaluable ally to Schindler in his efforts to shelter his extended family of Jews from discovery and harm. Time and time again, his secret was almost found out.

This is the stuff of adventure—and it's not surprising that **Thomas Michael Keneally**, with his 14 expression, wrote the 1982 best seller *Schindler's List,* a book on which **Steven Spielberg** (12/18/1946), with his 14 life path, based his 1993 Academy Award–winning film with the same title. **Liam Neeson** (birth name William John Neeson), with a 14 soul urge, was nominated for an Academy Award for his portrayal of Oscar Schindler. Steven Spielberg received the Oscar for Best Director for this movie. *Schindler's List* won the Academy Award for Best Picture, and overall received seven Oscars.

14 and Karma

"There can be no freedom (5) without self- (1) discipline (4)."
> —**Carl Gustav Jung** (14 letters in his name),

14 is said to be the great destroyer on the physical plane because of a misuse of the physical, of the five senses, in a former lifetime. It is also said to be related to bitter changes, loss, sudden sickness, accidents, delays, and even sudden death.

Many 14s like to take risks, like the amazing stuntman

motorcyclist **Evel Knievel**, whose birth name, Robert Craig Knievel, adds up to 14. However, the converse is also true. Because 14 adds up to 5, the goal is always freedom, but the 4 in 14 can indicate obstacles, guilt, caution, and fears that keep people from making changes when they should.

As numerologist Florence Campbell has said, there is a lesson for all 14s to learn: to have, to hold, and then to let go. 14 must learn the law of change; 14 must gain and use freedom rightly.

14s, though, need to learn that freedom comes from within. Some 14s are always changing the externals of their lives when the changes they should be making are internal. Some 14s unconsciously feel that the way to be free (5) is for the self (1) to always be in control (4). Often they will split (5) from any situation where they feel they are not in control (4). Some 14s are threatened by the new (5) and insist (1) on keeping their own defense mechanisms (4); while others are rolling (5) stones (4) who gather no moss (4).

14 and Accidents

On August 16, 2003, **Randy Smith** (14 expression)—Randolph E. Scott (14 letters in his name)—was motorcycling down Moody County Road 14 when his cycle crashed into the rear door on the driver's side of Bill Janklow's speeding Cadillac. Randy was thrown from the bike and instantly killed.

I don't know Randy's birth date or his full name at birth. What I do know is that he commonly went by names that had the number 14 prominent in them and that former tour-term governor of South Dakota, **William John Janklow,** was born with a 14 expression.

Accidents sometimes play a role in the destinies of some (*but not all*) 14s. The writer **James (Rufus) Agee**—who was born with a 14 soul urge and 14 letters in his name—was six years old when his father died in a car crash. He spent the rest of his life trying to understand his father's absurd end. This quest ultimately led Agee to write the book he is best known for, *A Death in the Family.* Definitely partly autobiographical, the book explores how the death of the head of the family in a car accident affects those who are left behind. Agee himself died at the age of 45 of a heart attack.

Irving Berlin was born on May 11, 1888, with a life path of 14. To write both the songs "God Bless America" and "White Christmas" must have qualified this gifted composer for sainthood—for certainly these two songs have brought happiness to millions of people and will continue to do so till the end of time.

Technically, Irving Berlin doesn't belong in this section, but I include him here to give you an example of a 14 who lived to the ripe old age of 101 and whose life was not snuffed out by an accident. That was not the case, though, for the 14s listed below.

Death by Motor Vehicle Accident

   14 Soul Urge
   (Andre) Brandon de Wilde, actor
   (Ralph) Dale Earnhardt, race car driver
   (Paul) Jackson Pollock, painter
   Ernest Edward Kovacs, comic
   14 Expression
   Grace Patricia Kelly, actress
   George Smith Patton, U.S. general
   Thomas Edward Lawrence, writer
   14 Life Path
   Bessie Smith, singer (4/15/1894)
   Albert Camus, writer (11/7/1913)
   Billy Martin, baseball star (5/16/1928)
   14 Letters in the Name
   James (Byron) Dean, actor
   Jayne Mansfield, actress
   Mary Jo Kopechne, political worker
   Jessica Savitch, TV news personality

Survivors

Some 14s have survived serious accidents.

Singer **Gloria Estefan** was born on September 1, 1957, with a 14 life path. A crash while on tour left her with a broken back. Country singer **Barbara Mandrell** (14 expression) was involved in a major car accident in 1984. Music legend **Bob Dylan** (Robert Allen Zimmerman, 14 soul urge) had a nearly fatal motorcycle accident, after which he withdrew from public life for a time of seclusion.

For some 14s, an accident may serve as a catalyst for a major change in consciousness, often setting them in a new life direction. Rap star **Tracy Marrow**, aka **Ice-T**, was born on February 16, 1958, with a 14 life path. He was injured in a car accident in 1986, when his Porsche 914 was broadsided by another vehicle. The accident served as a turning point in his life, after which he focused his attention on rapping and producing albums.

14 and Sex

"A prayer for the wild at heart, kept in cages."
—from *Stairs to the Roof,* **Tennessee Williams**
(Thomas Lanier Williams), 14 soul urge

A myth that relates to the number 14 and the letter *N*, the 14th letter of the alphabet, dates back to Greek mythology. Souls awaiting reincarnation that had misused the principles linked to 14 in a past life drank from the waters of Lethe and lost all memory of the wrongs that they had committed in past lives. Later, when they were reincarnated, they tended to repeat the very same mistakes that got them into trouble in the first place.

Just as 14 is said to be overly concerned with the five senses, many 14s are especially prone to make mistakes where sex is concerned. Some 14s have lost track of the sacredness of sex and have wrongly interpreted sex laws. Others are *love 'em and leave 'em* types who meet their biggest challenges through letting their sex lives run (or ruin) their lives. Often they leave in their wake a host of brokenhearted lovers.

14s have trouble learning from their experiences. Indeed, it is usually the jilted lover who learns the very lessons that 14 should have learned. To be involved with some 14s is like having a date with karma. Maybe you don't deserve to have your feelings toyed with, your heart shattered, and your life devastated—unless, of course, you were a 14 in a former life and are now learning how the shoe feels on the other foot. Too often, a 14 willy-nilly goes off to a new conquest never even thinking about the pain and suffering he or she caused. But that is par for the course, for many 14s simply do not take responsibility for their actions. Talk about cold. For such reasons, some 14s are considered to be *femme fatales*.

Marlene Dietrich

It was this kind of 14 that **Marlene Dietrich** was called upon to play in her early film career. Indeed, she defined the role of *femme fatale* for movie audiences the world over during the 1930s. **Maria Magdalena Dietrich** was perfectly cast, as her birth name adds up to 14 and she was born on December 27, 1901, with a 14 life path.

As critic Jim Ridley has noted, legendary Lili Marlene, in her first major film, *The Blue Angel* (1930), established a pattern that would be repeated with variations from film to film. Whether on purpose or not, she was always a heartbreaker. The men who pursue Dietrich's characters in her early films end up dead, ruined, or made fools of— but as she said in *Shanghai Express* (1932), "It took more than one man to change my name to Shanghai Lily."

The Not-so-Private Life of a Screen Goddess

John Wayne called her "the most intriguing woman I've ever known." However, he ended their affair in 1945 with the remark that he "never liked being part of a stable." Legendary filmmaker Josef von Sternberg, a onetime lover of Marlene, once said, "Dietrich is something that never existed before and may never exist again. That's a woman." Ernest Hemingway said of her: "If she had nothing more than her voice she could break your heart with it. But she has that beautiful body and the timeless loveliness of her face."

The 30 letters between Hemingway and Dietrich, written between 1949 and 1958—which were donated to the JFK Memorial Library—will be made public in 2007. Marlene said she never slept with her good friend "Papa," but she was very proud of the fact that she had slept with three members of the Kennedy clan, Joseph P. Kennedy and his sons Joe Kennedy Jr. and JFK.

Marlene was bisexual and had love affairs with various women as well, including Edith Piaf and Barbara Stanwyck. In July 1932, Greta Garbo and her girlfriend, screenwriter Mercedes de Acosta, had a lovers' quarrel, and Garbo went home to Sweden, leaving Acosta heartbroken and alone in California—but not for long, for soon after she began a torrid romance with none other than Marlene. This affair lasted until Garbo made up with her estranged lover eight months later. Acosta would always remain deeply attached to Marlene.

Although married only once (to Rudolf Sieber), Marlene had innumerable romantic relationships. Known for her "bedroom eyes" in high school, she had her first affair with her violin teacher at age 16. Her last affair with a man was with composer Burt Bacharach, a relationship that began when Marlene was 57 and ended when she was 62. At age 70, she was still involved with her last female lover, singer Marti Stevens. In between these relationships, she had countless lovers—both male and female. Below is a partial list.

From A to Z: the Lovers of Lili Marlene

Brian Aherne, Burt Bacharach, Cecil Beaton, Yul Brynner, Colette, Ronald Coleman, Gary Cooper, Lili Damita, Mercedes de Acosta, Robert Donat, Kirk Douglas, Douglas Fairbanks Jr., Eddie Fisher, Jean Gabin, James M. Gavin, John Gilbert, Howard Hughes, Joseph P. Kennedy, JFK, Burt Lancaster, Fritz Lang, Burgess Meredith, Edward R. Murrow, George S. Patton Jr., Edith Piaf, George Raft, Erich Maria Remarque, William Saroyan, George Bernard Shaw,

Frank Sinatra, Barbara Stanwyck, Marti Stevens, Adlai Stevenson, James Stewart, Mike Todd, Josef von Sternberg, Raf Vallone, John Wayne, Orson Welles, Michael Wilding . . . et al.

In the 1950s, in a discussion with her husband Rudi Sieber and cinematographer Stefan Lorant about her many liaisons, Dietrich asked:

"'Who do you think I loved more than anyone else?' 'Jean Gabin?' suggested Rudi. 'Gabin, yes,' she replied. 'Certainly, Gabin.' And in 1963, when Robert Kennedy met Dietrich and asked who was the most attractive man she had ever met, she replied, 'Jean Gabin.'"

—**Donald Spoto**, *Blue Angel: The Life of Marlene Dietrich* (New York: Doubleday, 1992, p.169)

But what about her many other lovers? … and why so many? …and what did they mean to her? We can gain some insights about these matters from her grandson, David Riva who said, "She would fall in love with a song, with Paris, or a beautiful woman or a powerful man, and she would pour all her passion in that direction for as long as she wanted to." (Variety, May 26, 2004).

Marlene Dietrich summed up her life as follows, " I have a child, and I have made a few people happy. That is all."

Giovanni Giacomo Casanova

Has anyone in history had more lovers than Marlene?

Yes—the legendary Venetian adventurer **Casanova,** whose birth name Giovanni Giacomo Casanova adds up to the number 14. Thanks to Casanova, we have the word *casanova* in our dictionaries. If you'll look it up in *Webster's,* you'll find that it means "lover, esp.: a man who is a promiscuous and unscrupulous lover."—and that is exactly what Casanova was. He was also the quintessential 14.

Giacomo Casanova was born in Venice on April 2, 1725. People born on the 2nd make good secretaries, and Casanova often served in that capacity for luminaries of his times. With a life path number of 3, he ultimately found his purpose in life as a writer. He was the author of several novels, poems, criticisms, translations, and plays, but is chiefly remembered for his memoirs, which recount his adventures with 122 women as well as offering an intimate portrait of the manners and life in the 18th century. His memoirs also describe in detail what it's like to be a person born with a name that adds up to 14.

Casanova was an extremely charming man, and women found him irresistible. His sexual appetite, though, sometimes got him into trouble. As a young man, he was studying to be a priest, but when the authorities found out about his sexual escapades, drinking, and generally dissolute behavior, it created a scandal; he was expelled from the seminary. Throughout his life, his sexual exploits cost him several important social and professional posts.

At times in his life, Casanova fell deeply in love. While in Naples in 1744, at age 19, he met Donna Lucrezia, a married woman, with whom he had a torrid affair. In 1749, while in Cesena, at age 25, he became deeply involved with Henriette, a mysterious adventuress who was one of the greatest loves of his life. They traveled together for five months, but then she reluctantly returned to her family. He fell in love again with Caterina in 1755, but this relationship came to a halt when Casanova was arrested and sent to prison. In 1761, while in Naples, he met, wooed, and proposed marriage to 17-year-old Leonilda. However, when Casanova met Leonilda's mother, she turned out to be Donna Lucrezia. He learned from Lucrezia that his bride-to-be was in fact his daughter. This knowledge put a quick end to Casanova's plans to wed Leonilda, but it did not keep him from having one more night of passion with her mother.

Like many 14s, Casanova was an inveterate traveler. He visited the major cities throughout Europe, but these sojourns were not always of his own volition. Several times he was exiled from cities by the authorities for one scandal or another; sometimes he had to flee his creditors, and a few times he was imprisoned, once for black magic, another time for bad gambling debts.

14s, though, have a way of extricating themselves from difficult situations. That is why they often don't learn from their mistakes—*and why they so often repeat them*. After Casanova was imprisoned in Venice in 1755 for practicing black magic, he engineered an escape the next year, fled to Paris, wrote a book about it, and became a celebrity. The following year, he helped invent the French state lottery and became wealthy. Soon after, he sold his interest in the lottery, but then made a bad business investment and was accused by his partner of fraud. It was time to skip town again.

Like many 14s (for example, baseball star **Pete Rose**), Casanova had a penchant for gambling. Wherever his travels took him, he always relied on personal charm to win influence and on gambling and intrigue to support himself.

A toothless Casanova spent his final years (1786–98) in Bohemia as a librarian for the Count von Waldstein. There he devoted time to his writings. Among his last lady friends were Cecile, a 22-year-old canoness, and Elise, who sent him food and wine. At various points in his life, Casanova had bouts with venereal disease (skilled in medical knowledge, he was always able to cure himself). On June 4, 1798, however, he died from a urinary infection. He had lived by the sword, so to speak, and he died by the sword.

Tennessee Williams

Not all those who have 14 prominent in their names or birth dates are sexually promiscuous. Some 14s *are sexy, but inhibited*. The 4 in 14 can indicate inhibitions, guilt, or other sexual problems that can impede the freedom and joy in sexual expression that the number 5 promises. Karma for these 14s manifests as complicated emotional relationships due to sexual problems and the intense feelings that these problems arouse in the individual and the people around him or her. Indeed, sexy but psychologically disturbed people abound in the plays of **Tennessee Williams** (birth name Thomas Lanier Williams), who was born with a 14 soul urge on March 26, 1911, a birth date that also adds up to 14.

Sexuality often has tragic consequences for those who misuse it in his plays. In *Sweet Bird of Youth,* the play ends with the gigolo hero being castrated for having infected a southern politician's daughter with venereal disease.

Central to the plot of *Suddenly Last Summer* is the deceased homosexual Sebastian, whose history of sexually victimizing Mexican youths results in his being murdered and cannibalized by them. But there is more to the story. Catherine, who witnessed Sebastian's violent death, was traumatized by the experience. Her aunt wants to have her lobotomized, so that she won't go around telling everyone the truth that her son was a homosexual. She makes it quite clear to the brain surgeon who might perform the lobotomy that if he doesn't agree to do it, she will not establish a foundation to subsidize his work. What we see is that the consequences of Sebastian's sexual behavior do not affect him alone—there are spin-offs that involve and affect everyone in the play.

This is also true in *Cat on a Hot Tin Roof*. At the core of this play is the main character's impotence, but his sexual dysfunction relates to truths that he cannot face. Not only does this impact upon his wife, but it also affects his relations with himself and his whole family. We see here that the workings of karma in the hands of a writer like Tennessee Williams are indeed complicated.

Perhaps Tennessee Williams's best-known play is *A Streetcar Named Desire*. To summarize this masterpiece with a few sentences is to do it injustice—my apologies to the reader and to Tennessee Williams. Blanche's sexuality and sexual history are tied in with other aspects of her life. Years ago, Blanche caught her young husband having sex with another man. He felt guilty about it and committed suicide, and Blanche has since felt responsible for his death. The combination of her husband's infidelity and her guilt about his death have led her to a life of self-destructive sexual behavior. All this occurs before the play begins. She is forced to leave town and ends up being taken in by her sister, Stella, and Stella's husband Stanley. After a series of confrontations with Stanley, she is raped by him and driven to the brink of insanity. Once again, guilt and a history of sexual irresponsibility lead to a tragic end.

A *Streetcar Named Desire* was first performed on the Broadway stage in 1947. Philip Kolin, author of several books on *Streetcar,* once said, "Williams absolutely invented the idea of desire for the 20th century. It was a play that dealt with for the very first time on the American stage, female sexuality and male sexuality."

Unanimously praised by critics and loved by audiences, *A Streetcar Named Desire* was subsequently awarded both the Drama Critics Circle Award and the Pulitzer Prize. **Jessica Tandy** received critical acclaim for her creation of Blanche DuBois, for which she received a Tony Award in 1948. A young **Marlon Brando,** at age 23, attained stage stardom with his astonishingly brutal, emotionally charged performance as Stanley Kowalski. Like Tennessee Williams, both Marlon Brando and Jessica Tandy were born with a 14 soul urge. Perhaps this perfect casting was partly due to the fact that **Elia Kazan** (birth name Elias Kazanjoglou), the director of *A Streetcar Named Desire,* was also born with a 14 soul urge!

The Number 16

Crucifixion of the Self on the Cross of Love

"Because it is bitter and because it is my heart."
—Stephen Crane, 16 soul urge

Nathaniel Hawthorne and The Scarlet Letter

The writer **Nathaniel Hawthorne**'s birth name was spelled Nathaniel Hathorne, which adds up to an 11 expression. When he began his writing career he added a W to his name—a 5—and became a person with a 16 expression. Though he would always retain the inventiveness and genius of his number 11 birthright, his writings reflect the themes of the number 16. Of special note is his *Scarlet Letter,* which deals with the themes of adultery and ostracism (7) of the self (1) from the community (6). Could we not say that with an 11 expression, Hawthorne became a channel, a medium for voices from higher planes to get across the meanings of 16 to humanity? For 16 is the number associated with illegitimate love in a former lifetime—with adultery!

In the novel, Hester, a mother with an illegitimate child, is sentenced to wear a scarlet *A*, signifying "Adulteress," as a token of her sin. The community shuns her, but during her period of ostracism she develops sympathy for other unfortunates, and her works of mercy gradually win her the respect of her neighbors. Here we have a moral tale of sin and redemption, or, as the great numerologist Florence Campbell might have put it, 16 equals crucifixion of the self (1) on the cross of love (6) in order to attain a more spiritual (7) approach to life.

To be in love with someone who isn't free (actress **Katharine Houghton Hepburn,** born May 12, 1907, with a 16 life path, in love with the married **Spencer Tracy**) or who is unable to reciprocate your love (singer **Judy Garland,** birth name Frances Ethel Gumm, 16 quiet self, in love with gay actor **Mark Herron**) is sometimes the fate of those with 16 prominent in their names or birth dates.

The British poet **A. E. Housman** was born March 26, 1889, with a 16 life path. While a student at Oxford, he developed a homoerotic attachment for Moses Jackson, who was his roommate, but who did not reciprocate his feelings. Housman, though, never fell out of love with Jackson and often told him that he was the reason he wrote poetry. They remained lifetime friends, but their relationship was never consummated.

F. Scott Fitzgerald, Princess Di, and Arthur Miller

16 in its simplest meaning is a *broken heart,* such as that experienced on more than one occasion by writer **Francis Scott Key Fitzgerald** (16 soul urge) in his marriage with zany Zelda Sayre, or that experienced by playwright **Arthur Miller** (10/17/1915 = 16 life path) in his relationship with **Marilyn Monroe** (6/1/1926), herself born with a 16 life path. And could we not say that **Princess Di** (Diana Frances Spencer), with her 16 life path (7/1/1961), also was crucified on the cross of love?

If there truly is a karma associated with 16, can we not say that **Judy Garland**, in her heartfelt singing ("Over the Rainbow," et al.); Princess Di, with her humanitarian work; and F. Scott Fitzgerald (see his *The Crack-up* and *Tender Is the Night*) and Arthur Miller (see *The Crucible*), in their writings have, so to speak, paid back their karma by giving us a better understanding of the principles associated with the number 16?

Ingrid Bergman

In any case, for some 16s, illegitimate love and the subsequent moral outcry from the community was a very real thing for them to cope with in their lives and not merely the stuff of fiction. Witness the example of legendary screen actress **Ingrid Bergman** (16 quiet self), who left her husband and child to have an adulterous affair with Italian filmmaker Roberto Rossellini in 1949. Keep in mind that Ingrid had played the role of a nun in the film *The Bells of Saint Mary's* in 1945, and that of a saint in *Joan of Arc* in 1948. From saint to sinner in the public's eyes, the scandal forced Ingrid to return to Europe, exiled from Hollywood. Not until her marriage to Rossellini ended in 1956 did Ingrid return to the United States.

Charlie Chaplin

Another Hollywood legend who was exiled from the community for moral behavior that outraged the public was film star **Charlie Chaplin** (4/16/1889). In 1918, he married 16-year-old Mildred Harris, and in 1924 he wed another 16-year-old, Lita Gray. Both marriages ended in divorce. His third marriage, to actress Paulette Goddard, was clouded by rumors that it had never been legalized. During World War II, he was suspected of communist leanings, and in 1952, while in London, he was denied a reentry visa to the United States. Chaplin was literally exiled and moved to Switzerland. Not until 1972, 20 years later, was he allowed to return to the United States.

Oscar Wilde, Douglas MacArthur, and Richard Nixon

Crucifixion of the self on the cross of love and subsequent ostracism from the community was the fate of celebrated writer **Oscar Wilde** (10/16/1854), whose homosexual relationship with Lord Douglas led to his arrest and a prison term of two years of hard labor. *Loss of name, power, and position* is occasionally a fate for 16s whose behaviors are at odds with the moral values of the community. That was certainly true in the case of Wilde, who upon his release from prison was bankrupt, and went into self-imposed exile to France. Sometimes it is pride that can lead to a loss of power and position, as in the case of **Douglas MacArthur** (16 letters in his name), who was relieved of his command by Harry S. Truman in 1952. And then there is Watergate. U.S. president **Richard Milhous Nixon** was born with a 16 soul urge, and the Watergate break-in lead to his subsequent resignation and ostracism.

Salman Rushdie

Not all cases of exile from the community and the number 16 relate to politics and illegitimate love. The Anglo-Indian novelist **Ahmed Salman Rushdie** (16 soul urge) was condemned to death by leading Iranian Muslim clerics in 1989 for allegedly blaspheming Islam in his novel *The Satanic Verses*. Rushdie went into hiding under the protection of Scotland Yard, not to surface publicly again until 1998, the year the Iranian government announced it would no longer seek to enforce its decree against Rushdie.

16 and Religion

Emily Dickinson and Gerard Manley Hopkins

People with 16 prominent in their names or birth dates tend to be either very *spiritual* or *agnostic,* and possibly atheistic. This faith or lack of faith may relate to a past lifetime in which there was either a positive or negative religious experience. Some people with 16 in this lifetime have their quarrels with God (**Emily Elizabeth Dickinson,** poet, 16 expression) and their dark nights of the soul; think of poet **Gerard Manley Hopkins,** with a 16 soul urge—"Of now done darkness I wretch lay wrestling with (my God!), my God."

Mother Teresa and Mother Seton

16 as an expression for **Mother Teresa** (Agnes Gonxha Bojaxhiu) became a life dedicated to community service, helping those isolated from the community either through poverty or sickness. And America's first saint, **Mother Seton** (Elizabeth Ann Bayley), also with a 16 expression, experienced loss of name, power, and position when her husband went bankrupt and soon after died. She was born into an aristocratic family, yet she devoted her time to helping those in need. Subsequently she founded the Sisters of Charity. Her original group consisted of 16 people.

Atheism and Agnosticism

Thomas Henry Huxley, English biologist (born May 4, 1825), had a 16 soul urge, a 16 expression, and a 16 life path. He is best known both as a promoter of Darwin's theory of evolution, and as a coiner of the word *agnostic* (note that the soul urge of this word adds up to 16). **Robert Green Ingersoll**, American politician and orator (8/11/1833), with a 16 life path, was known as "the great agnostic." **Katharine Hepburn**, not a person to mince words, once said, "I'm an atheist, and that's it. I believe there's nothing we can know except that we should be kind to each other and do what we can for each other." Here we have atheism mixed with compassion.

But what are we to make of **Madonna**, born on August 16, 1958? The crucifix-against-the-crotch imagery that accompanied the video of the song "Like a Virgin" seemed blasphemous to some people, yet subsequent recordings have spiritual references. Is she another 16 who was crucified on the cross of love, only to subsequently obtain a more spiritual approach to life? Did the material girl become a spiritual girl?

Alcoholism and Drug Dependency

Isolation from the community for some 16s occurs through the misuse of alcohol and drugs. Of course, just as people from all walks of life may become dependent on drugs or alcohol, people with any number can become addicts.

When a 16 abuses drug or alcohol, however, there are often tragic consequences. Listed below are the names of some prominent and beloved celebrities with 16 prominent in their numberscopes who experienced problems with drugs or alcohol.

16 Soul Urge
John (Adam) Belushi, actor
F(rancis) Scott (Key) Fitzgerald, writer
David Janssen (David Harold Meyer), actor
River Phoenix (River Jude Bottom), actor
16 Life Path
Marilyn Monroe, actress
Nick Nolte, actor
Dylan Thomas, poet

16 Letters in the Name
Robert (John) Downey, actor
Lorenz (Milton) Hart, lyricist
Elvis (Aron) Presley, singer
Jimi (John Allen) Hendrix, rock star
Daryl Strawberry, baseball star
Kurt (Donald) Cobain, rock star
16 Expression
(Clarence) Malcolm Lowry, writer
Dorothy (Jean) Dandridge, actress
(Harry) Sinclair Lewis, writer
16 Quiet Self
Judy Garland (Frances Ethel Gumm), singer-actress
Drew (Blythe) Barrymore, actress
O. Henry (William Sydney Porter), writer
Chet Baker (Chesney Henry Baker), jazz great
16 Birthday
Corey Feldman, actor (7/16/1971)
Eugene O'Neill, playwright (10/16/1888)

Alcoholics Anonymous

William Griffith Wilson (16 soul urge) had a recurring problem with alcohol abuse. However, while incarcerated for the fourth time at Manhattan's Towns Hospital in 1934, Wilson experienced a flash of white light and a liberating awareness of God. This led to his recovery and subsequently to the founding of Alcoholics Anonymous and Wilson's revolutionary 12-step program.

Five sober months later, Wilson went to Akron, Ohio, on business. The deal fell through, and he almost relapsed. He wanted a drink and stood for a while outside the bar at the Mayflower Hotel. Suddenly he became convinced that by helping another alcoholic, he could save himself. After a series of desperate telephone calls, he found Dr. Robert Smith, an alcoholic whose family persuaded him to give Wilson 15 minutes. Their meeting lasted for hours. (This was the first-ever AA meeting.) A month later, Dr. Bob Smith had his last drink, and that date, June 10, 1935, is the official birth date of AA—*a day that adds up to the number 16.*

Betty Ford

When President Richard Nixon resigned in 1974, **Betty Ford** (Elizabeth Ann Bloomer), who was born with a 16 soul urge, became the nation's first lady. Shortly thereafter, she was diagnosed with breast cancer and underwent a mastectomy. Suffering from a pinched nerve and the aftereffects of her illness, Ford became so hooked on painkilling drugs and alcohol that in 1978 she entered a hospital to kick the habits. Inspired by the experience, in 1982 she founded the Betty Ford Center for Drug and Alcohol Rehabilitation in Rancho Mirage, California. The center was one of America's first prominent centers devoted solely to such recovery, and today it is regarded as the premier treatment facility in the nation.

Betty continues to be active in her efforts to cure and

treat alcoholism and is a shining example of a person who puts her 16 to good use.

Conformity Versus the Need to Be an Individual

Sinclair Lewis and Arthur Miller

The Nobel Prize–winning author (Harry) **Sinclair Lewis** was an alcoholic, and he was also crucified on the cross of love with two marriages that ended in divorce. Like many people with 16 prominent in their name or birth date, he (1) was a top-notch critic (7) of society (6) and its values; his novels give us important insights about the nature of 16, the number of his expression.

For some 16s, the 6 in 16 becomes all-powerful, resulting in individuals (1) who, in the process of subscribing to society's conventions (6), become spiritually and intellectually impoverished (7). This was the subject matter of Sinclair Lewis's first successful novel, *Main Street*. His next novel, *Babbitt* (1922), is a portrait of an average American businessman, a Republican and a Rotarian, whose individuality (1) has been erased by conformist (6) values.

Arthur Miller's (16 expression) *Death of a Salesman* is the tragic (7) story of Willy Loman, an ordinary man (1) who is destroyed by his false values, which are in large part the values of his society (6). One must have the courage to follow the dictates of one's own conscience (7) despite society's (6) pressures to conform (6), and this is the subject matter of many other works by Miller.

16 and Ethics

Sinclair Lewis's satirical novel *Elmer Gantry* was written in 1926. It was made into a film in 1960, with **Burt Lancaster** (whose first name adds up to 16) receiving an Oscar for his portrayal of a con-man preacher who's a liar, a womanizer, a hypocrite, a boozer, and a seducer. *Elmer Gantry* chronicles the rise and fall of this Pentecostal evangelist, who reaches the heights of his profession only to experience a subsequent fall, triggered, in part, by pride and sexual indiscretions. In this novel, Lewis skewers evangelists who abuse their ministry for materialistic ends.

Perhaps if ex-reverend televangelist **Jim Bakker**, with 16 letters in his birth name (James Orsen Bakker), had read this book, he would have learned from his fictional counterpart the folly of tempting fate with reckless improprieties and wouldn't have lost everything — his job, his fortune, his wife, his reputation, his freedom, and his self-respect.

The same can be said of another defrocked televangelist, **Jimmy Lee Swaggart** (with a 16 life path and 16 letters in his name). His downfall came in 1988, a year after Jim Bakker lost his ministry and fell from power due to his affair with his secretary Jessica Hahn and the subsequent disclosure that he had bilked his supporters out of $158 million.

In Swaggart's case, photos taken of him with a Louisiana hooker spelled the beginning of the end. He was asked by his superiors to stay off TV for a period of two years. When he refused and stated with overbearing pride that his TV ministry couldn't survive without him, the church that had ordained him defrocked him.

The number 16 seems to be ever-present at significant junctures in Jim Bakker's life. The sexual rendezvous with Jessica Hahn on December 5, 1980, occurred in hotel room 538, which adds up to 16. Jessica received hush money to keep silent about their tryst, ending up with $265,000. Part of that money was paid by the PTL, whose board members agreed to pay her $115,000 on February 27, 1985, a day that adds up to 16. It took the U.S. government 16 months to complete its investigation of this case; Jim Bakker was subsequently indicted for fraud on December 5, 1988, a day that adds up to 16. Jim Bakker began his prison term on October 24, 1989, another day that adds up to 16. He did not serve out his 45-year sentence but was paroled in 1994.

But the saga of Jim Bakker and 16 continues. In 2003, nearly 165,000 people who sued Jim Bakker in a class action suit 16 years earlier received $6.54 each. The money came from $3.7 million placed in a settlement fund by former PTL accountants.

Jim Bakker returned to Christian television with *The New Jim Bakker Show,* which broadcasts from Branson, Missouri, and made its debut on January 2, 2003, *exactly 16 years to the day* after his last broadcast of *The PTL Club* on January 2, 1987. It now airs on more than 32 stations in 20 states, as well as more than 200 cable stations; it is also broadcast via satellite in 93 countries.

16 and the 16th Tarot Card: The Tower

Insights into the meaning of the number 16 can be gained by a look at the 16th Tarot card, sometimes called the Tower. Depicted on the card is a lightning-struck tower, with a man and a woman with a crown on her head falling headfirst from the top of the tower. These falling figures represent the loss of name, power, and position that can suddenly occur to individuals who misuse the principles of 16.

There is also a large crown knocked from the tower by the lightning flash. The crown represents the mistaken notion that matter and form are the ruling principles of existence. As Florence Campbell has noted, only the power of the spirit can keep the tower from falling.

O'Henry, Clifford Irving, and Martha Stewart

All people with 16 in their names or birth dates must strictly adhere to the straight and narrow in their business dealings. Unethical behavior leads to strict retribution in the guise of loss of name, power, and position.

The writer **O'Henry**, with 16 letters in his birth name (William Sydney Porter), perfected his writing talents while serving time in prison for embezzling funds. Another writer, **Clifford Irving** (Henry Dieter Irving), with 16 as his quiet self, also was sentenced to jail for his fraudulent biography of billionaire Howard Hughes.

Even the hint of scandal can prove deleterious for 16s, as in the case of entrepreneur **Martha Stewart**—whose birth name, Martha Helen Kostyra, adds up to 16. With an 8 soul urge and 8 life path (8/3/1941), she had created a billion-dollar enterprise, yet she was forced to resign as head of her own company and experienced a subsequent loss of much of her fortune when she was accused of trading stock on the basis of insider information. On July 16, 2004 she was sentenced to five months in prison for lying about the stock scandal.

The Number 19

Misuse of Power

To tell persons with 19 prominent in their names or birth dates that they have a karma of misuse of power in a past lifetime is liable to evoke feelings of hurt, surprise, and possibly anger, for most 19s are reform-minded and are anxious to make the world a better place to live. All 19s, though, will meet with tests involving the use of power. Some will fail to meet the test, while others will rise to the occasion.

George Herbert Walker Bush

Take, for example, former president **George Herbert Walker Bush**, whose birth name adds up to 19. His greatest test came when Iraqi president Saddam Hussein invaded Kuwait and then threatened to move into Saudi Arabia. Vowing to free Kuwait, Bush rallied the United Nations, the American people, and Congress and sent 425,000 American troops. They were joined by 118,000 troops from allied nations. After weeks of air and missile bombardment, the 100-hour land battle, dubbed Desert Storm, routed Iraq's million-man army.

Bush's decision not to go it alone in Iraq, but to enlist the cooperation of other nations, was a first in history and established a precedent that his son would later follow. With power in his hands, President George Herbert Walker Bush used it judiciously. Indeed, his skillful construction of a coalition of Western European and Arab states against Iraq was probably the most significant diplomatic achievement of his presidency.

Napoleon Bonaparte

Born on August 15, 1769, with a 19 life path, **Napoleon Bonaparte**, French general, first consul (1799–1804), and emperor of France (1804–15), is one of the most celebrated personages in the history of the West. As noted in the Encyclopedia Britannica, he revolutionized military organization and training; sponsored the Napoleonic Code; reorganized education; released the Jews from the ghettoes; and established the long-lived Concordat with the papacy. His many reforms left a lasting mark on the institutions of France and of much of Western Europe. He truly fulfilled his 19 destiny as a reformer and as a leader (1) of the people (9).

His driving passion, however, was the military expansion of the French Empire. His desire to conquer the world is an expression of the dark side of 19. In this instance, 1 + 9 combines to mean *me* (1) *against the world* (9). Unlike **Hitler** (14 life path) and **Stalin** (13 life path), Napoleon was an "enlightened despot." He was tolerant and had a respect for human life, but he had a tragic flaw—a lust for power that is revealed by the hidden 8 in his 19 life path (found by subtracting the 1 from 9 in 19). His great rise to power was followed by a subsequent fall, which ultimately ended with his exile to St. Helena, where he died a lonely and defeated man. Of 19s who have misused power, the numerologist Florence Campbell has written: "We may find ourselves stripped at the end of the race."

1972: A 19 Universal Year

The Universal Year 1972 adds up to 19 (1 + 9 + 7 + 2 = 19), a clear indication that issues concerning the abuse of power would be in the headlines of the world's newspapers. An assassination attempt was made on the life of Governor **George Corley Wallace** of Alabama—with 19 letters in his birth name—by Arthur Bremer. An Arab terrorist attack at the Israeli compound at the Olympic Games in Munich resulted in the death of 11 members of the Israeli Olympic team. In recognition of a life devoted to exploring the effects of World War II on the people of Germany, **Heinrich Theodor Böll** (19 quiet self) received the Nobel Prize for Literature in 1972. That same year, Mafia gangster **Joey Gallo** (19 Key) was shot to death. Somehow it seems symbolically appropriate that the film *The Godfather* was first released in our theaters in 1972, as **Mario Puzo**, who wrote the screenplay and the novel from which it was adapted, was born October 15, 1920, with a 19 life path. However, in addition to the horrific increase in the high-jacking of aircraft by terrorists, the biggest story involving the abuse of power in 1972 was Watergate.

The Number 19 and Watergate

On September 15, 1982, two former White House aides, **Everette Howard Hunt** (10/19/1918) and **Gale Gordon (Battle) Liddy** (19 expression), were among the seven men indicted in Washington on charges of conspiring to break into the Democratic headquarters in the Watergate complex on June 17, 1972. Hunt was one of the members of the White House "plumbers," the secret team assembled to stop government leaks after defense analyst Daniel Ellsberg leaked the Pentagon Papers to the press. A former CIA operative, Hunt organized the bugging of the Democratic headquarters in the Watergate as well as a break-in at the office of Ellsberg's psychiatrist. Hunt's phone number in address books belonging to the Watergate burglars helped investigators—and reporters—connect the break-in to the president and his reelection campaign.

For his role in the Watergate scandal, which he coordinated with E. Howard Hunt, Liddy, a former FBI agent, was convicted of conspiracy, burglary, and illegal wiretapping and served four-plus years in prison before being pardoned. Approval for the break-in, though, had to be obtained from **H. R. Haldeman** (10/27/1926), who was born with a 19 life path. Both Liddy and Haldeman were born with names that add up to the number 19.

The necessary financing for the break-in operation was approved by then–attorney general **John Mitchell** (9/5/1913), who was also born with a 19 life path. Both Haldeman and Mitchell were later indicted. Also involved in directing the Watergate break-in was **John Daniel Erlichman**, White House chief of staff, who was born with 19 letters in his name. He, too, was indicted with his fellow conspirators.

Judge **John Joseph Sirica**'s (3/19/1904) order that tape recordings of White House conversations about the Watergate break-in be made available to prosecutors precipitated President Nixon's resignation in 1974. The tapes revealed that Nixon had approved plans for the Watergate cover-up six days after the break-in at the

Democratic National Committee's headquarters in the Watergate complex.

Sirica's original suspicions that there was more to this case than a simple burglary were more than amply borne out. In all, *19 officials of the Nixon administration went to jail.*

Richard Milhous Nixon was born with 19 letters in his birth name. Facing impeachment proceedings in the House of Representatives, he announced his intention to resign on August 8, 1974, a day that adds up to the number 19. Of the three possible charges that would have been levied against Nixon, one was the abuse of power.

Judge Sirica (3/19/1904) was not the only person involved with Watergate who lived up to the positive aspect of 19, which is correcting abuses of power. **Martha Mitchell**, wife of Attorney General John Mitchell, also deserves mention. Her name at birth, Martha Elizabeth Beall, adds up to 19. Her late-night telephone calls to various reporters claiming that President Nixon was making a scapegoat of her husband helped keep Watergate in the news. Reportedly, Richard Nixon once said, "If it had not been for Martha Mitchell, there would have been no Watergate scandal."

Carl Bernstein and **Bob Woodward** were the *Washington Post* reporters who stumbled on this story. Both Carl Bernstein and Bob (Robert Upshur) Woodward were born with names that add up to 14, the number of the revolutionary and the champion of freedom. In addition, Bob Woodward's (3/26/1943) life path number equals 19. It was on June 19, 1972, when Woodward made his initial phone call regarding the Watergate break-in to his secret source, Deep Throat, whose identity was revealed in 2005 as FBI associate director, **W. Mark Felt**, a name that adds up to 19.

Subsequently, Woodward and Bernstein co-authored *All the President's Men*, which later was made into a film of the same name starring **Dustin (Lee) Hoffman** (19 expression) as Bernstein and **(Charles) Robert Redford** (8/18/1937 = 19 life path) as Woodward. For this story of abuse of power, it was perfect casting to have two men with 19 prominent in their numbers in the leading roles. **Hal Holbrook** (soul urge 19), who was born on February 17, 1925, with a 19 Success Number, was cast in the role of Deep Throat.

Knowing that Robert Redford has a 19 life path, we can understand why this project was so dear to his heart—why he bought the rights to the book, why he coproduced and starred in the film, and why this man has spent a lifetime promoting environmental causes. We mustn't forget, either, that 19 adds up to 1, the number of independence, and that Redford's pioneering efforts to promote independent filmmakers are also a reflection of his 19/10/1 life path. Indeed, he epitomizes this trinity of numbers, as he expresses the initiative of 1, the authority of 10, and the leadership qualities of 19.

The Fight Against Organized Crime

Eliot Ness

Eliot Ness was born on April 19, 1903. He was 26 years old when, in 1929, he was hired as a special agent of the U.S. Department of Justice to head the Prohibition bureau in Chicago, with the express purpose of investigating and harassing gangster Al Capone. Ness and his Untouchables raided breweries, speakeasies, and other places of outlawry. Their crime fighting made newspaper headlines and turned Eliot Ness and his Untouchables into heroes. The Untouchables' infiltration of the underworld secured evidence that helped send Capone to prison for income tax evasion.

In 1935, shortly after his crime-fighting days in Chicago ended, Eliot Ness become Cleveland's safety director. There he rooted out corruption in the police department, smashed gambling rings, tamed violent youth gangs, upgraded fire protection and traffic safety, and instituted other reforms. Eliot Ness was a true 19.

Estes Kefauver

U.S. senator **Corey Estes Kefauver** was born July 26, 1903, with a 19 life path. He achieved nationwide recognition as chairman of the Senate Crime Investigating Committee, whose partially televised hearings in 1950–51 dragged organized crime out of the shadows and brought it into the glare of television lights. Americans were spellbound as Kefauver gave the nation its first look at organized crime. Prior to the Kevaufer hearings, the majority of people had no idea that such a thing as the Mafia existed. Now they were seeing mobsters being asked probing questions by committee members before their very eyes. Names like **Frank Costello** and **Lucky Luciano** suddenly became household words.

Kefauver arguably left his most enduring legacy in the area of consumer protection. As chairman of the Senate's Antitrust and Monopoly Subcommittee in the late 1950s and early 1960s, he conducted several highly publicized investigations into such abuses as administered prices in the steel, electrical, and drug industries and into the inadequacies of federal drug safety regulations. Until his death in 1963, Estes Kefauver was the nation's foremost defender of the public interest.

Two years after Kefauver's death, the mantle of consumer-advocate-cum-laude passed to **Ralph Nader** (2/27/1934), who gained fame with his first book, *Unsafe at Any Speed*. Like Kefauver, Ralph Nader was born with a 19 life path, and, like Kefauver, he has been an outspoken critic of corporate abuses of consumers and the environment.

Robert Francis Kennedy

Robert Francis Kennedy (19 expression) was the first attorney general of the United States to make a serious attack on organized crime. During his brief tenure as attorney general, prosecutions of organized crime figures reached levels never before attained. Kennedy expanded the Justice Department's Crime and Rackets Section from 17 to 60 people, created investigative bureaus in six cities to collect data on over 1,100 racketeers, and authorized seven anticrime laws that were approved by Congress. A month before his brother's assassination, in October 1963, Kennedy persuaded mobster Joseph Valachi to testify under government protection. He was the first-ever Mafia informant. His testimony revealed for the first time the intricate, secret working of the so-called Cosa Nostra crime syndicate and described how the continued operation of the Mafia depended on payoffs to local police and politicians.

Bobby Kennedy had first emerged as a national figure years earlier, in 1957, when, as head of the team investigating the trade union movement, his investigation of **James (Riddle) Hoffa** (19 expression) was televised. Kennedy claimed that Hoffa had misappropriated $9.5 million in union funds and had corruptly done deals with employers. A jury, however, found Hoffa not guilty. After Bobby Kennedy became attorney general, he resumed his obsessive investigations into Hoffa's activities. This time Kennedy was successful. In 1964, Hoffa was found guilty of taking money from the Teamsters Union pension fund and was sentenced to eight years in prison (later to be pardoned by Richard Nixon in 1971).

Bobby finally got his man—or did he? While Bobby Kennedy was still alive and Hoffa was still in jail, the FBI questioned Jimmy Hoffa for alleged comments he had made to a fellow inmate on May 30, 1967. According to the informant, Hoffa told him, "I have a contract out on Kennedy. And if he ever gets in the primary or gets elected, the contract will be fulfilled within six months." Of course, when agents asked about this, Hoffa denied ever having said it. On June 4, 1968, Robert Francis Kennedy, with his 19 expression, was assassinated by Sirhan Sirhan, who was born on March 19, 1944.

Understanding the Dark Side of 19

Lizzie Borden, O. J. Simpson, and Nicole Brown

Did accused ax murderer **Lizzie Borden** (7/19/1860) really chop up her mama and papa in Massachusetts in 1892? Though she was acquitted in one of the most famous murder trials of the 19th century, doubts still linger about her guilt or innocence. The same can be said of **O. J. Simpson**, who in 1997 was acquitted of killing his wife, **Nicole Brown**, in the most famous murder trial of the 20th century. Was he guilty or innocent? Perhaps someday we will know. What we do know is that Nicole Brown, born on May 19, 1959, was the victim of a hideous death, and that her husband, Orenthal James Simpson (7/9/1947), was born with a 19 life path.

Truman Capote, Joyce Carol Oates, and Edgar Allan Poe

What causes a person to kill in cold blood? This was the question that **Truman Capote** (9/30/1924 = 19 life path) examined in his novel *In Cold Blood,* a chilling account of a multiple murder committed by two young psychopaths in Kansas. The same question was asked repeatedly by **Joyce Carol Oates** (19 soul urge) in her many novels, which often portray characters whose obsessive behaviors and intensely experienced lives end violently, sometimes due to larger forces beyond their control. Another purveyor of the darkness that can grip a person's soul was writer **Edgar Allan Poe** (1/19/1809).

George Lucas, Ice Cube, and Ice-T

The latest *Star Wars* trilogy by film director-writer-producer **George Lucas** (5/14/1944 = 19 life path) examines how Darth Vader came to embrace the dark side. Gangsta rapper **Ice Cube** (birth name O'Shea Jackson), composer of "America's Most Wanted," was born with a 19 soul urge and a 19 life path (6/15/1969). Fellow rapper **Tracy Marrow**, composer of "Cop Killer" and considered to be the father of gangsta rap, chose the perfect pseudonym *Ice-T,* which adds up to 19. Both of these songwriters have given us insights into the criminal consciousness.

Not all 19s are criminals or reform addicts, but all 19s must come to terms with the fact that good and evil are intrinsic parts of human nature. This point is drummed home in the novels of British writer **William (Gerald) Golding,** who was born with a 19 quiet self on September 19, 1911. Most people are familiar with his first novel, *Lord of the Flies* (1954), a story about how a group of innocent schoolboys revert to primitive behavior and savagery after they are shipwrecked on a deserted island in the Pacific.

19s must confront humanity's dark side—and that is exactly what Golding did in his fiction. In his view, the first step that must be taken to confront humanity's dark side is to become aware of our own capacity for good and evil. All 19s have powerful emotions, any one of which, if not watched, can threaten to usurp the whole personality and lead to destructive behavior. This is what happens to negative 19s like Oklahoma City bomber **Timothy McVeigh**, who was born with 19 letters in his birth name. Any natural function that has the power to take over the whole person is what psychologist Rollo May and others have named the "daimonic"—what Goethe called the "power of nature." To quote Rollo May, "Violence is the daimonic gone awry."

The daimonic is paradoxical in nature, however, in that it is potentially creative and destructive at the same time.

The 9 in 19 can be the power from the depths that pushes the 1 to a new level of selfhood (10—that is, 1 + 9 = 10), or it can be the power of nature gone awry as the blind rage that takes possession of the whole self. Negatively, 19 is the individual (1) pitted against the universe (9); positively, it is the daimonic (9) personalized (1), resulting in an individuality that is both unique (1) and universal (9).

Understanding Karma and 19

The 1 and 9 of 19 add up to 10, a number that indicates a higher level of selfhood than 1. In its highest state, 10 is man (1) beside God (0): It is the individual (1) who achieves a higher state of consciousness by getting in touch with the Christ within (0); it is the person who dies to his or her old self in order to be reborn at a higher level of being. (See the 19th Tarot card, the Sun.)

The path to reaching such an exalted state for 19 is through the 9—the number of humanity. All 19s have to come to terms with the 9 in coming to terms with the 1—that is, to embrace all of humanity, the world, indeed all of creation, which 9 represents. 9 is not only human nature, with its capacity for good and evil, but also Nature (mosquitoes, too) herself.

To be a 19, in the words of poet Delmore Schwartz, is to be "a citizen of the world and thus a citizen of no particular time or place. . . . The world as such is not a community . . . it is the turning world in which the human being, surrounded by the consequences [karma] of all times and places, must live his or her life as a human being." All 19s have to acknowledge their role in the larger scope of things. In coming to terms with their humanity, 19s can be reborn to (experience) their divinity. 19 relates to the resurrected Christ. Just as Christ had to descend to hell before he could ascend to heaven, so 19s must face the darkness before they can embrace the light. 19s must follow the example of Christ and do their part to redeem the sins (karma) of humankind. This is what I think numerologist Florence Campbell meant when she wrote, "The final karmic debts must all be paid before the completion of the life cycle." 19s are heirs to all the ages, to the psychic debris of all times and places. It's their job to help dispense with the karma of the human race, so that a new and more enlightened kind of humanity can be born.

Chapter 12

THE NUMBERS OF COMPATIBILITY

"*You are my last love, I will love you till the end of my days.*" **Humphrey Bogart** wrote these romantic words to **Lauren Bacall** in a letter shortly after they met on the set of the film *To Have and Have Not*. Within months they were wed, and they were apart only once in 12 years of marriage, during which they made four films together, had two children, and took active roles against the anticommunist witch hunt of the 1950s that was spearheaded by U.S. senator Joseph McCarthy. True to his word, Bogart loved Bacall till the end of his days—his death from cancer occurring in 1957.

What can numerology tell us about this fabled Hollywood romance? Were Bogie and Bacall in fact soul mates? A comparison of their birth names reveals that they both shared the soul urge of 2, the number that, perhaps more than any other, longs for a loving relationship that will be the end-all of existence.

$$\frac{15/6}{3 \quad 57} + \frac{16/7}{565} + \frac{7}{61} = 20/2 \text{ soul urge}$$

HUMPHREY DEFOREST BOGART

$$\frac{12/3}{57} + \frac{7}{61} + \frac{10/1}{5 \quad 5} = 11/2 \text{ soul urge}$$

BETTY JOAN PERSKE (birth name of Lauren Bacall)

To determine compatibility between two people, first look at their individual soul urge numbers. You will want to know what makes your partner tick, his or her motivations and deepest emotional needs—and these are all revealed by the soul urge.

If your soul urges are the same number, you'll undoubtedly have much in common. You can often read each other's thoughts, and you'll view many of the issues that arise in life from the same perspective. You will be supportive of each other and will work well together as a team.

When you first meet, you'll be amazed that you don't have to explain yourself to this person. He or she will fathom your meaning before you even complete the sentence. You may even feel that you've known each other in a former lifetime. Instant compatibility—without you having to work to make the relationship work. It all seems too good to be true.

However, the fact of the matter is that life—and relationships, especially—are seldom this easy. As time

490

goes by, your similar approach to living could turn into a dull sameness that could turn stale for either party. Picture this conversation between you and your mate:

"It's a nice day, dear."

"Yes, it is," your other half replies.

"Shall we go the movies?"

"Yes, I'd like that."

After a while, you may feel that you're sharing your life with a parrot and not a lover. This does not mean you should shy away from a potential romantic interest who has the same soul urge, but it does mean the two of you will have to find ways to stimulate and challenge each other. Then you'll both grow as individuals and your relationship will continue to renew itself, so you'll always have that freshness and excitement that was there when you first met.

Numerology has a way for you to achieve this end. Add your two soul urge numbers together; the sum is called the *soul urge essence*. In the principles associated with this number, you'll find the best ways to keep your relationship alive and fresh—to make it endure. In the case of Bogie and Bacall, both having a soul urge of 2, their soul urge essence is 4, the number of work—and indeed, this legendary couple worked together, costarring in four Hollywood movies.

How to Get Along

If Your Soul Urge Essence Is the Number:

1: Recognize the uniqueness of your bond. Don't go by what others say a relationship should or should not be.

2: There's a definite need for give-and-take. Neither one of you can be boss—but together you can be king and queen, corulers.

3: Be sure to keep the lines of communication open between you. Talk to each other—in a lighthearted way. A sense of humor always helps.

4: Work together on a project.

5: Be sure to go out for fun times. Add variety to your life. Take trips together. Sex is a must. Be spontaneous. A surprise now and then helps.

6: A shared responsibility brings out the best in both of you.

7: At times, you both need periods of time by yourself. Don't invade each other's space. Yet at the same time, know how to share the silences. You may spend time analyzing your relationship.

8: You must have a shared ambition, a goal that you both are willing to work hard to achieve.

9: Become involved in a cause that's bigger than both of you.

11/2: Some self-sacrifice will be needed in this relationship—that goes for both of you. Have a shared dream. Write poems to each other. (Also see soul urge expression 2.)

22/4: You both are dreamers, visionaries, but focus on practical ways to implement those dreams. (Also see soul urge expression 4.)

If Your Soul Urges Are the Same Number

There can be an overdoing of the traits of that number. For example:

1–1: With two strong egos who like to have their own way here, something's got to give. There could easily be a constant power struggle.

2–2: You can't spend the whole day in each other's arms. If one of you becomes moody, it could easily trigger the same reaction in the other. Get the hankies out if you both get depressed at the same time.

3–3: The two of you will talk a lot. Both of you may be inclined to scatter your energies. Who will do the housework?

4–4: Is one workaholic enough in one family? Take care that you don't become drudges. Remember the adage about all work and no play.

5–5: You both like to burn the candle at both ends, and you could burn each other out. Hopefully, one of you is responsible.

6–6: Two home-loving 6s together; will you ever leave the house? You both have strong moral principles.

Take care not to dwell in a house of self-righteous, smug conformity.

7–7: Two loners living together; who will be the first to break the silence? It will take you years to reveal your full selves to each other, but each time you do, you'll each grow in understanding. On the debit side, you are both prone to be melancholy at times—let's hope not at the same time.

8–8: Two souls anxious for money and power. Take care that an obsession with material concerns doesn't blind you to the other good things in life.

9–9: Two humanitarians under the same roof. One or both of you is going to have to learn that charity begins at home. Take care that strangers don't mean more to you than each other. Both of you are highly emotional and dramatic. If polarized negatively, there could be a soap opera in the making.

11–11: There's a highly charged atmosphere here: two idealistic, nervous-wreck, genius types living together. What if you both freak out at the same time? Also, is one of you willing to be the power behind the other's throne? (Also see 2–2.)

22–22: You are both larger-than-life figures. There will be electricity between you. You're both prone to nervous tension. Together you can be a power for universal good or—if polarized negatively—a potentially destructive force. It all depends upon the ideals the two of you share. Together, will you be Bonnie and Clyde—or Pierre and Marie Curie? (Also see 4–4.)

If Your Soul Urges Are Both Odd Numbers or Both Even Numbers

You'll have similar but slightly different perspective toward life. 1, 3, 5, 7, 9, and 11 are compatible, as are 2, 4, 6, 8, and 22. For example, a person with a 4 soul urge has a desire to work hard and enjoys work for its own sake. These values are not the same as 8's desire for recognition and financial gains, but they are compatible. 4's ability to apply his or her talents to the job at hand will be an asset to 8 in his or her climb to the top, whereas 8's ability to see things in the large picture will help prevent 4 from becoming narrow-minded or limited in vision. The positive interaction of 4 and 8 can benefit both parties as individuals—and the relationship as well. Some other combinations:

1–3: 3's sense of humor can keep 1 from taking himself or herself too seriously. 1 can give direction to 3, who tends to scatter energies and time.

1–5: 5 broadens 1's horizons; 1 gives 5 purpose and direction.

1–7: Ideally, 7 can teach 1 to think before acting, whereas 1 could encourage the laid-back 7 to act on his or her ideas—to practice what is preached. Negatively,

1's ego may not take kindly to 7's natural tendency to criticize.

1–9: 9 is humanitarian in outlook; 1 tends to be selfish. Yet 9 can broaden 1's outlook, and 1 can give impetus to 9's ideas. If each would become just a little bit like the other, then we would have two individuals who are both unique (1) and universal (9).

1–11: 1 gives 11 direction and purpose; 11 inspires 1; both are creative thinkers. (See also 1–2.)

2–4: 2 will always be willing to give the hardworking 4 a helping hand. 4 gives 2 a strong shoulder to lean on. 2's sensitivity will keep 4's practicality from becoming too hard-boiled. 2 has the sympathy, companionship, encouragement, and love that the sometimes depressed 4 needs. 4 is methodical, while 2 works well with details.

2–6: Both are peace loving and family-oriented. 6 will appreciate 2's cooperative spirit and won't mind 2's occasional tendency to lean. In fact, 6 relishes the role of comforter and adviser. Both have a strong need to love and be loved.

2–8: 8 organizes and thinks big. 2 won't mind taking care of the details. 8 can make the money to buy all those collectibles that 2 desires. 2 is a natural for the role of guy or gal Friday to the executive 8. Though 2 is a leaner, it will be 8 who with each passing year will come to count on 2's help, loyalty, love, and support.

2–22: If 2 is willing to be a spoke in 22's wheel, they

can get along. 2 takes care of the details that 22 often ignores, but when 22 operates in its impersonal mode, 2's feelings are often hurt. Visionary 22 thinks big and may find 2's concern about little things to be unimportant. Sometimes empathetic 2 can ameliorate 22's nervous tension; sometimes not. (See also 2–4.)

3–5: Both are outgoing, friendly, and pleasure loving. 3 has a way with words; 5, a way with people. 3 can be charming and flirtatious; 5 can be adventurous, seductive, and exciting. Together the two have much in common.

3–7: 3 is a master of small talk and likes to keep things light and breezy; 7 is serious-minded and doesn't care for idle chitchat. 3 is gregarious, and 7 has a need for privacy. Though opposite in many ways, each has what the other needs. 3's good cheer is an antidote to 7's occasional melancholy; 7's seriousness and depth can keep 3 from embracing the frivolous. Both usually have writing ability, and the mutual capability to talk things over can offset many potential conflicts.

3–9: 3 may seem immature at times to 9, yet 9 benefits from 3's youthfulness and endless enthusiasm.

3–11: Both share artistic interests and social skills. 3's lighthearted approach will help 11 get a message across to others, whereas 11's idealism and fervor will inspire 3 to expand horizons.

4–6: Both are home loving, conservative, and responsible. They have much in common, but need to be careful not to get bogged down in a rut.

4–8: See the lead paragraph to this section.

4–22: Visionary 22 benefits from 4's practicality, though 22 can find 4's lack of vision limiting. The two work well together in business, but can get on each other's nerves in a personal relationship.

5–7: There can be a lot of nagging here, as 5's need for constant social activity conflicts with 7's need for privacy. Yet each has what the other lacks. 7 needs to get out more to offset a tendency to be reclusive; 5 needs to take time out from partying for reflection and introspection. Each can learn from the other.

5–9: Apt to have similar interests. Both are adventurous, outgoing, and interested in people. 9 inclines to be more romantic than the sensual, self-indulgent 5.

5–11: 11 lives in the clouds and hates to keep appointments, and 5 is sometimes irresponsible and undependable—a deadly combination where practical matters are concerned. Both of you, though, thrive on change, innovation, and all that is progressive.

6–8: 8 will invite all the important people over to the house, and 6 will make them feel right at home. 6 will respect 8's ambitions, and 8 will love 6's ability to work well with groups and be a good host. Both are responsible, practical, and stable.

6–22: Visionary 22 may find 6 to be conventional in his or her thinking. Whereas 22 wants to change the world, 6 is content to stay right at home. However, 22's humanitarianism meshes well with 6's sense of social responsibility.

7–9: 7 often has a wish to retreat from the world—the very world that 9 reaches out to embrace and comfort. 9 can broaden the vision of 7.

7–11: If 11 acts like a clinging 2, 7 could feel a bit smothered. Both numbers are prone to escapism—hopefully not at the same time. 11 can inspire 7.

If Your Soul Urge Is an Odd Number and Your Partner's Is Even, or Vice Versa

Your relationship with each other is likely to be difficult, requiring both of you to make adjustments in order to get along. For example, a person with a 2 soul urge needs assurances that he or she is loved and needed. This may not sit well with a 1 soul urge type, who is self-reliant and, at times, doesn't think he or she needs anybody. 1 is pushy and assertive, whereas 2 is gentle and accommodating. 1 is a leader, 2 is a follower. 2 has a need to express and share feelings, whereas 1 does not. Are these irreconcilable differences? Perhaps, and perhaps not.

Because 1 in numerology is associated with the male principle and 2 with the female, what we have here in the conflict between 1 and 2 is the age-old battle between the sexes. Note the following:

- The word *man* $(4 + 1 + 5 = 10/1)$ adds up to 1.
- The word *woman* $(5 + 6 + 4 + 1 + 5 = 20/2)$ adds up to 2.

Numerologically, in the case of 1 and 2, opposites do indeed attract! Just as man and woman do find ways to get along, the same applies for relationships between 1 and 2 soul urge types.

The dichotomy between male and female principles as signified by the numbers 1 and 2 applies to partners in same-sex relationships as well. Also, sometimes it's a woman who has a 1 soul urge and her male partner who has the 2 soul urge. In this instance, the woman is liable to wear the pants in the relationship.

Let's turn our attention now to some other potentially challenging soul urge combinations:

1–4: 4 won't take kindly to 1's need to dominate, and 1 may feel stifled by 4's rigidity and need to control. 1 can be impetuous, and 4 can be overly cautious.

1–6: 1 could easily misinterpret 6's genuine concern as meddling. 6 likes to help out, but 1 often feels he or she doesn't need anyone's help. 6 can be put off by 1's self-centeredness.

1–8: May be a contest of wills. Each of you likes to have your own way. Who's the boss?

1–11: 11 can inspire 1, and 1 can give 11 purpose and direction. Both are creative and original thinkers. (See also 1–2.)

2–3: 3 can be flirtatious, causing 2 to feel jealous or insecure. Variety is the spice of life for 3, and at times 3 may become bored with 2's desire to share and maintain the status quo.

2–5: 2's need for security inspires a love of the status quo, whereas 5 thrives on constant change. 5's sometimes wandering eye could put 2 in a state of perpetual emotional insecurity.

2–7: 2s wear their hearts on their sleeves, and 7s do not. 7's natural tendency to criticize could hurt 2's feelings—and 2 crying about it won't help matters out, either. Constant togetherness is not 7's bag, as 7 needs time alone.

2–9: Both are emotional and loving. 2's forte, though, is personal love, whereas 9's is universal love. 2's desire and need for constant togetherness may conflict with 9's interest in the greater world at large. 2 simply cannot have 9 all for himself or herself.

2–11: 2 can give 11 moral support and encouragement, and 11 can broaden 2's vision. The combination can be very harmonious, though both can be indecisive and overly sensitive. (Also see 2–2.)

3–6: 6 can stabilize the extravagant 3 and won't mind 3's need for the limelight. 6 is the parent, and 3 is the child. The question is, Will 6 spoil the child, or will 3 act like a spoiled child and rebel? Both, though, are sociable and artistic. 3's vivacity keeps the relationship fresh, and 3 can always count on 6 to handle more than his or her share of the responsibilities.

3–8: 3 has the salesmanship skills and the social contacts, whereas 8 has the power to think big and to get ahead—an excellent combo for business. In a personal relationship, 2 may feel that 8 is too focused on business, whereas 8 may find 3 to be immature and superficial. 8 is organized; 3 tends to scatter energies and to be all over the place.

3–22: 3 motivates 22 to have fun in life and to give more attention to artistic and social interests. 22's vision enables 3 to make better use of creative gifts. If 22 reverts to being a 4, however, there will be conflicts; see 3–4.

4–5: The serious-minded, self-disciplined 4 could easily clash with freedom-loving 5.

4–7: 4 is practical, 7 is theoretical. 4 works hard, and 7 thinks deeply. 4 can help 7 put into practice what he or she preaches. You may lack emotional understanding of each other's needs. Neither one is much help to the other when one is depressed.

4–8: 4 is down-to-earth; 9 is emotional, humanitarian, and compassionate. 4's conservatism may clash with 9's broad love for humankind. 4 may resent 9's outside interests, and 9 may find 4 to be a bit cold and rigid.

4–11: 11 is a dreamer and an idealist; 4 is a realist and practical. Possibly 11 can keep 4 from being earthbound, while 4 can keep 11 from becoming lost in the clouds—then again, possibly not. Each has what the other lacks. (See also 2–4.)

5–6: 5 is a partygoer, and 6 is a stay-at-home type. 6 is duty-minded while 5 may be irresponsible.

5–8: 5 thrives on change and can take ups and downs in stride. However, 8 may find 5's need for freedom to be a way of not dealing with responsibility. 8 is goal-minded, whereas 5's goals may shift with the wind. In business, however, 5's expediency and people skills will help 8 get ahead.

5–22: Both love the new and the progressive. However, 5 may want to play at the very time that 22 wants to work. If 22 acts like a 4, there's bound to be disharmony: see 4–5.

6–7: The adage *at sixes and sevens* immediately tells us that all is not right with this combination. 6 centers attention on home and family, whereas 7 often prefers to be alone.

6–9: 9 will have to learn that charity begins at home, for family always comes first for 6. Still, this is a good combination for business, marriage, and friendship. 9 teaches 6 to expand the concept of family to include all of humankind . . . in other words, an extended family. 6 can teach 9 to follow through on idealistic promises.

7–8: 8 is practical and materialistic, whereas 7 is intellectual, philosophical, and sometimes spiritual.

7–22: This is a powerhouse combination for engaging in mental work. 22's originality combines with 7's in-depth thinking to produce powerful results. Each, though, is inclined to be eccentric at times in his or her own peculiar way, so there's a need to adjust to each other's idiosyncrasies. (Also see 4–7.)

8–9: 8 has the business know-how to make 9's ideas workable, and 9 can expand 8's vision and scope. 8, though, is a materialist; 9, a humanitarian.

8–11: 8 is materialistic; 11 is an idealist. 8 has the practical know-how to make 11's dreams come true, whereas 11 can inspire 8. Still, the clash between idealism and materialism remains. 11 may be too soft in 8's eyes, whereas 8 may seem too insensitive to 11. (See also 2–8.)

9–22: 22 can give practical form to 9's ideas; 9 can add the element of compassion to 22's vision. Both are humanitarians. 22 may not live up to 9's ideal of romance, however, while 22 may find 9 to be overextended emotionally with his or her interest in so many individuals and groups. (See also 4–9.)

11–22: A dynamic duo! 22 brings practicality to 11's visions and ideas. (See also 2—4.)

Other Factors

- If one person's soul urge is the same as the other's expression, the soul urge person will attach himself or herself to the other, because the other has what the soul urge person wants.
- If one person's expression is the same as another's life path, the expression person will play a signifi-

cant role in helping the other meet the requirements of his or her life path. Here we have the relationship of teacher to student; there's no guarantee, however, that the student will like being in this position.

- If you are missing a number in your name, and your partner has this number in his or her name, this person will be good at something that you're not. From one perspective, this person can help you overcome your karmic lack. Conversely, however, he or she could prove to be an irritant if you're not ready to deal with the assorted problems that your missing number represents.

- If two people share a Success Number (1st pinnacle), they will always have the same Personal Year, Personal Month, and Personal Day each year, month, and day of their lives. Having to experience the same vibrations at the same time gives these individuals a lot in common.

Further Considerations

- The number comparisons listed above for the soul urge also hold true for comparing two people's expressions, birthday numbers, and life paths.
- Compatibility between expressions is favorable for business partnerships. Compatibility between birthday numbers is a sign of sexual compatibility.
- Compatibility between life path numbers often means a shared destiny.

Example: Napoleon and Josephine Bonaparte

In his final exile on St. Helena, Napoleon wrote:

> *Josephine is the only woman I have ever truly loved. She reigns in my heart and I mourn for her.*

Years earlier, as Napoleon carried out his brilliant Italian campaign, he bombarded his new wife, Josephine, with a flood of passionate, emotional letters. In a letter to his brother, Joseph, Napoleon wrote of Josephine:

> *I must see her and press her to my heart. I love her to the point of madness, and I cannot continue to be separated from her. If she no longer loved me, I would have nothing left to do on earth.*

Napoleon was born August 15, 1769, with a 19 life path. **Josephine** was born June 23, 1763, with a 19 life path.

Index

If you liked this book, you'll love all this series:

Little Giant® Book of "True" Ghost Stories • Little Giant® Book of "True" Ghostly Tales • Little Giant® Book of After School Fun • Little Giant® Book of Amazing Mazes • Little Giant® Book of Animal Facts • Little Giant® Book of Basketball • Little Giant® Book of Brain Twisters • Little Giant® Book of Card Games • Little Giant® Book of Card Tricks • Little Giant® Book of Cool Optical Illusions • Little Giant® Book of Dinosaurs • Little Giant® Book of Dominoes • Little Giant® Book of Eerie Thrills & Unspeakable Chills • Little Giant® Book of Giggles • Little Giant® Book of Football Facts • Little Giant® Book of Insults & Putdowns • Little Giant® Book of Jokes • Little Giant® Book of Kids' Games • Little Giant® Book of Knock-Knocks • Little Giant® Book of Laughs • Little Giant® Book of Magic Tricks • Little Giant® Book of Math Puzzles • Little Giant® Book of Mini-Mysteries • Little Giant® Book of Optical Illusion Fun • Little Giant® Book of Optical Illusions • Little Giant® Book of Optical Tricks • Little Giant® Book of Riddles • Little Giant® Book of School Jokes • Little Giant® Book of Science Experiments • Little Giant® Book of Science Facts • Little Giant® Book of Side-Splitters • Little Giant® Book of Tongue Twisters • Little Giant® Book of Travel Fun • Little Giant® Book of Travel Games • Little Giant® Book of Tricks & Pranks • Little Giant® Book of Visual Tricks • Little Giant® Book of Weird & Wacky Facts • Little Giant® Book of Whodunits

Available at fine stores everywhere.